Seasons of Life
and the Altar Call of CHRIST

Shanna Florene Pittman

Florenehucklebysgranddaughter

Copyright © 2021 by Author Shanna F. Pittman

All rights reserved. No part of this publication may be reproduced, distributed, or transmitted in any form or by any means, without prior written permission. Publisher's Note: This is a work of fiction. Names, characters, places, and incidents are a product of the author's imagination. Locales and public names are sometimes used for atmospheric purposes. Any resemblance to actual people, living or dead, or to businesses, companies, events, institutions, or locales is entirely coincidental.
Please contact author at e-mail below for permissions and speaking events.

Shanna F. Pittman/ pittmanshanna@yahoo.com
Published in the US
Florenehuclebysgranddaughter
Cover design
Tiny communications LLC
Editor Felicia Cauley

Seasons of Life and the Altar call of Christ
ISBN-978-17733868228
LCCN-2021901414

Contents

Introduction: The Seasons Of Life And The Altar Call Of Christ 1
Chapter 1: Honors Ball 3
Chapter 2: Challis Longs for his Wife 11
Chapter 3: Will China mention Challis's Swinger days 22
Chapter 4: Unwelcomed Guest 28
Chapter 5: The Switch 43
Chapter 6: Too Much to Sort Out 54
Chapter 7: Get Your Own Business 73
Chapter 8: No Excuse 81
Chapter 9: The Lion's Den 92
Chapter 10: Isolation 106
Chapter 11: New News 127
Chapter 12: Responsibilities 140
Chapter 13: Rape 146
Chapter 14: Hello Daddy 159
Chapter 15: The Past Returns 168
Chapter 16: Dead or Alive 177
Chapter 17: JayBird meets the Family 209
Chapter 18: Where is Gracie 223

Chapter 19: Principles to Live By 229
Chapter 20: Attackers 238
Chapter 21: No respect 253
Chapter 22: Time to explain... 261
Chapter 23: Pageant... 273
Chapter 24: Dinner Guest... 290
Chapter 25: Worship.. 294
Chapter 26: School 297
Chapter 27: Fashion show 322
Chapter 28: Challis Seeks God 328
Chapter 29: Halloween 340
Chapter 30: Christmas surprise 351

INTRODUCTION

THE SEASONS OF LIFE AND THE ALTAR CALL OF CHRIST

The Seasons of our life is thought of as a calendar, we choose to live by this system of an organizational kaleidoscope of days, rain, or shine jarred in us, a mental note of usage that are embedded among our social, religious, commercial, or administrative genre.

This is vowed by giving sub names to periods of onset made up of time, typically days, weeks, months, and years. Our dates of the designations of our singular, specific days, we believe in such a system.

We use a calendar as a physical record of such a systematic conclusion. It also presumes calendars as a list of planned portrayed events, such as these; court calendars or a party, or a fully chronological list of peoples or administrator's documents. They also devise a calendar of man or woman's wills.

Christ intended this for us to indulge our minds on and live according to.

Ecclesiastes 3: A Time for Everything

[1] For everything there is a season, and a time for every matter under heaven:
[2] a time to be born, and a time to die;
a time to plant, and a time to pluck up what is planted;

³a time to kill, and a time to heal;
a time to break down, and a time to build up;
⁴a time to weep, and a time to laugh;
a time to mourn, and a time to dance;
⁵a time to cast away stones, and a time to gather stones together;
a time to embrace, and a time to refrain from embracing;
⁶a time to seek, and a time to lose;
a time to keep, and a time to cast away;
⁷a time to tear, and a time to sew;
a time to keep silence, and a time to speak;
⁸a time to love, and a time to hate;
a time for war, and a time for peace.

The Old Testament has captured the embodiment of the core of the true calling of Christ's meaning of unwavering sacrifice; they established an altar where sacrifices were offered. So, the name "altar call" refers to the meaning of a true believer "sacrificial offering" as to one's self on an altar to God. One's soul is truly the essential sacrificial offering as in Romans12:1 (KJV). "I beseech you therefore, brethren, by the mercies of God, that ye present your bodies a living sacrifice, holy, acceptable unto God, which is your reasonable service." It's apparent we live this mundane life day after day going this way and that way, but only through the chastity of the vigor of the onset of Thee, we arrive at the volume of Thee.

John 14:6 (ESV) Jesus said to him, "I am the way, and the truth, and the life. No one comes to the Father except through me.

CHAPTER 1

Honors Ball

As the soft overboard of music with surround sounds, and an unknown celebrity singing the Temptation's song, "Christmas Jingles" plays low, soft, and soulful as the CD plays in the background. The family gets ready to attend the Honors Ball. "Honey, where is my Christmas seasonal Chest?" Jamarion Calms-way Senior, who is a two-time Mayor, yells to his wife, "baby come on we're going to be late for the Senator's Annual Honors Ball."

"Where else could it be baby?"

Where it always is, in the garage up in the loft where all your holiday seasonal stuff always is."

"I thought you were finished, Senator."

Solace, yes, I am, but those other candles, any way you know I like to switch it up, as she sashays her dress to impress her husband of 40 years.

"Baby, he grabs her, kisses her.

"Now let's go, we're going to be late."

He gathers her white mink coat and helps the love of his heart with joy on her. He takes another glance at her and he sees a tear or two falls slightly down her feminine, delicate natural face.

"Now what's wrong," Solace is concerned about something, but he shakes it off as if nothing is wrong.

"I just pray Challis will come home for Christmas this year," finally.

"Well, the last time I spoke with him, he sounded pretty upbeat after all he has been through."

Jamarion Senior, "I'm sure he is coming home for Christmas."

Solace, "Three days till Christmas, but okay, God please rest upon my youngest son." she whispered to herself for Challis's soul. She puts on her suede and leather fitted gloves, the phone rings.

"I got it," she said to her husband. She picks up the phone.

Rea, "we're here!"

Already? "We're on our way," Rea, "Okay; we're seated at your table, right in the middle, in front."

Solace, "okay."

Rea, "oh and old ugly fake dread wearing Benny and Quetta were trying to make the ushers switch tables with theirs from the back, with your table."

Solace, "I'll have a few words with his and her busy body."

Jamarion Senior, "honey."

Solace, "anyway, we're on our way." She hangs up the phone, but rings again."

Jamarion grabs his wife's hand, and they both hurry down the steps outside. The car service has just arrived. Their oldest son, Mr. CIA Mike yells, "Mom!"

He has on a bad designer tuxedo. His dad, Jamarion Senior, Mr. FBI was also wearing a tuxedo too. He says, "Come on, just leave your car there."

Mike and his wife Cindy, who is wearing beautiful long chiffon glitter formal flowing dress, with accessories to match, and a fox-fur accordingly.

Jamarion the II was wearing a matching black and white tux, and his wife, Karen, who has on a body fitting sequence, with a very long split up dress, which slid up her thighs drove up and parked right at the top of the curve of the round.

Around the driveway, in his parents' gated community, where people are most accustomed to showing I D.

The security guard, Don Worth, usually uses a buzzer to buzz each resident, and any guest desired to check in, but because of the renovations, we now require individuals to do a pass code to get in at the gate. Many residents and guest have expressed this process has been a pain though.

The Calms-Ways and their wives were all in attendance, they all used same car service, which was a stretch Bentley limousine. Driver Ryan Lumpkin is the family's usual driver to high-profile events such as this. Ryan made sure The Calms-way family arrived on time.

Lights Camera Action limo driver Ryan parks the limo but keeps it running. He gets out, goes around and opens the door.

Senator Solace gets a call as she is about to step out; she stops to answer her phone and sees the number. It is her baby boy.

Solace, "Son?"

Challis, "Mom, I'm so sorry I have to work over, no one else can do this."

Solace, "Yes, I know, you're the executive producer, take lots of pictures! I see you right now on TV, at the set, you look beautiful. Okay, no matter what son, make sure you are home for Christmas."

"Things are better in my life, but I'll let you go, so you can work that red carpet, love you so much mom," Challis said.

Jamarion Senior gets out of the car first, then helps his wife out.

There are plenty of news and magazine photographers taking pictures of each celebrity recipient, and they set the décor on point.

They dressed huge beautiful Christmas trees in such huge gorgeous bulbs in plain and Gold, plus see through glass. Their sons and their wives follow forward, the camera's flashes as they all smile.

The ball room has one Christmas tree, which adores the huge grand hall and is all white tree with pearls for trim and rhinestones and gold and glass bulbs, with all ivory white inlays and brass trimmed walls.

There are also church-like huge picture windows in accenting color patterns, which all go through the enormous glass and brass doors and ivory doors into a huge foyer in which only the great honoree's line the walls.

But after tonight, someone will be 'The Senator District 10 West Virginia's Honoree' of the year. Solace Calms-Way's will be there, as several other nominee's will all line the great honors wall after tonight, soon.

Senator Solace notices her table, but Benny pimps right up to her. Benny Marbury is the Senator for District 6 in Detroit, Michigan Representative.

He snaps his fingers to the soft Christmas jazz, and dances up on cool to her. Jamarion, "hey he is wearing a crush velvet burgundy tuxedo, he does his belt while he added hang with me. You know they are going to call my name first. I'm still the best Walter Wright Champion of the world."

Then he spins around like he is Michael Jackson and the moon walks, singing out aloud, 'Tonight, Tonight, "come on",' as he does the running man in a small space.

Jamarion II, "This nigga never changes."

Mike, "Hell no."

Jamarion Senior, "damn is he stuck in time,"

Jamarion II, "what does he have on? Is that a." Karen gets interrupted by her husband.

Jamarion II, "a big ass fake rhinestone, big ass gold chain, and his belt he won by default in 1974 boxing Walter lightweight champion, he wears that belt around his waist with his double, triple pimp daddy suit on."

Cindy, "OMG, with rings and sheer knee highs to match. She could see this because he had one suit leg cut short to the knee, the other one is long."

Senator Benny, "Senator Solace, switch tables with me, hater and my baby, because we have to leave early."

Solace, "Jesus, help me, get there,"

Jamarion Senior, "no baby, okay Benny, we will see you all."

Benny, "no file, you know wherever I am there, is always Prime Time." He does his hands thing and then the half splits.

Jamarion Senior, "this motherfucker."

Benny, "oh it's cool."

Jamarion Senior, "come on baby let me get my honoree to her appropriate table."

"All their sons and wives speak to Benny, he stands trying to be cool, and he fist bumps her sons."

Benny, "excuse me, what's cracking now? You all little niggas grew up."

Mike, "yelp, something like that."

Benny in gangster style stands in his double-breasted outdated and style white with crush velvet tux matching tuxedo shirt tux with matching bow tie and red patent leather shoes to match and his accessories.

Solace shakes her head as she glances over at Benny's wife, Quetta.

Solace, "now she got on an all-white patent leather short too young looking for her back out and patent leather drumbeater major boots with feather fringe and a matching cowboy hat. I will be damned."

Rea hears that they have reached Solace's Honoree table. Rea, "wait till you see Benny and Quetta?"

Solace, "I just saw his trifling behind." Rea, "him and Quetta look ridiculous."

Solace, "that's only half of it, I declare both of them a hot ass double mess, and I need a nice tall glass of champagne."

They both laughed as their husbands' high fives and fist bumps each other, and they all sat down.

Time goes by, the host announces the first Honoree, he shows his life on big close circuit mega screen and before the man could announce him, Senator Benny ran up, with his wife following him, almost skipping behind him with her and her white crush velvet scarf yelling, "you did it, baby."

Solace, "honey, please more champagne."

Jamarion Senior, "here comes the server."

Ivan, "champagne!"

Jamarion Senior, "yes, he stands and takes two, one for him and one for his wife." The rest of their table-guest follows.

Benny moves the host commentator out of the way after he takes his nice silver and gold, huge plague, then he goes to the podium and takes out a wrinkled piece of notebook paper and he goes on and on about carpet affair.

Challis and his grandmother Constance are getting out on their last paparazzo, everywhere on the front and outside of the red carpet. Solace's phone rings. Jamarion Senior, "honey," as he looks at her. "No, wait," as brings out the phone. As several cameras clicked, she checked the caller and its Challis. She answers it.

Challis, "hello," she said and listened to him, "love you too." They hang up; a teardrop on her face.

Jamarion Seniors, "he cannot come?"

Solace, "whatever," she struts on with a smile on her face.

DE LaRue Magazine representative, Pilar Pota, "Senator Solace Calms-way, whose design are you wearing this evening?"

Solace, "the Madame Solae 'a Solace of course," as she walked the soft glitter chiffon red rhinestone straps flowed at every stride with her red rhinestone stilettos and with a soft tone.

She is a redbone classy woman that can turn it up when she chooses. Her hair is in soft highlights of red, with a red and rhinestone hair clip to one side of her shoulder-length hair tonight.

Before they know it, they are all being escorted to Solace's table. As she turns, Jamarion Senior, "baby, come on, it's your night."

He grabs her hand and escorts her on. Solace, "wait."

Rea, "don't you look gorgeous," as she stands to greet her older sister by one year and 2 months.

Solace, "thanks, you look beautiful as well, this silver glitter formal fitting is lovely."

Rea, "I try, you know, The Madame Solae," They hugged and kissed.

Frank, "you look fantastic."

Solace, "I knew I always liked my brother-in-law."

Rea, "Greetings has ceased. A ceremony of honors is being given out one after the other, while Thelma has lost a lot of weight. She looks good though."

Solace whispers to her sister, "You know she had that surgery last year."

Rea, "I knew she did something," she whisper back.

Time goes on, there is presenter after presenter. Then suddenly, she cries a little and stares at the presenter.

Solace, "wait one minute."

Jamarion Senior, "I knew he would not miss this."

Rea, "Doesn't he look so good and mommy looks gorgeous and my boy so handsome?"

Challis is dressed in a designer tux, just like all the other fellows present.

Challis, "It brings great honor tonight to give this well-deserved honoree award to my 30-year term mother, Mrs. Solace LaRue Calms-Way."

Mommy Constance, "Oh mommy," Mike, "yes I'm here."

Rea smiles and shakes her head and blows her mother a kiss. Solace's other son's walk her up and help her get up on the stage. She is already crying buckets of tears. Challis hugs his mother; she hugs him back; she hits him playfully then she hugs her mommy.

Constance kisses and hugs her daughter.

Solace, "wait, where is daddy?"

Constance, "at home with Tina and Jasper, you all know he fell on the ice over at Isaiah's and Delores."

Solace and her son, Challis, "oh, okay."

Solace wipes back tears with her hankie, then she steps forth and, "the Lord has been so good to me." She places her hands on the nice size glass honoree award, "so many times I wanted to dial back my service when my boys were much younger, but the Lord just let me know he is who he is, as also to my husband, thank you, baby."

Jamarion Senior looks at his wife of 40 years and just smiles. Rea lets a few tears flow because she knew how hard it was for her sister to get on the train every week and leave.

Solace, "In the first year, I really tried to stay in D.C, but I just wanted to be home every day, so yes, that was life." "I say this to you young couples out there, its work in marriages and in careers," she cries, "but if you keep God first, I'm telling you that at the end of it all, there will be a nice pot of gold at the end of the Rainbow."

Challis, "mom you did alright.

Solace, "if you work hard, anything can happen." As Solace smiles and shows compassion within her face for him, then she looks at her honoree stature.

Time goes by and the Calms-Ways have had great fellowship and a nice delicious entrée. The night goes on, now all have returned home except Challis, he is staying at his parents'.

CHAPTER 2

Challis Longs for his Wife

Challis, his mother, and his father all sit in their screened-in back room with all the windows open and the outside air abreast to each in their night attire.

Challis, "mom, dad, things are changing in my life for the best."

Solace, "Well, you know you can't bring her back."

Challis, "I know it's the dandiest thing, I still miss her, but I don't."

Solace, "That's good; when you're ready you'll find someone, I believe that!"

Mama Constance, "baby, where the hot chocolate is?"

Challis, "Mama I got you, what about some popcorn?"

Mama, "yes."

Time goes on, they all chat till morning. Challis leaves for his brother's and wives' Christmas party was in two days. They have the party every year, but he had some other things to do first once he got in Manhattan, New York.

Two days sailed by and after the party morning came in.

Mac, "baby," as he was kissing his wife, he was Challis' brother from another dad and mother. To him, his wife was still as gorgeous as the day they had said their vows.

He became consumed with his thought process of his wife; it was just like she had not aged at all, except like a freshly poured wine or The Monet.

She truly had maintained herself to look almost the same as the first day he first saw her strut across Broad and High. As all their party comers and couples had indulged in different paths of matrimony, but those 7 couples plus one who had not been in attendance had all remained the closest of friends.

Challis C notes Calms-way, 6'6, their wounded soldier of life, their comrade, who had lost his wife of 10 years.

Cancer just 3 fresh years ago had stolen her from them all. Mac and China Casaco and their dearest friends did everything together.

They never missed a beat, dinner, plays, trips. They both hurt for Challis's purple heart and his wife, Jabra, although most of them did not particularly care for his bride, nor how he ever took her as his bride.

China and Jabra were not childhood friends or adult friends, and all these years were not two shades of sisters in crime. China bore another sister, each dedicated in life to one another,

they were truly the closest to one another. After all, Giselle had taken a different route than her. They had barely anything in common. They still had a love for one another that few could ever reckon with.

Some years go by, the two lost touch but never lost each other. They still stayed in touch wherever in pure, decisive optimist.

Her boys are grown, and her life seemed to transcend, but she needed her bestie to pull it through, for she had no plans.

But she knew that just one sister girl talks and all else would be history. Anxious, but she considered her hubby a close combative friend to assist her. But this to China was more than ever at a time difference and she, deep down, needed her sister.

The truth though, she knew that she and her hubby both loved each other and cared deeply for each other. However, having spent a century with him, and all the nonsense they felt for each other, had gone down the roads of life.

Around and around they went, missing each other, but so be it China still had her husband, and that daily living together keeps gathering them closer and closer, till they realized that till the end of time, that their togetherness would always bring them through.

He had done very well for their family and their selves in life. They had married straight out of college in their twenty's. Mac had a college grad with Challis and then pursued his Navy Seal Officer's career.

While China had a college grad in Marketing, and for nearly 20 years has been a stay at home mom.

She started her magazine with her sister, Giselle Che La. According to her, that's where they had started her business and hadn't called home for over twenty years.

Truly, her Giselle had done all the work to get her established, but once China took the ball and run. Thank loving God.

Long ago she chose Giselle in elementary school to be her bestie, but nowadays, China called home a Penthouse perched right in downtown Manhattan.

Both embodied their home now, they thrived with their essential lavish within life itself, a doorman filthy rich community. By day and night, everywhere she went thinking all is made of money, she lingered though on that she had. They had raised all their children.

Mac was cool. Although China wanted to define some more self within an older age. Hear her out not over their lives or upscale life works. Wow, it captured her embodiment within the crest of their marriage.

She felt they were sane even though two of their sons are gone. Life is coming next fall, but days ran and ran, soon Christmas would fall with all its pleasures and love.

By mid-morning, the snowstorm had not let up and their friends had all evacuated; the cleaners cleaned the entirety of their dwelling and put up the entire extra's, and locked up their Pent; after they did everything they let their selves out.

One party regular lingered over; Mr. Challis C-Note Calms-way who has a key had let himself in.

Though they were not in the slightest bit bothered about him; because they had grown extremely concerned about him.

China sashayed in her gorgeous kitchen, which all over the windows cascades, all around on each side over the Hudson River, which is one attraction that captured them.

She hurried as she grabbed a cup of morning Joe black, two sugars, and no cream. Challis had stirred. He had scared her a little, and she did not know why, since she knew he was lurking around somewhere near, because his wife is gone.

When she was alive, they always had a major holiday only spot. He spoke with comfort and her as well, China felt regular.

Challis grabbed a cup of black coffee and sat on the counter, and then he poured for himself as Mac entered with a cup.

Mac, "Well, good morning stranger."

Challis, "you know I do not have time for them."

China, "well, they love you also, and we had," as she danced with her 5"5 petite self in her robe and stiletto high heel slippers, with pink fur.

Mac is 6'5, and as he pours himself a cup of black joe.

Mac, "so what do you have to talk about to us?"

China, "yes."

Challis, "now let me just plead my case."

Mac, "the floor is yours," "well, God knows I love and miss my wife dearly."

They both nodded, "yes, we miss her too," But China truthfully did not, and Mac had his doubts.

Challis, "I have searched my thoughts and my heart, and I've concluded,

Mac, "What?"

Challis, "I'm head over heels in love right now with a woman that has the core of the entirety of my heart. God has purely indulged my mind, body, and soul. I say this, because yes, she is the one I have married this day the Lord has made, to care for, to cherish, to give every state of my being too."

They both agreed.

Challis, "now, I'm in love very much, so I'm going to marry Giselle."

China with coffee in her mouth almost blurted it all out over the floor; she had to put her hand over her mouth.

China, "Giselle who?"

Challis, "Your sister."

China "let me go before I say something." She makes to leave, and her husband stops her.

Mac, "no," stopping his wife from leaving.

China, "no, you are something else."

Challis, "overall this time I said nothing, nor did she."

China, "yes, she did not want to, I begged her to check in on you since you were staying right down the street from her publishing warehouse."

Challis, "every day, I enjoy and miss her; something happened, seriously, my heart is hers."

China in an angry mood, "no, what did you do to her. I told you over and over the last year that you're a swinger. No, used to be! I never wanted that. But you went right on along with it."

Mac grabs her, "baby."

Challis, "she is so kind, so breathe taking too, so sweet and so trusting."

China yelled, "hell we know all that."

Challis, "We made love, and we…"

China Interrupts, "OMG! An abomination against God, she was a sold-out virgin, no she was vulnerable, you're a filthy animal. Nothing is sacred to you, no, you know you dislike her and she has never given you a reason to after college, out of all the women in the world she never bothered you, she always has treated you with the utmost respect, get the hell out my house. I never want to see you."

She cries and puts her face on her husband's chest.

Mac, "baby let him, don't cry, I'm sure he's genuine."

Challis, "yes of course I love her, it's been 6 months to date since we have been together, or I've seen her. I miss my kitty boo boo…"

China, "Lord before God."

Mac, "Maybe he does, do you?"

Challis, "she can have everything I got, and it still would not be enough just for her to be my wife."

China, "no let me call my sister, I am so damn sick of you, she has been through enough and you want to stick it to her some more? Men are just complete dogs."

Mac, "honey what?"

She gets out her cell phone and calls her sister. The call gets disconnected. "Wait a minute, let me call her again." She dials again.

Challis pulls out a huge 12 karats engagement ring.

China, "God please where is my sister?" She hits Challis over and over; her hubby grabs her, and she cries.

"Of all the nasty trifling women in this world," she breaks down again, her hubby picks her up.

Challis, "she's mine I love her, and I care about her interest; she's mine, I will go to the ends of earth for her."

Mac, "let me see this!" reaching for the ring. He gives it to him, "baby this is real."

Challis follows as Mac tries to show his wife. She is so distraught, he gives it back and goes to put his wife back to bed, she says, "no, no."

Mac, "stop it, stop it," she cries more.

China, "he is going to destroy her just like all his call girl women."

Mac, "stop it, I think he is being sincere, you know how hard it is for him to love someone."

She is all alone somewhere by herself, as she cries more, and her husband consoles her. Giselle is a renowned New York best Seller twice.

Mac, "baby you have not seen Giselle recently since your spa retreat."

China, "we talk every day, except you know how she gets when she's writing."

Mac, "well, I have seen her. I told you, on the train with my dad last year."

China, "yes?"

Mac, "she looks confident and really well to me. I told you that it was the best I have seen her in a very long time since her mother and father got killed. She's a good 70 lbs., and lighter too."

China, "when I spoke to her, she said she was swimming and running 4 miles a day. Hell, she looked damn happy also to me. Honey, let me call Professor Nova, she is probably over there."

Mac, "baby stops bugging out Calms-way down. This is a blessing. We know both and I'm happy for both."

China, "Hello Professor Nova?"

Professor Nova, "hello, are you okay? Sounds like you have been crying."

China, "I'm fine. Have you seen my sister?

Professor Nova, "she has been right here for a couple of days, I'm a bit under the weather but I'm better now; she looks great to me, but she has been a little down since she has been here with a terrible stomach virus. I had it too, mine went on for weeks."

China, "please you take care of yourself, Professor."

Professor Nova, "child, I feel way better than I did, but that mess has to run its course. I asked her months ago to do a Christmas writing seminar for me at the College. It's been going on for the past semester today, Christmas eve is the last day; every one of my students is in love with her and mark my word, just wait to you see her, she looks the best, she has lost all this weight, toned all up. She has attempted to pick up, and she has done such an outstanding job. She's doing well by taking good care of herself."

"She has been wearing some bad clothes she made by herself, all kinds of stuff. I tell you I have never seen her like this ever, but I like it on her."

China, "do you mind if I come down there for a couple of days?"

Professor Nova, "child it's Christmas Eve, now you know me, and your mother have ours after Christmas Volunteers honors New Year's charities dinner there next week, the Friday after next, so we will fly out there tonight."

China, "yes, now you know both of you are staying with me; I have to call my mom, so cancel your reservations."

"Child now have your Christmas Eve; I will come by Christmas day for your 5-star feasts. I can't wait to see your tree; I have mailed all your gifts to you I have so much to do. I know now you know I will help you but come you can have my entire love; you know what I need is a brief vacation. Where are you staying?"

"Mandarin Oriental, they have the best Christmas after decor where the event is held every year." China, "ok let me call."

Professor Nova, "no China, I got the Presidential Suite. You know they sponsor me and your mother and everything the charity does for free; this is going to be a nice time."

China, "okay, but I will be right there also?"

Professor, "come on, there will be plenty of room. We will arrive at the hotel at 8 pm."

China, "okay, call me and I'll meet you all at the hotel."

Professor, "okay, love you all, bye."

China, "love you also," then hangs up.

Then she gets out of bed and yells, "Honey, I'm going to mommy and Professor's Volunteers for the next week, but we're still doing our Christmas and New Year's stuff."

Mac, "Okay baby, have fun."

Challis, "all hell yes, my future wife is helping with that."

China, "get away from my beautifully designed Christmas tree, and no, she is not getting here till Friday. She is on a cruise."

Mac, "Baby, do not interfere."

China, "I am; she is my sister. She is going to be there, if she didn't want C note, she would have not changed her number, no I will be damned if you stalk her and my mommy, the Professor is going to be there."

Mac, "baby, where your dad?"

China, "He is coming, but he is going to be late, you know he is at ice fishing every year by this time of year."

Challis comes into their room right then, "God swears. I love her with all my heart."

"You did not even give her two looks when she was fat," China said.

Challis, "I have never considered her fat."

China pushes him away, "get out of my way."

China, "baby, have you seen…" She runs around, "oh never mind, it's right here and get the hell out of our house and room," as she puts on one high heel blue suede shoe.

"Honey, please baby, we are evicting Challis," she says with one blue suede shoe on.

Challis sees a news segment of Giselle at Ohio State University's new upcoming authors' Christmas seminar.

Mac, "See, she looks good."

Challis, "Good as hell, that is my baby."

China jumps over the bed and looks for the remote to change the channel.

Mac, "baby, stop this, it is all for the best," he grabs the remote.

His wife cries again, "I don't know what to do." She drops to the floor.

Her husband gets down on the floor with her and says, "it's going to be all okay."

Challis, "what the hell do you want me to do? I love her; shit, I'm settled."

China gets up and smacks him!

Mac, "what the hell!" he gets up and grabs her, and says, "what's wrong with you?"

Challis, "she's frustrated, but that is cool."

China, "this is horrible."

Challis, "I want to share the rest of my life with Giselle, there is nobody else within this world that I love and desire night after night, day after day, but her. She is my wife, my kitty booboo baby."

China goes sits on the edge of the bed, "we are all going straight to hell."

Mac gets up, "no, we're not."

She cries for a while, and then she stops. "Wait a minute, what happened to Bishop?"

Challis "sit the fuck down!"

China, "wait, he really liked her?"

Challis, "right, I saw that mother fucker at her warehouse talking to her all crazy because she will be gone for a couple of days on her book tour, and he had to work or some bullshit like somebody cares, he went to bounce, I stretched your boy straight out cold 1,2."

Mac, "that's what I'm talking about." They fist bump each other, slap hands and hug.

China, "she is done with him."

Challis, "yes, and I finalized it. Now my peeps hurry, I want to go see my future wife."

China, "he loved her."

Mac, "How? Because he calls here all-day, whining to you, no she is out of his damn league."

Challis and Mac fist bump again, "anyway, look and it's about that time."

A couple of hours have flown by.

Instead of China meeting Giselle and Professor at the hotel, her hubby and Challis wait at the airport and around 2 more hours go by and like a breath of a soft season of life wind, they see Giselle and the professor.

CHAPTER 3

Will China mention Challis's Swinger days

Mac, "see? I told you, damn my sis, she looks incredible, but really, she was always beautiful to me, but damn, damn. Doesn't she look happy all smiling fresh and natural?"

Suddenly she jumps up and down and Challis yells, "I love her just like that, come to Papa my baby."

China, "wow over here."

Giselle pulling a luggage cart and Professor Nova is smiling and coming towards them.

Giselle, "Our luggage." Challis runs to her, he grabs the cart, "we got it."

He then picks her up and kisses her.

Mac, "okay baby, he loves her, it looks like he does to me."

China, "he better."

Challis, "why did you disconnect your phone?"

"I didn't, I just canceled the line. I needed some time to think," she puts her head down.

Challis puts his arm around her. As they walked, everyone else followed.

China and Mac hug Professor.

Challis, "do you have a phone yet?"

Giselle, "no, I have just been buying burner phones."

Challis, "Why not?"

Giselle, "nothing, I'll get one soon."

Challis, "no wait, is that mother fucker bothering you?"

Giselle, "yes, he came to my office a couple of days ago, the dean told me he was looking for Giselle, it's nothing I'll handle it," Professor Nova said, she throws her hands up, "he's harmless, show him your neck."

Giselle puts her arms down, touches her neck, "It's fine."

Challis to Giselle, "show me."

Giselle, "it's all right," she puts her arm in his arm and, "that is our luggage."

Challis, "it will come back around now."

Giselle spins around, "it's a beautiful night, let's not ruin it. What is done is done, I'm good!"

Challis grabs two, Mac grabs two, and Challis grab the other two.

Challis, "you are going to need more than this because you are staying here with me."

Giselle, "all right," She turns and hugs her sister, they walk shoulder to shoulder.

China, "Just look at you and your hair," she touches it, puts her hands through it.

Giselle, "I feel so good about myself."

China pulls her back so they could talk alone.

Giselle, "I lost 105 lbs. Dr. Lip scum got in my ass. He made me drop 70 lbs., and then I got the surgery for my tummy tuck, arms trimmed, bags tucked, Botox and my girls nipped couple places to stand."

China looks at her closely, "no bra,"

Giselle, "I don't have to but of course, I have one on."

China, "I want this dress."

Giselle, "I got me and you all kinds of amazing stuff; I have been staying a lot at mommy's dress shop."

China, "I thought that's where you were but Challis…"

Giselle, "I have loved Challis all these years. I just never thought he would love me back." She cries.

China, "well, he does. I'm just glad that you can finally the true woman that you wanted to be."

Giselle cries a bit more.

China, "see your damn face."

Giselle, "OMG! I got several facial peels; it hurt so bad at first, but ta- da magic,"

China, "yes, but it freshens you, hell yes, appointments here I come."

They give each other a high five.

Giselle, "I just hope this is all true."

Challis, "she is dead. She died, and we all went to her funeral, but I know the truth, she never really loved Challis as he loved her, and our God is perfect and the more I think about it he's best for you, his life is who he is."

Giselle, "I know that he really loved her."

China, "yes, but look at God."

They sit and hug.

China, "damn you smell damn good as well." Giselle opens her bag and pulls out a perfume; she sprays it on China, on each of her arms.

China, "yes, it's still nice, but it smells potent on you."

Giselle, "I made it for me particularly."

Giselle hands a bag to her sister, China, containing perfumes, huge bottle powders, lotions, body butter, soap, body wash, and shimmers.

Giselle, "I'm promoting my line," China opens a bottle and smells it.

China, "oh yes, this is my stuff."

Giselle, "yes, I went to Jack's lab, and I gathered some leaves, flowers and liquefied them, and then made it."

China kisses her, "this smell so good."

Giselle sprays it all over herself and then, "my other stuff?" I "It's made just for your body chemistry, see if I put it on." She does, "see it does not scent," she lets China smell it.

China, "that's why I needed a cup of your bath water sample."

China, "you have discovered me; I love it."

She puts it all on again, "and all this shimmer, I'm going home to bathe again."

They both laugh.

China, "now hurry, they are coming, did you get your treasure repaired also?"

Giselle, "yes, it's like a virgin."

China, "that's what I'm talking about Mac did not know what hit him, he's going to have to go get a penile to fool with me."

They both burst out laughing.

Professor, "they are both so crazy."

China, "I think I want some girls."

Giselle, "go for it."

China, "I must get some."

Giselle, "no, they use fat from your body."

China, "My thighs, yes."

They gave each other high five again.

China, "them double Dutch girls and those legs and ass is fucking Challis's up, you got all that naturally and now improved, oh yell, Jabra did not have all that brick house, and he knows it and no matter what you improved, you already had all that, so know you are toe to toe with his ass, you are worth him."

Giselle, "yes I feel it, but since last year I have put back on 30lbs I don't know how."

China, "all in your behind and breast, you are still banging, keep his ass working, don't stop all your shit, because I want you to help me write a book or two and let me be in on fragrance building." Giselle, "partners, but look we will see, have your dad draw up the papers for fragrance."

They both get up and dance around and laugh and smile.

Giselle, "we are about to blow up."

Challis, "come here, damn I missed you."

He grabs her, picks her up, and kisses her again. Mac pushes the luggage cart.

China, "I am so glad to see you, where is your husband?" And hugs Professor.

Professor, "now you know those two fools are ice fishing, both are going to come back sick as a dog."

China, "that's right."

Challis who keeps kissing Giselle, "I missed you."

Giselle, "I missed you a lot also," as she looks at him face to face, "but it was important for me to do some things I have wanted to do and settle for myself."

Challis, "I never knew you had all this hair," he runs his fingers through it.

Giselle, "I always took care of my hair, I just hated the maintenance part of it, but now, it's really easy like this."

Challis, "I like it on you and all your natural highlights," he kisses her again.

Mac, "he wants her."

China, "I can clearly see."

Mac, "and I can too."

Professor, "Me as well."

Mac, "and they both look damn good together and happy love is an adjective, nobody can ever get too old to give that."

Professor, "Amen to that."

Challis, "It's almost Christmas, come on baby, let's marry tomorrow Christmas Eve, I love you," "I don't want to live another day without you."

Giselle, "I…" Challis cuts her off, "no words, right? We're getting married; you deserve a beautiful wedding like every other woman."

Giselle, "yes, I want."

Challis, "do you love me?" He twirls her around.

Giselle cries a bit, "definitely I love, and I've been in love with you for a very long time."

He kisses her, "let me see." What is that on your neck? She shows him her neck.

Challis, "I'll fuck him up."

Giselle lays her head on his shoulder and, "please, let's just leave."

Challis turns her around and puts his arm around her and, "definitely."

Some more hours go by. Professor and all of them are out to eat at a luxury restaurant. In the hotel, Challis put Giselle's engagement ring on her finger.

China, "let me see this."

Mac, "that looks like 10karats to me."

Challis, "something like that."

Giselle, "I can't wear this."

Challis, "yes you will all 12 karats of it."

All their mouths drop open.

Mac, "upgrade baby!"

China, "yes and I know this, but let me see again, that is so gorgeous."

Professor, "that color, butterscotch yellow is your favorite color."

China, "yes, it is, way to go, brother."

Challis, "I know my kitty boo boo baby."

China smiles, she thinks, 'well it's real.'

Mac, "let's toast to new beginnings."

They all toast with their first balled up in the air. Night falls, all the ladies are at the hotel; when there's a knock at the door.

CHAPTER 4

Unwelcomed Guest

China, "who is it?"

Bishop, "Me."

China, "What do you want? "Challis and Giselle are engaged."

Bishop, "I just wanted to see her and give her the gift I got for her before Christmas, I know it'll be the last time I will see her."

China, "that's not possible, Challis will not like that."

Bishop, "Fuck Challis."

China, "have you and Giselle been sexually active in a relationship?"

Bishop, "no fuck, that bitch lied to me, she told me to my face she was saving herself for God, and I see her, and she told me she and Challis made love and her…"

China, "okay, right then, no spilled milk, they are in love, move the fuck on, damn."

Bishop, "I am, I just want to give her the gift I got her and tell her something."

China goes grab her cell phone, "let me text her. Bishop, "Stay where you are."

Bishop is here, "I'll send Challis for you, text back."

As china is texting Giselle, Bishop leaves quickly and gets on the elevator.

Bishop sees Giselle, and pushes her back on the elevator, and yells, "text her back,

We are just going to take a ride."

Giselle, "look, we have nothing, no more violence. I'm in love."

Bishop cold cocks her and stops the elevator. He pulls in the service cart, takes a sheet off the other cart, puts it in the cart and some more sheets and towels and puts her inside, and puts the stuff over her.

Then he goes to the employee closet and puts on a serviceman's outfit, no one pays any attention, and he wheels her right through the kitchen through the service entrance into his SUV, Candy apple-red with Ohio plates.

China, "Ok, she texts ok."

Bishop, "I just dialed the cops and calling security, no answer." She looks out, peeps hole, no.

Bishop, "ok, she called the police, and let the hotel manager know."

Todd Winters, "I just a few minutes ago and saw her go up on the elevator."

China runs while on the phone screaming, "he has her, Professor is coming up."

She, "Lord, what's wrong?"

China is crying; pushes her back on the elevator, "Bishop, he has taken…" she cries again; she can't get it out, he has Giselle."

Cops arrive, China runs over to the cops, and Lt. Detective Baldwin, and his partner Detective Sergeant James.

Marine hotel manager comes over, "we have a monitoring room that covers the entire hotel."

Detective Baldwin, "show me." Baldwin says both detectives go with the hotel manager.

China just cries, "let me call my husband and Challis, come on, baby."

Mac, "hello my beautiful wife, I miss you."

China crying, "he took her."

Mac, "wait, took who?"

China, "Bishop took Giselle."

Mac, "Challis, Bishop took Giselle."

Challis, "What the f**** Where did they go?"

Mac, "where are you?"

China still crying, "at the hotel, the police are all here."

Mac, "baby stay where you are, we're in route."

They hang up "Mother fucker," Challis swore, he calls Tears." Hello."

Challis, "listen, Bishop has my Giselle."

Tears, "what do you want us to do?"

Challis, "place an advert on the streets, that there is a 1million dollar bounty on his head if they bring my Giselle and him alive."

Tears, "oh yell, listen up, Challis just offered 1 million dollars for Bishop's head alive and Giselle his wife, we got you."

They hang up.

Mac gets out and turns off the car, "here we go."

Challis, "video cameras," they both go into the camera room.

China runs to her husband, "he is in a Candy Red SUV with Ohio plates."

Challis goes ahead.

Mac, "baby," he kisses his wife, "stay here, I'm going."

China, "we're alright, to go!"

They both leave.

Challis, "let's stop by my place and pick up a few things."

They run on to Challis's Penn House, which is right down the street from their spot and the hotel. They grabbed out of a private room and Ozzy 2 and 357 magnums 2 and plenty of ammunition.

Both change into work boots and Navy combat fatigues and bounce. Challis is a Navy Seal, same with Mac.

They arrive in 10minutes. Challis owns several planes and choppers, and they get in the Cobra Chopper.

The cops and the city all have heard about the bounty on Bishop, they both take everything and get in. Mac pilots and within minutes on 71 they see the candy apple red SUV pulled to the side of the road.

Mac, "We can put down in that field and foot it."

Challis, "because this bitch is in these woods, he's going to his cousin, Comer's hideaway spot."

Thirty minutes go by, Bishop is carrying her while she is still knocked the fuck out.

Comer says to Bishop, "Nigga, why did you bring her here? Challis has offered a million on your head."

Bishop, "I just want to fuck her real good, and he can have her after I have had her."

Comer, "okay and mother fucker gets to it, so I can collect the money for rescuing her in there," as he points to a dingy bedroom with no sheet on the bed.

Bishop then takes her and throws her on the bed as he tries to wake her, he shakes her, but she is still out cold. He comes back and undresses her.

Comer and his cousin, Randy, show him the TV, "look on the TV, all the cops are closing in on you. Bishop runs back and starts to unzip his pants.

Challis to Mac, "there it is," they signal to each other, each one goes to each side of the house.

Challis runs up, looking in windows until then he sees his future wife knocked out, naked and straddled across the bed, and Bishop undressing.

Two Rottweiler dogs greet Mac, he shoots them with his gun that had a silencer, then he kicks in the back door. Randy and Comers are both sitting in the room, they both point to the master bedroom.

Challis goes in through another window, by now, Bishop is in a fucking zone, he is saying, "damn, you are beautiful." Just as he gets ready, with a soldier hard to penetrate Giselle, she wakes up and kicks him right hard in his privates.

He falls back and acts like he's in no pain and then he explodes and throws a lamp at her, it hits her on the head. Then he grabs her and grabs a long hunting knife and points it at her, "bitch move!" he said to her, he pushes her, "get down bitch on your knees."

Giselle screams and he smacks her, then he puts the knife to her throat. She still says no.

Challis bursts into the room at that minute, Bishop aka Clarence grabs her harder, holding the knife close to her throat.

He goes by the window, "I'll cut her limb to limb."

Mac hears what's going on; he goes back out of the back door and runs to the window.

Challis shoots Bishop right in his elbow, he screams, "mother fucking cunt!" He drops the knife.

Giselle runs to Challis, crying. He grabs her and wraps a blanket around her.

In seconds, the cops pulled in, with several guns out.

They entered, "put it down, Challis!"

Challis does as they command him. They arrest Bishop and his cousins. Mac runs back to the chopper, which was not too far away, and takes flight. Challis goes with Giselle to the hospital in the ambulance.

After a while, Challis calls Mac and China and the Professor. They arrived at the hospital, and then Doctor Curtis comes out, speaks to all of them, but more personally to Challis.

They had been Navy Seal buddies, he, Mac, and the doctor.

Doctor Curtis, "Giselle she is doing well, and her four fetuses are coming along a little distressed, but it's fine, they are just what our hospital needs, four Christmas bundles of joy."

Challis, "what are you talking about?"

Dr. Curtis, "oh I'm sorry, she is 24 weeks pregnant, she was very surprised herself and she has a concussion too."

China, "Jesus, Professor is praying."

Dr. Curtis, "and her right and left rotary cups is torn and her right and left biceps has a complete tear,"

China, "God, no more!"

Dr. Curtis, "you all can go see her in a few minutes; she needs to see you right now because, at midnight, we are preparing her for labor and delivery."

Challis, "What? Why?"

Dr. Curtis, "she has had a placenta abruption, where the babies have moved away from the wall of the uterus because of trauma. This is a severe medical risk."

Challis, "I want her moved to the Challis wing, Presidential floor."

Dr. Curtis, "I'll have her moved immediately."

Challis, "and all her care is covered under me."

Dr. Curtis looks over at the entry desk, he saw no one, "give your information to the medical clerk at the entry desk when one of them returns."

Challis, "okay."

Dr. Curtis leaves.

Detective Baldwin, "Doc, I know it's Christmas Eve, but we need a paternity test, in case Bishop says they are his."

Dr. Curtis, "Excuse me, Challis, I have to swab you for a paternity test, for the police."

Challis, "Okay then."

Detective, "Okay, we need to speak to her, is she awake?"

Dr. Curtis, "In 3 minutes."

Mac, "You want me to run grab you anything?"

Challis, "No, but thanks. Let me call Morgan," he gets out his cell phone and dials.

Challis, "Hello, I'm at the hospital downtown."

Morgan, "Okay, I'm right down the street, I can grab you a few things."

Challis, "Okay, get the red Ralph Lauren double bag it has everything packed in it already, I'll be up at the Challis wing, Presidential floor."

Dr. Curtis, "Giselle, the police are here, and I need to swab you," She opens as much as she can, and then he leaves.

Detective Baldwin, "now please tell us what happened."

Mac, "We're crashing here too."

Challis, "24-hour cafeteria."

Dr. Curtis and nurse Tamia come back with the documentation of the results and give it to Challis. He opens it and reads it.

"Yes."

China snatches it from him, "Let me see, "she goes through it and reads out loud, "oh yes, 99.9, you're the father!"

Challis, "Yes."

Mac, "Well, congratulations."

Challis, "I'm going to be about my wife and our children's business."

China, "Both of you need some kids." They all go to eat except Challis, who goes to sit with Giselle.

Mac, "Bae, remember what I told you?"

China, "What?"

Mac, "Teresa and Jabra."

China, "Oh yeah."

Mac, "He did not like any of that shit for his birthday, but he went along with it, he did not like how much his wife was into it all, then she suddenly got serious cancer, this is an incredible day, excuse me, babe."

China, "Okay."

He goes to the restroom, and as he comes out, he sees something, but he doesn't know what.

Mac went to his wife, "bae I'm going to pack us some stuff because we are going to be here as well."

Professor, "Me too."

Mac leaves, he walks down the street to their Penthouse.

Right under the lights he dodges behind a building and pulls out his camera, and then he realizes that he needs to get closer, he does so, as

SEASONS OF LIFE AND THE ALTAR CALL OF CHRIST

many people walked by, he drops in front of a parked car and holds out his phone.

He is standing behind a car, close enough to Jabra and some woman.

Nedra, "Let's get in and out because of my baby Teresa, she will land tomorrow morning and I want to have all the cash ready by 5 pm, which is the time we are supposed to leave and give it to her."

Tonya, "The bank does not open till morning; we can't get any more out tonight," the lady with her.

Jebra, "Let's go before someone sees me," she puts her cap down, "people know me."

Meanwhile, Mac has been taking pictures all along, picture after picture; he had moved closer and had been recording them both all along.

He checks his recording and pictures that he got. He waits till they dry off and then he gets up and runs home. He packs two bags for himself and his wife and runs back to the hospital, and as soon as he gets there, he shows his wife the pictures.

China, "Yes, that is her and her cousin, what's her name… Tonya."

Mac, "I just sent you this stuff, let me tell my brother, I have to show him his wife."

He leaves, he reaches the hospital's 7th floor, and he calls Challis. They both go sit down.

Mac, "I got this today, but I have to show it to you," he plays the recorder. Challis watches and listens, and he is extremely pissed.

Mac, "What do you want to do?"

Challis, "Just what I'm doing, I felt this, but now I see it clearly, text all the clips to me."

Mac does that.

Challis, "And all is good, I love my kitty booboo, I gave her the fucking world, and she plays me for 100 million to lie up with her and her dyke bitch, thanks," he fumed, "let me send this to the correct authorities, here let me see."

He hash-tags it and sends it to the fraud unit, FBI, CIA, AND the LOCAL POLICE AUTHORITIES, HE then LOCATES PICTURE OF TERESA'S ASS AND WRITES LETTER EXPLAINING what happened AND SENDS IT all out to every news circuit.

He then sends pictures to the fraud unit, Dover Insurance, that settled the case, and then he sent it over 50 states and countries and uploaded it on Facebook, Twitter, and Instagram.

Mac, "I am not mad at you, God knew, Giselle she's loyal."

Challis, "I heard her, he had a knife to her throat, she still kept on saying no, that's going to be my wife."

Challis, "I am good, Jabra was never happy because we had no children, I told you I thought something was up with me, it turns out nothing was wrong with me, went getting all tested and shit with Jabra, no I don't want to know, anyway I'll be a father with the woman I love."

Mac, "Yeah, I'm happy for you, man. "They fist bump and hug each other.

Challis and Mac rode the escalator down to one officer.

Challis, "Will it be a visible protection?"

The cops, "Oh yes, on your floor and overnight."

Challis, "Thanks, I want to pay private duty cops round the clock after your regular shifts are over."

The cop, "I'm Dan Rather, and I will put the word out," they shake hands.

Dr. Curtis comes out, "we have to take them now."

Challis, "Can I go in?"

Dr. Curtis, "Yes, but she will not be awake during the cesarean, and Dr. Shaunae will do the delivery."

Challis, "Is she good?"

Dr. Curtis, "The best in her field."

Time goes by; his people are all up in the baby room that overshadows the surgery room. Challis is in scrubs, and there is no cesarean because Giselle opted for natural instead.

So, they induced her labor, and they reached eight and they then said, "push."

Giselle is in tremendous pain but did as best as she could. Challis was too shocked. Mac filmed it all.

Giselle pushed again.

Dr. Shanae, "Come on, our Christmas babies, yes, okay, push one more time, I can see his head."

They pull him out and Challis kisses Giselle, "you are doing well."

He squats down to see his first son born. Challis gives Mac and everyone in the room thumbs up.

Challis, "Damn son, you're huge and tall."

Dr. Shanae, "Yes he is." The nurses grab him and tag him, 'baby A.'

Then the nurses clean him all up, "will you cut the umbilical cord?" they asked him.

Challis, "Yes," Challis replied, he goes takes the shears and cuts them.

Mac, "He is tall and hefty."

China, "Yes he is and so beautiful," she cries.

Then baby boy B came straight out, no push.

Challis, "I am your dad, and you all are my huge, tall, lookalike babies, thank you."

Giselle, "Let me see them, please."

The nurse brings them over and Giselle kisses them and cries and then the babies both screams.

Dr. Shanae, "Okay now baby girl push."

Giselle does so.

Challis, "Come on baby," she pushes again.

Dr. Shanae, "Stop, wait, let me see," as she looks on the screen, "they are holding hands and the umbilical cord is wrapped around both their necks."

Giselle prays immediately. Challis said a prayer also, then he goes up to her, "we're alright, God has brought us this far."

China, "What's wrong? What's wrong?"

Professor, "Looks like they may be twisted up."

They all just pray.

Dr. Shaunae puts her hand up Giselle and slowly turns the girls then she eases them both out. China screams.

China, "Look, they are so beautiful, all that hair!"

Giselle, "Are they alright?"

Dr. Shanae, "Just calm down," she brings them both out, and then she slowly unwraps them.

Challis, "Girls, my daughters, our baby girls, we got them all girls and boys, baby I am so ecstatic." Dr. Shanae, "Four healthy Christmas Day births, mom and dad."

Challis, "That's alright, thank you, God."

Mac, "They have to be girls."

China, "Yes, all that hair, and damn the 2 ham hocks."

Dr. Shanae, "Dad, you want to cut the Umbilical cord?"

Challis, "Yes," he goes and the nurses clean both baby girls, then dad cuts baby C and Baby D.

Dr. Shanae, "Okay, 14 lbs. 2oz boys and 5 lbs. 2oz girls."

Challis, "Huge daddy's little tiny boo boos."

One of the nurses, "Dad, we have to seal up mommy."

Challis kisses her, "You are the best and thank you and I love us."

Giselle, "I love us also and I thank you Lord so much."

Dr. Shanne, "Hi mommy, I can tuck your tummy back in and vagina, I can see you had work."

Challis leaves the room.

Giselle, "Please!"

And within 45 minutes she's all done and sent to the ICU. In the waiting room, Challis comes out, followed by Mac.

Mac, "How big are my nephews?"

Challis, "14lbs each 2ozes."

China, "I cannot believe that she did not know."

Professor, "I did the exact same thing with Steven, I had him at 24 weeks."

China, "I knew with our boys, I was sick."

Professor, "First time nothing."

China, "I cannot believe that we have babies."

Challis, "Where are they?"

The nurses bring them out, they are all bathed, and all babies are in incubators.

Challis, "Why do they have them on all those, and in that stuff?"

China, "They are premature."

Challis, "They are absolutely beautiful."

China, "Call your parents, your family!"

Challis, "I will, I'm just so stoked, this is more than I ever dreamed I would have."

Mac pats him on the back, "beautiful man, simply beautiful, you're a dad."

The nurse, "Dad, you can change, come in."

Challis looks at his kids, and he names them, "you came out first, Challis II, you are my big healthy son, I am so proud to be your dad."

"Now unto you, Caviar, my huge healthy son, he goes to his daughters and daughters; yes, brown, blue and gray eyes like mommy, his daddy's boo boo's, I love you both so much. He gets choked up, long hair down your backs and both your hair color is a sandy brown and black mix, Solace and Solae a, okay sleep."

Time goes by, Challis has contacted his parents and they have contacted all his siblings and they are all in a flight.

Mac, "It's about to be like the circus."

He and Challis gives each other high fives, handshakes and hug.

Challis, "And you know it."

Mac, "So what are we calling them?"

Challis, "Challis the II and Caviar."

China, "Oh yes, after Giselle's dad."

Challis, "And our baby girls, Solace and Solae a."

China, "I like that."

Then Challis goes into Giselle's room. She is out of ICU. He gets into bed with her, she is still sleeping, and she wakes up, "Hi."

Challis, "I love you so much, and nothing but the best," he kisses her.

Giselle, "I have… We have nothing, I did not know, and they need…"

Challis, "No worries, they will have more than enough."

Giselle, "But they need their own covers and stuff now and what oh so much, I don't know their names."

Giselle, "Challis the II and Caviar," smiles to her dad.

Dad likes that, and it makes her really cry while Challis consoles her.

Giselle, "She loves that," and cries, Challis hugged her she keeps crying.

Giselle, "This has been the hardest day ever but a blessed day also, I'm a mother. How awesome is that wow!"

Challis, "The best we are here, we are going to be amazing parents."

He kisses her again, "We are going to be husband and wife," as they both fall to sleep.

Mac, "Let's eat!"

China, "My mom texted me she is at the hotel."

Mac went to tell Challis. He goes in and tells him they're going to get bae's mom to eat.

Mac, "You want anything?"

Challis, "No but ok, how are my kids?"

Mac, "They're fine."

The nurses are in with them and told him they'll be back though staying the night. Challis signals ok, peace captain. Mac goes, night falls and morning comes. The floor is busy. Mac and his wife shower together, then

SEASONS OF LIFE AND THE ALTAR CALL OF CHRIST

China comes in and assists Giselle to bathe, while Challis goes and sees his kids and the nurse said they are not taking their milk.

Dr. Shaunae, "Mommy said she is going to breastfeed all of you babies."

Challis, "Definitely, I like that, it's better milk."

Dr. Shaunae, "Yes and it heightens their cognitive skills that's why they're all moving and looking around like they are full term."

Challis, "Yes!" As he smiles.

Dr. Shaunae, "Ok, mom needs to breast pump some bottles."

Nurse Jackie, "Ok, I'm on it, I will get the breast pump and I'll do as many as she can."

Mac, "What is she's going to breastfeed?"

Challis, "Yes."

Mac, "That's what's up."

Challis, "Please, I just want us to have a healthy marriage. Our home, yes we've got to get us a new huge house but for now, our Pent will have to do."

China, "Can I feed my nieces and nephews, doctor?"

Dr. Shaunae, "For now they all have to go with mom for feeding because they are all proper themselves and won't take any of our milk or bottles."

China looks right at Challis and rows her eyes, Challis hugs China, "Thanks and how else could they be."

A day goes by, and all his parents have come and all his brothers are Staying in the Presidential wing floor and busy but unknown to all, word has reached Jabra and Teresa has come in disguise to the hospital because an announcement was made and all the pictures of the babies of Challis and Giselle were seen.

Jabra, "Bae I love us, let's just go, we have ½ the money."

Teresa, "No, we're going to that hospital and hold that black bastards for ransom, whatever you want us to do I'm on board, Teresa my cousin is in their unit, and during the shift change we will snatch and put four babies that resemble them and let's do this," she hugs her wife Teresa.

Challis stuff came and he signs.

Mac, "What is that?"

Challis, "Our kid's bling, can you put this on our sons and these on our daughters?" "Doctor, I want our daughter's ears pierced."

Dr. Shaunae, "ok."

Challis, "Yes please."

Dr. Shaunae, "I will do that now and I can pierce, and let's do footprints and birth certificates."

Time goes and after 3 hours all their kids are jeweled up both boys with rings on and gold name tags, necklaces with their names on them and their daughters have on gold diamond necklace and diamond bracelets, gold bangles, and an ankle bracelet with their names on it. Just his daughters' tiny size. Giselle loves, bite, and kisses each of her babies.

Challis, "Look, our sons have my birthmark, see," he shows her black on his ankle, "our girls have this heart on their back just like you."

Giselle kisses him, "You noticed."

Giselle, "Yes, and all their jewelry pieces have GPS trackers."

Giselle, "They don't need that."

Challis, "They do and here I got you," he puts on her a beautiful white gold diamond choker cross necklace.

CHAPTER 5

The Switch

After taking several pictures of their children and then they all fall to sleep, night falls and they all go to their hotels. During the shift change, no one noticed that Teresa had help swap the babies. Not realizing, another hour or two goes by and they are in the wind with their babies, no pays attention because they are all sleeping. Around 4 am, the nurse brings in all the feeding babies, Giselle gets ready and takes her boy but he's not as big.

Giselle, "Wait, these are not our children."

Challis, "What?" he stirs, gets up, and looks, "no, these are not our babies."

The nurse "They are."

Challis runs and looks in the nursery.

Mayor Jamison Samian Calms-way Senior, "son what's wrong?"

Challis, "It's hysterical."

Mac, "What's wrong?"

Challis, "They got our children."

Mac, "What the f****, no."

Dr. Ombre comes in, "I just came on duty, and the nurses informed me just now that you say these are not the Calms-way children."

Challis said, "No, look our babies are not in here, look! Our daughters have sandy brown, auburn hair, blue-gray, green-brown eyes, our sons' deep-set gray-brown eyes, all our kids have dimples and our sons are way bigger and taller, they also have birthmarks like mines on both their right ankles". He pulls his right pants leg up, so they can see and shows the pictures he took of all their children.

Dr. Ombre, "I can see."

Challis, "I have more pictures, our daughters both have heart shape birthmarks like Giselle's." Here", he shows them.

Dr. Ombre makes the call code amber and they lock the hospital down.

Challis' mom, "Senator Solace Birdie Calms-way, "baby it's going to be alright."

Challis hugs and kissed her, "They need their milk, they are premature."

Mayor Jamison Samian, Calms-way's dad, "Who would do this right under our noses."

Challis, "It's Jabra."

His dad, "What, she's dead."

Challis told Mac to show them and he shows from his cell phone.

Jamison III, "FBI just says the word we're here."

His other brother Mike who is with the CIA, "What do you want to do?

Challis, "It's got to be a warrant already established for them."

Mike, "No when did you discover she was still alive?"

Challis, "Yesterday."

Jamison III, "I'm going to make a couple of calls she can't be too far."

Detective Baldwin comes and Detective Smoothers goes and talks to all the staff.

Detective Baldwin, "Did you see Jabra your wife?"

He said no but Mac recorded her earlier and he shows the recording to the detective and the pictures.

Detective sends all to his phone, "Ok, come let's look at the hospital's camera footage."

Mike, "I'm coming."

His FBI brother Jamison, "Where is the hospital feed?"

Detective Baldwin, "I remember you, Santana Fields."

Jamison, "Yeah."

Donald Detective, "Come on, we may need the FBI on this."

Jamison, "I've already called; they are in route."

These babies are our family, he pats his younger brother Challis on the back, Challis just nodes his head, his dad Mayor Jamison follows and Mac as well.

China wakes up, "What's going on?"

Mac told her their babies have been kidnapped and China runs to the nursery, Mac her hubby follows, she screams and cries, "OMG!"

Mac asked her to calm down, he hugs her, "They're going to be alright, go be with Giselle."

China runs; his mom walks, and Senator Birdie follow her, they all reach the camera room and the police are already on their fast track.

Challis, "Right there, see I know Jabra anywhere."

Detective Baldwin looks at his watch, "They have 2 hours on them."

Mike makes a call to lock down, Detective Baldwin goes in and he sees his superior, chief Jamison contacted CIA to lock down water, the air and buses. Jabra hid out with her bae Teresa at her cousin nurse from the hospital Bunny damn they already got the amber alert lockdown, and, on the news, they are searching everything, water, air, ground.

Teresa, "Shit burner, let's make the call cause if this jealous mother fucker doesn't bite to black baby market we'll go."

Chancellor Bunny's husband told them they're cops everywhere.

Teresa, "Nothing."

Chancellor, "you all went and did it, now we got to live here, baby."

Bunny, "they are leaving as soon as their ride gets here."

Teresa goes into the bedroom, comes back out and Jabra, "bae come," they came together, she gets up.

Chancellor, "Challis just offered 5 million bounties on your head, come on baby let's go to my mother's. We can walk; we are not built for this shit."

They locked up and bounced. FBI has arrived and set up shop to trace calls through Challis phone. Jabra called him, "hello."

Challis, "I don't have a fucking thing to say to you but where the fuck is our kids?"

Jabra, "we want 50 million dollars wired to an offshore account 54278911 or your children die." Challis, "Jabra I'm telling you just like this that there is nowhere you or that bitch can go if you harm one or shred on our babies' heads."

Teresa, "fuck him and his ugly ass babies, you got 1 hour to make the transaction or else."

They hang up and he asked the FBI if they got it and FBI Saunders said it's not long enough.

Challis, "wait, the jewelry they all have on has GPS."

FBI Saunders, "we can track that."

He goes to their set up equipment and in seconds, "ok they are staying at 1110 Park Avenue." Other FBI guy Bose said they just ordered pizza and a gallon of milk, Mike in CIA tracked the call and FBI.

Bose, "now you know who did, ok let's hit it."

Challis, "I'm coming, the money wire."

Mike, "They're going in and they will get them, they will not know what hit them, let us do our job."

Giselle was fully dressed, and China came out.

Giselle, "I'm going."

Doctor Ombre, "I'm your doctor, you're running a high temperature and your blood pressure is high, no."

Challis comes to her, he hugs her, "I'm so sorry, I promise you I will bring our children back healthy and fine."

Giselle, "this is not."

Challis, "listen to me, I promise I will bring them back!"

Professor, "come on child, let them go, there's nothing you can do."

Challis goes, they all shuffle into different cars and they stop at the Pizza joint.

The manager, "I just told them their veggie pizza was in route."

FBI Palmer, "he's going in and will need t-shirt and pants and asks the pizza guy, what size of shoe do you wear?"

Pizza guy, "it's 12."

Palmer, "It's his size, give them."

He is dressed in a hat on, he gets in the Pizza delivery car.

Jabra, "damn they are too cute, their hair reaches down their backs."

Teresa called her bitch and asked what she wants, and she held Challis. She smacks Jabra hard, "no don't!"

Teresa, "I'm sorry, but damn, I'm hungry, shower, we're going to be in here for a couple of days, we just buzz this mother fucker in, where is the money?"

Jabra, "Here, 30 with the milk."

She left and the cops and FBI reach the spot.

FBI Palmer, "he'll go in first so they should all get in position."

FBI Palmer buzzed and Teresa responded, and asked him to come on up to the condo. He hopes on the elevator and acts like he is on his cell.

Teresa opens the door to Palmer the Pizza guy, "$30, add the tax of 54 cents."

Teresa, "damn $30.54 shit!"

The Pizza guy, "how many times I got to tell you."

Teresa, "come here; fuck you people."

Palmer gives her the Pizza, she takes it, and then he bum rushes her with his gun.

Teresa, "I'm down, shit, fuck."

The gun was to her head and masses of FBI rushed in. They secure all the babies and they find Jabra showering. The cops toss her a robe, and they arrest her, Challis runs in,

FBI Palmer, "they're all sleeping."

Challis, "God, thank you!" He wraps each of them up.

Dr. Shaunae comes in with some hospital blankets, and stroller, "we will check each one of them out at the hospital."

Challis picks up all, puts their sons in the stroller, tucks them, then doctor picks up their girls and they both scream and cry.

Challis, "come, daddy got you all." He takes them and they stop crying, both look at their dad but sniffle.

Dr. Shaunae, "daddy's girls and all say definitely except the two stupid kidnappers."

Mike, "Hi, aren't you both so gorgeous?"

His bro Jamison III, "too cute looking all around, our mama is going to, I love you two."

Detective Baldwin, "No girls!"

Mike, "all boys, our mom is going to lose it."

Jabra has her head down as she speaks, I'm really sorry."

Challis, "I know, may God have mercy on your soul," and he leaves with his children.

They all arrive back at the hospital.

Challis, "no more nurseries for daddy's babies. We are moving into mommy and daddy's suite."

Dr. Shaunae, "fine, we will accommodate."

Giselle is still crying and just praying.

China, "Hi, look, here is your boo boo's mommy."

Giselle sits up and says out loud, "thank you God!"

Then Challis gives her their daughters, and she kisses them both right on the lips and looks all at them closely.

Challis, "Hi, my Bunkie Bunkie's."

China all up on the bed, "They know you, look they are all smiling."

Giselle said, "I hope so" and China gets ready to take them, they start crying, she puts them back down and they're quiet now." Challis picks them up and they just smile.

China, "what am I supposed to do, I'm your two's second mommy, you two beauties have to like me." Challis, "chill, they will, they have been through a lot."

His mom, "Birdie, let me see please, my beautiful granddaughters, He gives one of them to her." Challis, "that's our baby girl," his mom said, "oh yes, after me your Sugar, yes, she is smiling, and she likes you."

His moms, "oh my God, move home please!"

Giselle, "where is home?"

Challis, "Virginia, after all of this that sounds more and more like home, I'm a mom now, I don't want to raise my kids here."

China, "damn you're right, wherever you go we are coming."

Mac, "Ok, honey yes."

His mom Birdie walking with Solace, "they say it takes a village to raise these kids," she sits and rocks, "give me!"

Challis hands her, "this is Solace, oh yes! I like Solace yes, I'm about to retire, I want to be a Sugar at home yes, I do help take care of my granddaughter's, and woo you both smells, so good."

China, "their mommy keeps her smelling good."

His mom, "what is that wonderful smell?"

Giselle, "it's just light scented oil."

His mom, "Little crystals, nice sugar."

She just rocks them, closes her eyes and hums a gentle song from the gut of her soul to them she uses to sing to her own children and other grandchildren and Challis.

Giselle, "give me Caviar!" Challis does.

China, "they are both so heavy."

Giselle, "hi, wake up, he is just sleeping," she kisses him and lays him in her bed.

Challis gives her Challis the II he was straight awake.

China, "look at him, his eyes beautiful, he all strong looking."

His mom, "look at their hands, they're going to be big and tall just like their daddy."

His dad comes in Ex-2 term Mayor Jamison Samian Senior Calmsway, "hello, that's what I'm talking about."

He acts out, hut one hut two and Challis the II smiles and his dad, "they know whose they are, just look at him so alert and his hands and feet."

Challis gives his son to his dad, he takes him, "oh yeah, look at you all, strong looking, all this hair with light gray green-brown eyes, man just look at your legs, keep your fist balled up because in this world your momma kidnapped yesterday, today you all kidnapped."

His mom, "Lord, Lord! Get me my oil Mike, because the devil is busy!"

Mike goes in his mother's bag and hands the oil to her and she gets busy with it.

Giselle, "it's a lot, and she cries a bit."

Challis, "but we made it, we're all here baby."

His mother, "yes you all are. Giselle, now I know where I know you from, your mother Solae a décor."

Giselle, "yes ma'am."

His mom, "you look just like her, wow it's been a mighty long time, all these years and you and my son. God is so good."

Giselle, "Amen!"

Sugar, "she was making all of my suites, my dresses, formals last, all that good apparel I still have, it looks just like new."

Giselle Birdy flies over San Rodda Dee.

His mom, "yes she really did keep me together, you know why she uses to call me that all the time?" Giselle answered because you were always in a hurry flying in and flying out at the last minute.

His mom, "yes, I really miss your mother, she really cared about the essence of me not just my wardrobe, the quality, and she could really cook also the best food from scratch. Yes, that beautiful light fluffy biscuit bread. Lord I can just taste her fruit jelly's right now, she uses to just make me stuff all season long, clothes, wigs, everything, packs me up hot food straight from her table. I do fly in and get everything; she knew me and that is what's missing in shopping today. People just want to sell you anything and so many women wanted her to make stuff for them up on the Hill and she wouldn't, she would say don't send me anyone else because you are on the Hill is enough. I'm raising my daughter and I don't have time to think about all these people and she meant that too. I know you still sew and cook."

China, "that she does she everything to perfection."

Giselle smiles, "yes ma'am, I really love to cook and sew still also."

His mom, "yes you're a former principal dancer, author, movie creator, isn't you?"

Giselle, "yes ma'am and I think it provides an assured type of balance of one's self- worth, when you make efforts to intertwine one's belonging your- self as a craft."

Challis sits on the edge of the bed as a man with that creed.

His mom said, "it represents, it binds you to purpose, therefore I hope you will marry Challis." China, "of course, he proposed to you, where is your ring?"

Giselle, "she has it and China digs in her designer purse," and gives to his mom.

His mom, "very nice, this is gorgeous."

His dad asks him to take his daughters and his wife, "no, they are fine." She kicks off her shoes.

His dad, "I'm sorry," she tries on Giselle's ring, "oh yes, Giselle, you won't have your daughters often." She smiles at his dad.

His mom, "I don't care, I love all my grandkids, but boy, I need my granddaughters."

Dr. Shaunae knocks.

Giselle, "come in!" She comes in, "ok I got to check all babies and mommy."

Challis kisses Giselle and leaves. His dad follows, Mac as well.

His mom, "can I stay?"

China, "Me also!"

Dr. Shaunae, "yes if mommy does not mind."

Giselle, "they're fine."

His dad Mayor Jamison, "Son, Jabra."

Challis, "I buried her, she is dead. I have to speak to my attorney, I don't have time for this, enough is enough damn."

Challis, "his bro Mike is FBI, Mac. You're my lawyer, do I have to divorce her?"

Mac, "it's been years, but her crimes will resurface her back to life but her existence to you is null and void."

Challis, "I want to give her the wedding of her dreams."

His dad, "you need to have that down the road, we will all come and we will feel just like it's that day but to cover all your bases, you two need to marry right up in here," and Mac agrees.

Challis, "these filthy circumstances, all this stuff, I'm like damn 2 days shit I really want us to all pack the fuck up and bounce. Have a brand-new start; I don't like it here no more."

His dad said, "I know you both have a lot of stuff to settle."

Challis, "that's what he has staffed for."

His dad, "look come home and stay a year, build then go, you got premature children, your wife is to be is all jacked up, shit come home and breath, it's too damn quick here, slow that's what you want to raise your kids, you teach them quick not the world slow. You need her to be home."

Challis, "she is not Jabra running all around and doing not a damn thing but spending my money, she's different, very productive in many circuits and very well liked around the world and recently she's a 2-time New York best seller."

His dad, "she can write at home; good, the doctor is out. Come on sons, let's go!"

All follow and go in, Challis pulls the curtain back and huge open space couches huge plasma, he turns on low track and field is on and a full huge chef, kitchen and bedrooms.

Mac, "I forgot this room was all this big and had all this top of the line stuff."

They sit on the wrap-around couch suite side except for their dad and the women got in the recliner.

His mom just out the blue, "Giselle, what kind of house do you want?"

Giselle, "before I discovered I had children and a mommy of 4 in two days."

China, "right Giselle, I want us to have a home that is extremely productive." As she gets more under the covers,

His mom, "like how?"

Giselle, "I want to liquidate, it will take some time. I have been working on it, I hate to, but I have to, it's too much. It's hard.

CHAPTER 6

Too Much to Sort Out

My parents owned so many properties, so many office buildings, boat cargo business car, and truck dealerships, Grocery specialty stores still all going, strong free clinics across the world. I have not bothered with any of it till just a couple of months ago, but nothing in a sense has missed a beat to me."

China said, "your parents were the coolest business tycoons, I know, and they lived so humble and so modest."

Giselle, "thanks legacy, I will brand my parents' name and giving it to all chosen staff solely if they continue under my parents' name. I have dealt with most of the staff for years, which all are still quite active."

China, "Both of us."

Giselle, "I don't want to forget what my parents have instilled in me or built for me, but the task is extremely great, and I don't want to bother you now with downsizing my assets. Life is quick, I never thought my parents would be killed walking in the park as they have been for over 45 years after a sit-down family meal by a chased by the cops drunken driver, no one for days knew or cared where they were. The state declared them missing. Tell me it takes 48 hours. I started going in the wee hour of the night, I did not want anyone to sympathize with me, I went 2 am and 4 am night after night, and I walked the entire park for miles but nothing. I could not find them, I knew they were in there somewhere; I was looking through the bushes, yet nothing. I questioned God, I told him why he had forsaken my parents and me when my parents have served him all their lives. I told my God that he had destitute me, he had stripped me of my identity."

A tear rolls down her face.

China, "you have me and you are a consistent thriving forever millionaire."

Giselle asked her to stop. She continues, "it means nothing, you don't understand what I'm talking about. Listen to me, my parents are dead and they're never coming back. It has always been 3 of us against the world."

China, "yes I do, where?"

Giselle, "I discovered that both of my parents were knocked down in the biggest part of the ravine that stretched for quite ways around where the marigolds were at their best showing. I only noticed because I screamed to God where they are. I dropped to my knees and as I arose, I notice the park light glistened off my mother's wedding ring. I ran over and there they were, I could tell my father had rolled my mother over with everything. I believe he had my mommy on top of him because my mother's clothing had been torn; it exposed her when I found them. My father had buttoned my mother up inside with him, their blood drenched trench. I only unbutton it so I could see if they may have still been alive."

China, "I'm so sorry Butter, but still I do not know why you waited so long to tell me."

Giselle, "just couldn't take another."

China interrupts her, "what? I would have helped you."

Giselle, "she could not be of help to her because she knows nothing about it."

China, "I love you though I loved your parents."

Giselle said, "right, you loved my parents."

China, "Yes and you."

Giselle, "I know but that's one thing though: they were my very own parents, mine!"

She cries and China joins her and cries too.

China, "I was calling you calling you every day, never did you call me or say anything."

Giselle, "what was I going to say? That I'm sorry? That I can't bring myself to get out of the bed? Or that I keep asking God to let me stay asleep forever?"

China gets up and hugs Giselle, "I'm always here for you, I'm so sorry Butter."

Giselle hugs her, "I know."

China wipes her eyes, "I know you and your parents were very private."

Giselle, "yes, I had to get up though on my own because God just kept shining his light no matter how many sheets were put over the curtains and blinds, the Lords breath of life still steadily shinned through I kept hearing over and over, my God saying to me, they are not descent and in order over and over he would not allow me to sleep, no choice, I was so tired and just exhausted but regardless I had to get up because I knew deep down that I had to make sure for my parents sake and for my Savior that my parents were descent and in order."

China, "why was Tonya calling me and talking about you tearing her up? I could not understand her; I tried to call her back."

Giselle, "because I tore up her Forensic Laboratory."

China, "Why?"

Giselle, "because she had my mother on display with her dress up and she had all these internship students viewing my mother's autopsy because she had no consent to, I did not give her consent I told her interns to turn around so I could pull my mother's dress down and they did and I was trying but it was stuck and I had to end up." She cries and continues, covering my mother, my poor mother," she cries more and more, sniffs and grabs a tissue, "up with my coat because when I hugged my mommy, my precious mommy, she was so cold. I kissed and kissed, and I wrapped my arms around her, I rocked her, she was so light. I just could not get her

SEASONS OF LIFE AND THE ALTAR CALL OF CHRIST

warm. I told Tonya to turn the heat and Tonya said she can't and it won't come down because it's stuck to her skin and I asked her where my father was and who put my mother's dress up again like that and she said I don't understand and she could not tell me, she said it was confidential and I told her I was not leaving till I took both of my parent's home where they rightfully belonged. I ask her why she didn't keep them together, I told her they were always together she said she couldn't. I told her to give me my father's and mother's files, then the police came in and I told them I was taking my parents with me. I saw the drawers, and I started looking in each one and in the last one there lay my father exposed. I told her she was going to bust hell wide open, grabbed a sheet and she kept playing all this really loud music and I told her to turn that damn music down and she said it wasn't loud but it was so loud. I tried to see where it was coming from, I kept telling her they weren't descent and order why didn't she have them descent and in order, and that I was just going to take them where they belonged in the first place. I almost had got my dad onto the cart with my mom and the police stopped me. I told them that I was not causing any trouble and please turn around don't look at my parents. I told them someone had left my mother's dress up and that I just came to take my parent's home and they said they can't let me and that they had to stay and that they were going to quietly walk me out and I told them I couldn't leave my parents. I told them I promised my father and please I was just trying to leave with them, and they would not let me Commissioner Galvin came in and he had them put me in, holding under observation."

China, "What! Were you incarcerated?"

Giselle, "yes."

China, "How long?"

Giselle, "4 days, it was so peaceful."

China, "why, what did you do in there and the prisoners?"

Giselle, "they were all really the best, all so nice. I knew mostly everybody, and they were so gracious. I told them to please help me that I just wanted to sleep so the guards let them put together for me 2 twin steel beds with 2 extra mattresses with one big sheet, with lots of cover pillows and it was so comforting and I just slept and slept."

China, "In there?"

Giselle, "yes, it was so tranquil. Just what I needed and I thanked God for always taking care of me and my parents, then I went to court and Judge Dover let me out on probation, he said as long as I stay away from the county Forensic Facility and pay for all the damages and check in with him at court every-day for 10 days then the rest of my sentence would be time served. I asked him if he found out who left my mom's dress up and my father exposed and was my mom's dress still up and was my dad covered, he said he was sorry, but he did not know. I asked if I can take my parent's home please together and now but he said no and I said it won't be possible for me to meet his requirements because descent and in order is still not in play, he said if I want to go back to jail and I told him fine and he asked me why and I said, because I have shamed my parents and brought disrespect to my father's name and he ask me how? I said that I promised my father since I was a little girl that if he was not able I would always make sure that my mother was always taken care of and always present her myself as a living sacrifice to God's creed as to stand for what is always descent and in order. He said he was sorry about that but a restraining order has been filed and that I was to never go there again and I asked him, could I just start over and pay for my parent's to go home? and I would pay extra for every-thing I've done and he said no and asked, but are you able to sleep now? I said yes just in prison, but I can't at home. I told him I just can't go home without them; he said if you can't sleep, he assigned me to stay with his wife and mother for 10 days on their ranch."

China, "were they nice?"

Giselle, "yes, they were very spiritual, the best on their ranch. They have a creek out back and it sits opposite an open range and at 3a.m, as so many beautiful horses roam, they would wake me up to ride a mile or two and then as God's morning breath came in, we would cook breakfast outdoors on open fires and just sit and eat along the water and pray and talk about God and just watch the open range of horses run and God come in."

China, "they didn't have a kitchen?"

Giselle, "of course they did, and it was beautiful, Judge Dover told me time serve, he expunged my record though when I was released. When I got home, I went over to Tonya's house, she told me the best she could do is if I wanted them cremated she could do that and she would drop their ashes by my house, I told her ok then I went to the police station and I apologized to Lieutenant Jack, Sergeant Kenneth, Detective Rhonda, and Captain Phillips, they said all was squashed if I could just make them each a loaf of my mommy's biscuit bread and fruit jelly one day, I told them one day but not right now because my heart was just not in it and they all hug me and said it's cool then I went to the park same day and people were just going on like normal, still dogs pissing all over the marigolds."

China, "your mom loved marigolds."

Giselle, "Yes where her parents died."

China, "that people are so inconsiderate."

Giselle, "yes, because people were talking and complaining about how their children and pets would get in the flowers and get blood on them and it was my parent's blood. I went to the police, they had it all taped off, but they said they were still gathering evidence. They said evidence had seeped deep down to the core of the ground and it was going to take them a minute to gather it all up."

China said, "they're so trifling."

Giselle continued, "yes, so I went the next night when no one was in the park and I shoveled up all the evidence till it was a deep hole, I covered cart after cart of everything the dirt, flowers and grass and I boxed it all. I made all these satin bows for each and I had it all Fed Ex to the Columbus Ohio Police Forensic Department. They charged me with tampering with evidence and arrested me again; put me in prison a couple more days. It was fine, I just slept and when I went to court I asked Judge Dover if he would he like it if people kept trampling day after day through his dead parents blood where they took their last breath, I told him I wanted to buy the park and he asked me to elaborate. I told him I wanted to level it and cement the entire park, he said explain more and I told him it amazes me that my parents were a vital aspect of Columbus Ohio's society and I feel like if the city can't stop, that the park can. I told him people saw the tape off area and they just kept going on, their kids dogs pissing in the marigolds just like it was nothing, he told me that people have to keep living and though he offered his condolences but he suggest that I settle and leave Ohio for a while. I agreed and they dropped the charges, I went that night at 2 am and Judge Dover, his wife, sons and several cops came also by the park. I don't know why they were up in the area that late, I understood the cops but then I had brought all this stuff to restore the flower bed. Judge Dover said he should have the cops arrest me, but he thought I needed some help and he had his sons and the cops cement the area and they name the park and that area after my parents."

China said, "aww, lonely you," she gets up and hugs her, "dear sister, you know me, Mac and my boys would have helped you."

Giselle, "I know."

China, "No."

Giselle, "where is professor?"

Mac told her she took a cab to the hotel so she would be there to meet his mother in-law.

China, "Lord yes," she lays back down in the bed with Giselle and asks, "what are you going to do now with all your parents businesses you own, in abroad and in all the United States of America." Giselle, "I'm giving every- thing away over to my parent's faithful employees except two of the fabric factory's and the home builders. I informed them we hire felons now and teach them this trade." China, "that's nice but the other really for nothing, oh and how much did your parents leave you?" Giselle just shook her head, "my parents have left me over 95 billion in cash and 10 billion in CD's and my books have brought me in enough to leave our children a legacy."

China, "why free?"

Giselle, "because my parents would want it that way and my father always said **2 Timothy 2:15**[15] Do your best to present **yourself** to God as one **approved**, a worker who does not need to be ashamed and who correctly handles the word of truth. They have done that, and I already made up my mind." Giselle continued, "they can have everything except my mother's dress shop, I gave the house and the downtown corner dress shop to a lady named

Roma. I met her on the train, she was a seamstress, has twin daughters 5." Mac interrupts, "we left cards in a hat, with what we truly wanted."

Giselle, "yes and I got hers, her husband she said had been killed in the service and she said they were losing their home, she said she was a stay at home mom and she sewed and made a decent second income living but now that her husband was deceased she was going to have to get a job out of the home. I looked her up and I saw some of the blankets and shawls and wedding dresses she made, and I liked it. I bought quite a few and 5, I sent to you."

China, "they are gorgeous, I got them the other day."

Giselle, "she also loved how she was so attentive to her daughters and steadily teaching and correcting them. So, as they go, I had my parent's lawyer, Mr. Samuel, to locate her, and I had Judge Dover to investigate her, all was true. I signed our home over to her, I cleared out our home."

China asked, just like that? and Giselle said, "yes, I will never go back to Columbus, Ohio again. I gave out the majority of my parent's stuff and I had Mr. Bryant's paint and renovate the company and continue the upkeep for her. I also did a lot of updates". China said she was going to need furniture and Giselle said, "I gave her 50million dollars and $3 million trust, a piece for her daughters and when they turn 18, she gets 15 million more."

China, "For what?"

Giselle, "for whatever she wants."

His mom, "she can furnish her home with a fraction of that."

Giselle, "I just had her to sign also that if she ever chooses to leave, that she replenishes and play it forward for free."

China, "Why?"

Giselle, "because it's hers, they can live there the rest of their lives but surely there will be another woman that is in her same predicament."

His mom, "that's beautiful."

Giselle, "thank you but its God, the Lord told me to do it as so."

China, "I guess."

Giselle, "and I gave her both of my mother's new car, and her new show trucks and me and Gracie flew to India, Paris, Italy and Rome several days and I fully stock the dress shop and got Gracie major stuffs for the stores. I hired Gracie and Lynn, but I also gave her a 3 million and I bought Lynn a BMW and Gracie a Range Rover truck, 2 show transport trucks plus 10 million and I gave her 10 seamstresses. The condo's daddy owned, she lives in plus both their salary for the next 2 years and their salary to assist and Mr. Moraines will still do all of the upkeep on both still."

China said, "I do not know why Mr. Moraines with his millionaire self-does upkeep."

Giselle, "for one, he likes to help people, nothing wrong with that."

China, "I'm just saying, still she graduates Fashion College this year, right?"

Giselle, "it's a year plus, she gave her the show stores at both locations and the haul team and trucks."

China, "now I know she has some mad skills and nice pieces but how is she going to fill all that, it took you all years to do and create, how she is going to maintain that."

Giselle, "she will, all these years she has plenty of clothing, the entire get up full major masses of stuff in mommy's warehouse. She has really applied herself plus she won all her state and abroad competitions, she's legit, I went to all and I was very impressed plus you know she won Miss Teen and she designed all the stuff she wore to get her name out more."

China, "I saw Giselle and what do you think her and mommy were doing with her all these years, she has her entire line she'll do her first showing and commercials next year in the summer and fall and it's going to be spectacular for that lady also, and her daughter, yes."

Giselle smiles to herself and goes on talking, "her kids can go right down the street from their home and business right to elementary, middle school, I'm sure Roma and high school just like me and you after school amazing."

China, "my second mom was really the best," the thought touches her heart and a tear falls, she gently wipes it away, "the best."

Giselle, "Your mom, yes with her fly self."

China, "remember my mom camped out till your mom would dress us?"

Giselle, "yes."

China, "I was so embarrassed, we were just new friends in kindergarten."

Giselle, "yes."

China, "mommy came in there talking about the what, the what."

Giselle and China burst into laughter.

China, "your mom was like the color décor?" amidst laughter.

Giselle, "that was too funny,"

China, "she did not care, I was so embarrassed, she did not know a darn thing, thank God for The Madame Solae a Augustine Simonies."

Giselle, "yes," she cries a bit.

China gets up, grabs a brush and gets in the bed behind Giselle and brushes Giselle's hair up into braids, two long braids and wraps it, "remember what your mom was like with her Lebanese self she takes pins from her own hair and pins Giselle's hair up and then she takes it and swirls out, making her baby hairs to frame her face, then she says, "your mom, how do you want you all to look."

China, "just as she finished with the hair."

Giselle, "thanks."

China, "you know I love you, but my mom all up."

She goes to wash her hands.

China, "don't worry because it can't be about the money, shuffle talking about, make it rain all that money at your mom like she was a pole dancer."

They really laugh, "your mom was like, 'no, no, my daughter here, your daughter, no, she got the broom all sweeping the money out, saying you get out right now, you go, you never come back, I don't get down like that."

Georgianna, China's mom comes in, "Georgianna Debian in the house," she speaks, and then China and Giselle really laughed.

"Mommy we were just talking about when you made it rain on her mother," China said.

"Oh yeah, my sister, she was like, 'I don't get down like that and I always keep it descent and in order'."

They all really laugh. "your mama wanted no parts of me, thank God your daddy and Caviars started doing business together and you became best friends,"

Georgianna, "I wanted her to be my friend so bad, in church she comes in all sharp, you and her with her accent, I remembered your daddy and Caviar's had a deacon meeting after church, I was like, here is my second chance with your mother, I tried to run up to her but she was really quick, she was like, no, and I was like, please," she looks at the both of them, "I want to help you, but your behavior and demeanor detest me."

China was like, 'please Mrs. Simonies, please help my mom,' your mom was like, 'step back you're too close,' I stepped back, she was like, 'let me look at you,' she was so disgusted with me,' she was like with her accent for your Chi-Chi sake, only solely if you can check yourself at the door."

"I said that I will, your mom said, 'we must work on your demeanor next time and then recreate you not just your clothes,' she was like, 'we're going to breathe and simplify and upgrade your tone.'"

They all laughed.

Georgianna, "your mom, was something else, I just wanted me and my Chi Chi to look decent and in order."

China, "don't cry mommy," she gets up and hugs her mom.

Georgianna, "let me, where?"

China, "In there."

Georgianna, "your mother was so submissive to a tee but tough as nails, she told me you don't have to fight every battle, but you will win every battle if you listen to yourself and get in tuned with our Creator. My sister what a person, what a true woman of Gods very own breath," she sits, "I remember she came to our house after me my husband and Chi had eaten at your table so many times, I invited you all over when both your dads were over abroad on business, you come in, you took off your shoes, they always did that for respect and we showed you all over our house, then we sat down, and said grace. I gave you some box tuna noodle with some peas in it and a store salad, and a cake."

"Then your mother says, 'we will be going,' and I was like, 'what?' she got up and you followed, always so obedient, as you put on your shoes I said, 'I did all this,' your mother pulled out story beats and gave them to each of you, she said, 'I will finish what I have started with you,' and I said, 'okay, bougie,' she said, 'girls, go out on the porch for a second, Chi let me speak to your mother,' and you went out, she then asked, 'are your other children home?'

"I said, no our sons were with their father overseas and my other daughters are at my parent's,' she said, 'how did you get the only 2-million-dollar home on the entire block? And she stops, she went to get you and I said, 'no continue,' she said, 'you're a show, spending all your husband's money doing nothing of your own or for your daughters.'

"I said, 'what?' she said, 'you have no substance, and that means that your daughters are not going to have any, so I think it's best if you explain to your daughter that she cannot be friends anymore with my baby Butter.'

"I was like, 'oh excuse me, we take very good care of our children, my daughter is in everything that your daughter is in,' she said, 'you got all this dingy glass half done non waxed floors, and you think that you are doing something?

Rea, "I do not want to say but I am in this house and it smells."

I said, we live here, and she asked, "what do you do all day?"

I told her she's crossing the line now, "I had never heard her cuss, she said not a damn thing."

"you may get away with treating your husband and children like this but you will not disrespect me and my daughter and she said when I make it my personal business to give you and your daughter the best of us and you will not treat me and my daughter like this and she took her daughter and left."

China, "I tried my best to talk to you but Giselle, I'm sorry, I have to do what I have been told so we cannot talk, sit, and play together. I cried all the way home and every day."

"My brothers had to carry me; Georgianna couldn't eat or sleep that entire summer; we were both miserable and I went to the hospital at the end of summer to have Simian and they kept me for two weeks."

"I had a terrible infection and an after birth sickness, they wanted to keep me for one more week, my family was with me but your daddy had to go and finalize over abroad and Chi-Chi, all my kids had school and dance and other activities, so my husband Mr. Bison went behind my back and he told your dad and your mother and she came up to the hospital and said, "give me your keys."

"I just gave them to her."

"Come on children and Chi Chi and she cleaned the hell out of our home every single day and cooked all these meals from scratch. Your dad could not get back; he was going to hire some people. I got released and though I was fine, your mother stayed with me, bathed me, and took care of all our kids. Our baby boy was three weeks old; she totally revamped me and all our children."

"Your dad got back, and she left."

"I was way better then, and she had you all doing chores, looking after yourselves, reading the Bible, studying Spanish plus other subjects and I changed China."

"You did hell to fire Georgianna; I say all of that to say that your mama and daddy were good and respectful people of great integrity and your daddy helped Bison so much."

"He gives credit this day to your daddy."

China, "yes he does, his mom took him all over abroad that's how we own Chi Chi Bank and credit union all over abroad, in Dubai, the U.K and China."

Georgianna recall all about home and the language barriers he taught your daddy, he was not stingy.

"Remember I asked your mom why she didn't upgrade bigger."

"Why so my daughter, can't we live a normal life that we can't walk down the street, go to the park after dinner and be unique but normal."

"I genuinely loved everything about her, how she was, and all my kids still sent your mother a mothers-day card and gift every year's birthday, Christmas and you and me."

Giselle, "yes, I love her, mom we love you and I did love her truly."

"What a decent friend, what a true woman of Essence, Poise, and Grace cut from my Lord's very own hem Elohim."

"This is a hard one."

"Hello, all the men speak as she goes into the restroom, gets herself together, and comes back out."

China sits more up, "Mommy that's really nice I did not see all that Sugar."

That's lovely Georgianna turns around and says then runway and thanks, Madame.

China, "I figured Georgianna made me all this stuff last summer just out the blue."

"My only real sister is gone now, I saw her off and stood, then she cried with Giselle for a sec and as they wiped their eyes with a tissue."

"Georgianna you know I love you, your mama and daddy, what are we going to do? we've lost two good people"

Come here she goes and hug and kiss Giselle, "you know Butter, don't be shutting down and we don't hear from you, your mama and daddy are gone, you're going to have to do something else, at least let us know where you're going."

"Well I did not see you back there, they all say you're alright, well no funeral we have had my sisters and a good man's eulogy let me say hello they are huge and so handsome she tears up your Caviar he would be looking right down on you.

Giselle, "Now I know they got a daddy, but do you not tell these boys about their extraordinary grandfather, a good man."

China, "for sure that's Challis II, her mom can tell them apart."

"China looks like he has darker brown grey eyes and Caviar's is dimmer."

Her mom, "still can't tell the difference, right here."

Georgianna, "let me wash my hands dry, I'm not going to pick up your boys; I don't want to get a hernia."

They all laughed, and then she takes from his mom and her, "this is Solace."

"Georgianna gorgeous looking and pretty, your grand mom uses to say that all the time."

China and Giselle smile.

Georgianna, "every time I see you; I'm looking at you just like your mommy and grand mommy. She would have loved and dressed you."

She gives her back.

"This is Solace after me, Georgianna."

Challis mom called him;

Challis, "yes ma'am."

He gets up and hugs her saying;

Challis, Georgianna I did not see you over there now, these two look just like identical twins, and their eyes, all this hair, full lips, no Botox next babies all keep it descent and in order too, beautiful yes oh here go you're his mom Sugar."

"Ok Sugar, my second daughter Tonya told me that as soon as you got well, you cremated them."

Giselle, "yes ma'am"

"Ok I won't beat you up too bad about their service because I would not have been any good anyway but let me get back to the professor. You know I love you, Giselle."

Giselle, "yes ma'am and I love you too, but we know we will not have any help from Chi Chi with you laying up here China."

"Mommy, Georgianna, pretender Charlotte, and Hana are here."

"Good Georgianna let me go, your daddy will be here tomorrow, he isn't a bit good either, after all this, we're selling and moving China where her mom is, he said it's somewhere quiet and he's furious about them being left alone all those days in that park that they walked for over 45 years."

"If he sees Columbus, it'll be too soon, and Butter should have told me so that I wouldn't be going to the park suddenly and doing nothing."

"I'll tell my second dad when I see him, it was just too hard, and I didn't want to bother anybody." Georgianna, "ok, I'll let your second daddy talk to you, Butter truly I'm sorry."

Mommy, "you know daddy only likes 14 people."

They all laughed and let me see all his kids.

"I barely got in when Chi Chi's mom counts on her fingers. My parents, all back in the **cut** get up and hug her."

China, "He called me, and I tried to call him back."

Georgianna, "see Chi-Chi is Daddy's girl, she looks just like him. She doesn't give a damn about me but it's ok."

Chi-Chi, "mommy I love you but is daddy ok?"

"He's on silence but thank God that I have two other daughters."

Chi-Chi, "mommy please I still really want all my stuff."

Mommy, "Chi-Chi don't start I know Giselle, I had her 2 bags and I mailed them to her home they probably arrived today."

"Georgianna thank you so much what would I do without my Butter."

"China, have a wonderful time."

Mommy, "Giselle what are you doing with the rhinestone inlay chiffon cape, I'm going to wear that as a Host."

Georgianna, "The soft tea first, then the yellow buttercup."

Giselle "yes, both will be so pretty, and the flow will be sensational, take lots of pictures and send them to Chi Chi's phone, video too, though China I want a real 8X10 copy framed also."

Georgianna, "will do."

Giselle, "Have a blessed evening!"

Chi-Chi, "mom, one last thing, I will be home next month for 2 weeks."

"Didn't I tell you we are not going to be there, were moving but ok."

Chi Chi sits up, "mommy let me"

Mom winds her finger, "nope, I see right through you."

"Butter is limited now and you're going to need your little tone and speak for fall."

Chi-Chi, "yes but you know I miss my parents."

"Life is short; you better put your work in daughter because I am set."

"My sister did mine for the entire year and I know how to do it."

"Take time and put in the effort."

Mac, "Let me walk you over her."

Mom, "I always have loved my son in-law, they leave China."

"Anyway, did you get me anything else plus I need a material trip."

"I'm just all over the place, my tone you got to get me speech back together."

Giselle, "For what? You hate to listen and sew but I made you a lot of things, you're going to be too cute for the spring and summer but know this, I have told you my mommy has it over only for specialties."

"I got to work on how to get my own daughters' tone and speech together."

China, "a few oils here to bam their babies."

Giselle, "get out of my bed and get out of our room."

China, "this is all new to me, now you're going to be limited to me first."

Challis, "now Giselle, just say it and you're going to be right over there with your mother."

China, "Question, is Roma white?"

Giselle, "No and there is no difference, but she is black."

"I rode by there before I left, she and her daughters were just smiling and riding bikes in the park I felt so nice inside about that."

Mom, "I'm sure is ecstatic about them three, ooh oh and Judge Dover introduced her to the city's new Chief of police."

"He is a retired ex-pro boxer and he's a widower with a 3-year-old daughter. His wife texted, she told me that they did lunch and took all their kids for roller-skating and on a picnic to the park."

China, "what does he look like?"

Giselle, "I don't know, who cares but Judge Dover likes no one and he said he likes him for her."

China, "Right, that's why you've been doing all that stuff and you didn't know you were pregnant."

Giselle, "I guess."

China, "you have given everything away."

CHAPTER 7

Get Your Own Business

Giselle, "not the Publishing Company or Fragrance warehouse business nor some businesses across the world plus I'm boogying Solae a décor, I'm also taking my mama to 6 stores I'm opening come this fall for her across the world."

China, "You aren't sewing anymore."

Giselle, "No, but I hired 130 customized seamstresses from all over the world."

China, "you know I love you and thank you Jesus you know you're going to have to let me start a clothing line with you."

Giselle, No, the devil is a liar."

China, "Why not?"

Giselle, "You do not have any compassion for your fellow woman or man, let alone my mother's quality type of clientele. Her name cannot become a part of you, never!"

China, "I know how to dress."

Giselle, "Yes, just yourself, your husband and your kids, plus you are going to get sick of the high demand."

(Mac walks back in) China told him.

"Yes husband, I want my own store."

Mac, "No"

China, "ok, I'll ask my daddy and open it myself."

Giselle, "ok."

China, "Giveme10 of your seamstress."

Giselle refused.

China, "Why not?"

Giselle, "waste your money. My parents left you for one because I like all my seamstress, it took me a long time to form them."

China, "How much did my second parents leave me?"

Giselle, "Call attorney Salmon, you have his number"

China, "come on."

Giselle, "ok, close your eyes."

China (excited), "please just tell me."

Giselle, "ok, a 22 billion in cash"

China (she screams, gets up, does the running man in a small space and keeps saying yes! Yes!)

"You know my second parents loved me."

Giselle, "yes they did. Ok sit, I'm also going to do a kids' store line. I need all of them hand-picked for me."

China, "What?"

Giselle, "The Madame Solae and Sir Caviar infant to teens' apparel and décor."

China, "that's a lot."

Giselle, "well, I have to dress our kids anyway so the store will grow from there plus I'm not doing clients till our kids are 5 years old and still it will be very selective."

Chi-Chi, "What? Why? We got stuff to do."

Giselle, "No, by then I will know my kids well and mastered their tone and chemistry"

Mom, "that's smart."

Giselle thanked her.

China, "my books, I need you to publish my books."

Giselle, "write first, write, I thought about this and I think its best you write one and you're going to have to send the manuscript to 30 different company and when anyone needs you then I will publish you."

China, "I cannot stand you."

Giselle, "what are you going to write about? Please, not yourself."

China, "Yes, me,"

Giselle, "Nobody needs to know how to live a luxury lifestyle."

China, "yes, they do."

Giselle, "if you want to sell, you could write on how to stay married for 20 years or more since you have."

China, "No I'm writing luxury defined by me."

Giselle, "I guess maybe it will work. Look, my dad made me do that same stuff, it took me forever you know that, but I learned along the way and you need to take a few more college courses on creative writing."

China, "I don't have time."

Giselle, "They offer online courses."

China, "do you take any?"

Giselle, "Of course. Every year, I soak up as much writing and fashion knowledge as possible. Also, start reading and cut off all those reality show mess you got on your back yard and read."

China, "I hate to read except it's our magazine."

Giselle, "There are lots of authors out there with audio books. It will make you a stronger writer plus I think you have a beautiful voice."

China, "Thanks but I got this."

Giselle, "No, you don't and I'm not going to be around when you get your first rejection letter"

China, "No."

Giselle, "I have over a 100 rejections letters,"

China, "you would have quit."

Giselle, "yeah, but my dad told me to keep going."

China "and look at you now."

Giselle, "I got it. You have raised two vital young men to society, you and Mac can write about that."

Mac, "No, she's with you."

China, "That's too easy."

Giselle, "how to be a parent sells, write about it, you'll have an audience."

China, "If I write it will you buy it?"

Giselle, "Of course, that's one of two best features I think you have. China, what I've seen in you plus my mommy also thought you were an impeccable mother and wife."

China, "God, where are my parent's graves?"

Giselle, "Well, you'll have to charter a boat to the Atlantic Ocean, to the deep. I had both of my parents cremated and I took one of my parent's boats out and I said a little prayer and thanked them both as I threw their ashes over the Atlantic Ocean and spent the night in that spot."

China, "All night?"

Giselle, "yes, because I had to make my peace with God. It was so beautiful, quiet, and tranquil. All the stars were so beautiful and I apologized to my Lord and told Him that I was so sorry about how I had disrespected my father and both my parents and my Lord Jesus Christ because he gave me the best of the best and I thanked him and fell to sleep under the moon and the stars but I woke up and never- mind."

China, "don't stop now."

Giselle, "I know I was not dreaming."

China, "What?"

Giselle, "when I awoke, I was really wet, and it was pitch black and I didn't leave any lights on."

Mom, "you came to yourself"

Giselle, "yes ma'am and I became extremely very cold and really scared, I started screaming and crying hysterically because I had brought nothing to help me and I realized for the first time that I was really alive, totally alone and all a sudden I saw my parents and they said "you are alright Butter and we are always with you," I told my dad I was extremely afraid and scared to live this life all by myself and I started crying, my dad yelled at me. He said "stop it now, we have raised you for a time such as this and the Lord told us to tell you that He is with you and that your latter days will be better than your former days and help is on its way" and they disappeared but I still could hear them talking. I thought to myself, saying "are you alright?" I said; still I'm not and then the Navy Patrol guys said do not be alarmed and I said who are you all? They said we were going for our last run and we came onboard. We thought this ship was abandoned, they flashed their lights on me, I turned and said "will you all please help me, I don't know how to get back to the pier please cause I don't know what to do and they said that's alright we will take good care of you no worries."

China, "how did they take you?"

Giselle," they towed my parent's boat and they had me put on a jump suit, helmet and they gave me a pair of boots to put on."

China, "where were your shoes"

Giselle, "I had worn stilettos."

China, "On a boat?"

Giselle, "yes I wanted to look nice for my parent's funeral, so they hosted me up into a helicopter."

China, "to hell with a book on parenting I'm writing about you, how your parents loved you."

Giselle, "Yeah Ocean first chapter, they met on a cruise traveling in that water nice book. I thought it would be a fantastic way to end their love story so write on my bestie sister."

"You know get up time for daughters please."

China goes and washes her hands, gets them.

China, "me and you two are going to have a problem."

They cry, "see"

Giselle, "wash and dry give me."

China, "I still need your mother."

They cry more.

Giselle, "stop torturing my girls."

Mommy, "Chi Chi, Challis you're going to have to sleep somewhere else, Challis.

China, "I need them."

They both looked at her.

China, "Giselle why don't they like me?"

Giselle, "they will love you maybe as I someday, but right now bye already, I can feel that they don't want to be bothered with you. They closed their eyes when you move towards them, then open their eyes when you leave."

Giselle, "Challis, we need to eat, and I need God's help because I can't eat a lot of stuff."

Challis, "yes soup! Soft stuff."

Giselle, "I just love creamy basil tomato, and would love some crackers."

But Challis told her to eat slowly, 4 bottles of water, antibiotic and 2 100% pure cranberry juice, and asked people to leave that she wants to bath her kids and herself and sister and change the beddings.

China, "The house has 6 bedrooms we can stock up this kitchen, while the kids are sleeping with mum."

Mom, "I still want to know what Giselle is going to do now that she is a mommy."

Giselle, "I'll be my mommy."

China, "Work, stay at home and be cool because your mama put the C in cool and she was Hella fun just like you."

Giselle, "that for the next 5 years our kids have to learn how to swim and stuff so nothing I'm shutting us down a while."

Mom, "you're right."

China, "I'm ready to turn life up Giselle gets back up and said great."

Challis, "we need new friends with swimming babies and little active learning ones."

As China was helping her, she points at the kids:

China, "1, 2,3,4, you all are ruining my life."

They put the kids in the baskets.

China, "we're going be going on play dates."

Giselle, "no, me and my kids we're going to be going on play dates, swim dates, story time."

China, "You and these kids?"

Mac told her that she got nerves then gets up and starts to dance and says, "Giselle was superb, took our boys on cruises for summers, threw them to many count slam men parties, made them costumes year after year for Halloween , had them in a play house bed and room , clean the hell out of our home, dropped us 5 star cooked meals from scratch all the time, helped them design their very own race park which they still have today and kids would come from all over the world to participate, they still carry wardrobe signature design to this day. Week after week she never misses a beat, nothing of theirs throws down for us, and she was the bomb! Aunty we owe her big time."

Giselle, "and I got my nephews 30 tailors and 12 seamstresses."

Mac, "oh how we soon forget."

China, my boys will help me, can I use their seamstress?"

Mac, "no"

She picks up Solace and she cries.

Giselle, "come on trainee, you got some work to do and put all that hair up, you're getting all your hair in my baby's face and that's the problem."

China, "I need a scrunchy."

Giselle, "just braid it up"

China puts Solace down braids in all her hair in one then she sanitizes her hands and picks Solace back up and she does not cry.

China, "I guess I'll have to shave my hair bald."

All the men leave, as soon as they're out the room;

Challis, "I like Giselle a lot, she is going to be a very good mother and wife because she was raised by a dedicated mother and father."

Mac, "she's very religious also."

Giselle called Challis when he answered; she told him that their kids need a lot of onesies.

Challis, "I saw some in the gift shop I'll go."

Giselle, "wait."

China, "just get about 20 and nice baby soap shampoo lotion that's good cause we have to bath."

Challis, "I know it'll get better."

Giselle cries.

Challis, "it's not you, I just want our kids to have their own stuff, I hate all this cheap soap and I don't know what to do, I love you Giselle."

Love and kisses then they hang up.

His dad asked, what's wrong?

Challis, "I'll be bathing them a lot myself and I want them to have all their own stuff."

Mac, "it's a 24-hour delivery."

Mom, "Hey son!"

They all stopped talking, she asked him to feed them then go and gather some things for his kids and get some personal stuff like gowns and rob for her.

CHAPTER 8

No Excuse

Phone rings:
    Mac, "hello"

Jabra, "please I need Giselle's number."

Mac, "what do you want her number for?"

Jabra, "because I've been in a battered women's relationship and I kept their kids alive and safe, taking a chance with my own life in jeopardy. My public defender said if she would write me a letter, I might end up doing a 2-year stretch."

Mac, "you don't just have that; you do fraud and that's a federal crime. You pretended you were dead and that's a crime itself plus insurance fraud."

They all get on the elevator.

Challis, "Mac, who is that?"

Jabra, "my time is up, we were friends and I'll just have my cousin call her."

Mac, "no you weren't."

Jabra, "well, we know each other she can just get in touch with her at the hospital."

Then the phone goes dead. As they filed off.

Mac, "it was Jabra."

Challis, "what the fuck does she want?"

Mac, "she said she was having her cousin contact Giselle because they were friends, I told her not and she said she kept your kids safe and she has been in a battered women's relationship."

His dad said, "Jamison Samian Calms-way Senior, you can keep on playing around if you want to, but she is another type of ball game."

Mike, "Hell, yeah! Going to a park in the late hours of the night by herself."

Jamison, "I heard that, I was like shit, what are you made of steel?"

Mac, "I love her just like a sister; she is truly one of the best people."

As they get in line to order food.

Mac, "she has been friends' with my wife since elementary kindergarten, their mothers were best friends and their fathers too, are we going to eat here?"

Mr. Jamison Senior, "yes, we got time, they're bathing and stuff."

They all ordered and sit down with the food plus drinks to eat and drink.

Mac, "my wife is very selfish and extremely self-centered."

Challis, "what the hell is wrong with you?"

Mac, "right but see she is going to be really good to your kids and you cause see, as he eats, Giselle makes my wife to be accountable to her and she will not allow her to be anything different."

Mr. Jamison Senior, "we saw her braid up all that hair."

Mac, "see my wife really never expected nor did she want her truly to have this life this is why she was so furious about you."

Challis, "I know"

As he eats.

"I heard her say she was ready to turn her life up."

Mac, "yes all year since our youngest son left for college, she needs Giselle because she just eats and sleeps, now don't get me wrong, my wife is domesticated, she plans these retreats every single year. Thousands of filthy rich women come for it. It last for 2 weeks, my wife comes back, falls all out and screams; "I feel so refreshed" I'll be like what do you all do, she say they had guest speakers and spa then I'll be like what's all these leaves and rocks pinned to these boards for? My wife says "that's Giselle's stuff, oh please don't move it cause I got to give those boards to the Sherwin Williams paints rep and Cover girl rep" I asked for what and she said "cause Giselle is starting some-kind of earth tones paint line and some ole nail polish, lip glosses, hammer blush line; I don't know why she goes, she gets nothing out of it and I'm so tired of her."

Mac pulls up and shows them her paint line, lip stick gloss, blush and polish line.

"She still conducts her childhood Children's book line SEE Goo goo-go."

Mike, "my sons still have that book line somewhere."

Jamison II, "mine as well."

Mac, "she wrote as a teen, she wrote a 7-book series on Detectives are us."

Mike, "they had to read that in middle year at school."

Jamison, "wasn't that a movie?"

Mac, "yes, grossed a whopping 700 billion dollars at the box office ran for 5 months before DVD. She donated all the proceeds to hunger alliance to form free grocery stores, homeless homes built, medical junior entrepreneurs, arts, HBC colleges and the battered women's facilities and associations. I say all this to say to my bro that she is very nice but not at all street or book stupid and extremely feminine."

Challis, "I proposed to her, and she said nothing at first then she said I need to ask her father."

Mike, "did she say yes?"

Challis, "she said nothing, after that she told me she had things to do and I have not seen her since in 24 weeks nor was I able to contact her, she disconnected all her phones."

Mike, "what? What did she tell you?"

Challis, "nothing, she did not tell me she was disconnecting her phone or phones either"

Mac, "she shuts down like that."

Challis, "No! no! she will not be doing that unless we are together."

His dad said, "on that note you better get your first wife in check before Wonder Woman makes it up in her mind to raise your kids alone."

Mac, "She could do just that and fuck everybody else and never look back."

Jamison II, "yes her parents died, and she gave everything away except a couple of things."

Mike, "she said she will never go to Columbus, Ohio ever again."

His dad said, "that's in the past, she is going forward, you know that woman got kidnapped, beat up, injured on Christmas Eve, and had her kids born on Christmas at midnight, she didn't know about that and then her kids got kidnapped the next day and she's just sitting there, lost both her parents but just as sane, talking in her right mind and taking good care of your two babies, drawing mental lines in the sand, told your wife she would not be going. She wasn't just talking about play dates, she's talking about shutting down 5years to bring your kids up to speed in life, they're going to be swimming, reading and knowing math, probably a language when they enter kindergarten."

Mac, "yes because she speaks 5 languages fluently, Swahili, Chinese, Spanish, Italian and French, she is not fucking around, she means what she does and says."

Challis, "I love the hell out of Giselle, she knows it."

His dad said, well, you rescued her, and all your kids, so let's hope she takes all that and you into consideration. Know this son, you're on audition."

Challis, "No fuck that she knows me."

His dad yelled, "lie to her, deceive her one time and Lord help you. Forward, no goodbye, that's the only place she is going."

Mac, "that's how she has rolled forever, she does not waddle, she gets going. Jabra thinks she is going to help her, she better look somewhere else because she detests harming others for gain."

Challis wants to order their food; he gets up and throws his stuff away.

Jamison Senior, "see"

Challis, "him and Jabra taking extensive lavish trips separate, all I'm saying is its best to buy his ass a riding mower cause he's going to have to be in this life with her teaching, helping their kids cause her father was with her. This is all depending on him and right now she is."

Mac, "right cause the hospital is responsible to feed her, but she put it on Challis, that's how they're going to be rolling and a super clean ass productive fun house."

Jamison Senior, "Challis, write a couple more books and movies from home."

Mac, "Her mother was very submissive to her father, and she was very much so. I gave my father my word, 6 feet of snow, no planes, ice below zero. She drives all the way from here by herself to Ohio in 1 week at night. Her middle name is courage."

Jamison Senior, "Challis, better wake the fuck up right now because she got her own damn money, and she is beautiful in and out."

Mike, "she is growing it."

His dad commented, "I like how she gave that woman their home and her mom's dress shop."

Jamison II, "it was really nice, and it's time to help someone out there personally cause a lot of times we give to all these charities and most people never receive it."

Mac affirmed asking about the food, which challis said he had delivered. He brought back some oatmeal raisin cookies and milk and gave his dad the same.

Mac, "Jabra." Challis, "Dad, how can we get married tomorrow?"

His dad answered, "wait till Monday, which solely depends on if she'll marry you."

And nothing opens on a Sunday as it was still Christmas time.

Challis, "she will, then we can all go get a marriage license and a pastor and bam we'll be productively, happily married."

Mike, "Yes, because we need her shit, I'm thinking about something else I can do."

His dad said productivity and asked;

"Challis, what are you going to do?"

Challis, "right now, I want to marry the woman of my dreams and get my inner family healthy and the hell out of New York."

His dad, "Come on, we're going to all focused and be productive, in love and joyful cause after this year, I'm going to look at my own damn trees, dirt and rocks and see what the fuck I can make, then what son?"

Challis, "we're going to live, love, and once our kids get to 10, I'm running for President."

His dad, "Now you are talking right."

Some time goes by and they reach the room. It's all scrubbed and clean. A lady and her husband are there, his mom wearing a moo moo.

"Excuse me, please."

She shows her sons Mac and her husband back out.

"The white man is Jabra's attorney and these 2 are my cousins."

Challis, "I am sick of this"

He goes back in.

Jabra's attorney, "hello, I am Attorney Reed for your wife Jabra"

Challis, "we're not married. She dissolved that when she faked her death. Attorney, well on Monday morning we're establishing."

Mac, "I'll be filing a motion to block that Kisha lady but I just want you to realize Giselle that you have 2 daughters whom Teresa was trying to kill but Jabra stop her attorney, and the judge on the case he opens a file with a special judge being brought in from Ohio. Dover's man cousin

Timothy, "if you do not help her, they are trying to put her away for 20 years reoccurring time."

Giselle says nothing. All her kids are in the bed, clean with her. The room smells incredible, and they do too!

Giselle, "injustice then what time is it?"

China, "8 pm"

She looks right at all of them.

"At 10 pm our children will be awake for feeding and changing, I will eat now and then sleeping while my kids are asleep."

China showed her where the food is, on a tray and told her to be careful.

China, "It's really hot."

Giselle, "ok, I got it thanks,"

As she takes it;

Challis, "let's go."

They all filed out at his command, Mac, his best friend, and family in tow behind him.

Mac, "I'm going to file 5 restraining orders and notify the Police that your client is antagonizing stress upon victims."

Attorney Reed, "let the games begin."

Challis, "let Jabra know that her well-being is not any concern or importance to me or my intermediate family, and any if any of her peeps come on this floor again, I will file trespassing charges."

Mac, "tell my wife I'll be back."

Mike, "where are you going?"

Mac, "I'm going to file restraining orders."

Mike and Jamison II tagged along, and they left. Challis goes back in, gets his bag, and goes into one room. All rooms have cable, televisions, and phones, then he showers. His dad informed China that her husband went over to the police station. He then goes into another room and showers.

Giselle is all done, she goes and brushes her teeth, use the restroom to shower, oil light spray and she goes to get in bed.

Challis, "do we need bottle?"

Giselle, "No, but two towels, two sheets."

He gets them and Giselle bids him goodnight.

China, "I'm going to bed, I'll text Macie that we're in bedroom 1."

Mommy, "We will be in 2 and I'll text them to come in the second door."

Challis, "yes ma'am."

Then he pulls the divider and locks it and turns out all lights except one small night light.

Giselle, "two washed clothes were still wet and only one was dry."

She gives him a Ziplock;

Giselle, "put it in here, please."

He gets up and does so, then gets in bed at the back of Giselle. Challis hugged and kissed her, and they slept arm to body, but at 10 pm Giselle wakes and takes her gown off, lays towel on her lap, sits Indian style, and feeds their kids, girls first.

Challis sits.

Giselle, "you can sleep."

Challis, "no, I want to help."

Giselle feeds burps Solace then she lays her down and then Solae and feed burp her, lays her down then she grabs the wipes and wipes her breast, and then she changes each one, wiping their face and buts, oiling their butts and powdering it. Challis takes Solace and lays her up further and then he takes Solaea and did the same then he gets up and gets Caviars.

Challis, "he is heavy, we should bottle."

Giselle, "this is easier."

She takes her son and feeds him, burp him, and then she wipes his face, changes him, wipes oil powder, and then Challis gives her Challis Junior she feeds him, burps him, wipes his face, changes him, but wipes oil powder.

SEASONS OF LIFE AND THE ALTAR CALL OF CHRIST

She puts all soils in a Ziploc bag and throws them in the trash, wipes herself, sanitized her hands, puts her gown back on and they go back to sleep.

At 2 am, Giselle wakes and says; "ok" they repeat the process.

Giselle, "ok 4am is the next feeding."

Challis, "That's in 2 hours."

Giselle, "listen every-time we have woken them up is, 8pm, 12am, 4am, 6am and 10 and so on cause the next will be 8 pm, 12am and 6 am."

Challis, "Why?"

Giselle, "Because from 4 am swim, their day are tailored around that."

Challis, "wait how?"

Giselle, "we must have in our home a heated pool and a track by the time they release us, that's your job."

Challis, "ok, you know I love us."

Giselle just looked at him and lay back down.

Challis, "I love you."

Giselle, "Cha I know I love you as well."

Then he lays back down, and they both slept till 4 am, same thing, then 6am.

Giselle, "when it's 10 am and they're still asleep, you should go change."

Challis, "ok."

And they woke.

Giselle, "let's change and bath each of them, please changes the bed sheet and no feeding; let them sleep."

They slept and Giselle went and showered, Challis changed the bed sheet, threw out all linen and trash and then he put his kids in bed and showered also and got back in bed.

Doctor Shaunae came in to check on the babies and Giselle.

Giselle, "I need to make bottles."

And she left with Doctor Shaunae. Challis and their babies slept an hour longer. Giselle came back, and she showered again, Challis called her, "come baby", he put her over him and under the covers they all slept more.

His mom peeped in and she took a picture, she thought, they all look so cute.

By 4pm Giselle said to her babies;

Giselle, "Lazy look."

Challis, "look, they're all smiling."

Giselle, "Probably dreaming."

China came in, they were still asleep.

Challis, "That's a good sign you all can go home, they're probably going to sleep all-night till their swim time, you all should move it up till 6am."

Giselle, "no lifestyle when perk begins, 4am run, 5am swim, 6am dress for school, 6:30 I cook breakfast, 7am we sit for breakfast, 8 am to school."

China, "What about weekends."

Giselle, "it's free but for language tutorials, we will listen to it when they rise and before sleep."

China, "what time are you all going to be in bed?"

Giselle, "our kids will have 3:30pm after school, snack 4pm after-school activities, do their homework by 6pm, dinner by 7pm, swim by 7:30pm, shower or bath by 8pm, read the Bible, in foreign and English language one language also, prayers and in bed by 8:30pm."

China, "I hate you."

Then she leaves. Challis turned around to Giselle.

Challis, "I love you."

He really kissed her, and I am truly on board with all of that, wow! He kissed her again. That is going to be damn, and they're going to be strong in mind, body and soul.

Challis, "Yes, we are shutting the fuck down and at 3years old strength, training, and 4 boys' basketball and football."

Giselle, "girls, ballet, gymnastics, piano, but like what else at 3?"

Challis, "Pushups, crunches and leg lifts, jumping jacks."

Giselle" yes I like it and I'm starting now to speak to them in Spanish and English."

Challis, "I speak fluent Spanish."

A knock came.

Challis, "Come in."

Nurse Cheetah, "Ms. Giselle, Dr. Shanae wants me to take you to get a cat scan,"

Giselle gets up.

Giselle," The bottles Cha, are in the fridge warm."

Challis and she kissed again and again.

Challis, "I got them."

Giselle leaves.

Mike, "all hell no" hey! Challis! Challis!!

Challis, "Yeah."

Mike, "come in a hurry."

CHAPTER 9

The Lion's Den

Challis pulls back the partition and goes in, then Mike rewinds, his dad sits down and looks, Mike rewinds and starts it all over, they all look. His mom comes in and sits, they all see the news showing park pictures of Giselle digging up all the flower bed and carting all the stuff away then they see the huge hole she has dug then she takes a bundle and faints but gracefully she lands on it under her head and she literally does not wake up.

Mommy, OMG Jesus!

2 huge lions run and come and lay down, each one right beside her facing the opposite way, eyes open all night until the daylight comes in then the lions go behind the trees, each still in watch of her, then they see her wake up and sit up and she gets up, sweeps, packs, rests and drive the carts out of the park. They waited till she was gone, then they ran away.

His mom gets up shouting and saying that was the Lord Hallelujah! taking care of her.

Mike, "mom, it's back on commentary, and what a Navy rescue team we have in America and they show them approaching and rescuing Giselle from her parent's huge Carnival-like ship."

Jamison II," damn, what is she talking about, a boat, what the fuck Mike! Wow".

His mom was still shouting;

Mommy, "don't count my Savior out nothing but the blood of Jesus, come on in Lord, my mighty Christ."

His dad's "son, she is amazing."

Challis, "yes I know."

Mac, "it's remarkable."

Mike, "who the hell does that?"

Mommy, "a diamond in the ruff, don't allow Jabra's stifling behind to take what God has truly made just for you son, do you hear me?"

Challis, "yes ma'am, I know."

Mommy, "see, God heard her when she cried out, "I'm all in this life by myself."

Mike, "but she wasn't, Challis said he's pissed, that she could have called him, and he would come."

His dad, "no God was teaching her he was there just for her."

News again; "we just got word that some-how the 2 Lions escaped last night from the Ohio Zoo, they're both back safely."

Mommy, "Jesus."

Mac, "they did not even touch her."

Mike, "they laid down all night right beside her in watch."

Jamison II, "they would have torn anyone who messed with them up."

Mommy, "Jesus, he is worthy to be praised."

Challis puts his babies in bassinets lying next to the California King Hospital Bed, he then puts all their towel's and dirty laundry in huge laundry bags out in the hall for the staff on laundry duty then he goes and cleans their huge bathroom, he sweeps again dust and cleaned all the glass then he takes a big bucket of mop water and scrub, moved his kids, his family all starts cleaning up on the other side then Mac mops.

A knock came in and it was the delivery guy.

Mac, "come in."

Delivery guy, "I have several deliveries for Giselle Simonies from Challis Calms-sway."

Challis, "Right here."

The delivery guy pulls out a bag of 7.

Challis, "Ok, I'll take this one."

And pulls out all and makes up their bed then he gets all the extra pillows and puts those on the bed, goes and gets stuff out and hangs all up and puts it away in a huge closet in their room then, he opens another one, 2 more get filled to entirety but walking in space, he then takes around 40 towels and washed clothes, body wash specialty soaps and puts in bath closet.

China, "damn, did you buy the entire store daddy? It's just 3 days."

But Challis said nothing. A knock came on the door.

Challis, "come in."

Nurse Lacy, "Dr. Shanae wants the babies for test and check-ups."

Challis, "I'll get them."

He shuts the closet and goes.

China, "do you want my help?"

Challis, "they are all fine, thanks."

He checks each one of them, they're all dry and then he puts them in the stroller Cadillac bassinet he had thrown together.

Mommy, "that is nice, it's see-through and big enough for them to recline lay down."

He puts them with fur comforter and pillows for infants and then he grabs bottle warmers, diapers, wipes and wets, 4 washed clothes, takes 4 dry and puts them in separate Ziploc bags and bags all in stroller compartment with a big thing of wipes also and grabs for himself three cold glasses of water and goes. Nurse Lacy holds the door but 3 other nurses came as well and they all leave together, following the babies in tow.

Mommy, "Challis is not playing."

His dad, "I have never seen him like this."

Mommy, "he's been wanting to have his own kids for so long."

His dad, "he use to say just 1 will be fine."

Mommy, "well, four is better, 2 sons and 2 daughters."

Mike, "their four kids are magazine photo and very good looking."

Jamison II, "the ham hocks are going to be huge."

His dad laughs.

Mommy, "what's so funny?"

Daddy, "Challis told me so many times, I love my wife I'm in love with my wife, but I detest her."

Jamison II, "I hated how Jabra was the cause of when we first met her, all those times."

Mike, "she was sweet, but I saw straight through all that and I told Challis."

Mommy, "she was going to church with me all the time."

China comes in, picks her purse, and says, "bae, mommy, me, and Professor are going to our hair and nail appointment."

Mac, "ok."

China grabs her purse, kisses her husband, and says, "oh here,", she gets out her purse and says, "this was just delivered to me, this is the inheritance account and debit cards, we can transfer ourselves or keep that account. I don't want to take it with me."

Mac takes it and puts it in his wallet, she leaves.

Daddy, "she never truly loved Challis."

Mike, "she was the worst looking, worst dressing, worst wife, worst housekeeper, and worst cook."

Mommy, "well, she is with who she truly loved and wanted."

The phone rings.

"Hello!"

Rea, "Hello sister, where have you been? I've been calling you and calling you."

Solace's sister, "we have been through it."

Rea, "you see the Lord."

Solace, "he's here."

Rea, "yes but the woman in the park with the Lions, did you see her being rescued by it? Seems like the entire Navy, she drove her daddy's big ole ship out there and sailed all the way from Ohio."

Solace, "she is Challis fiancé /baby mama."

Rea, "What?"

Solace, "that's where she is, they just had premium quintuplets, 2 huge big ole boys and 2 absolutely beautiful, tiny colored eyes, sandy brown-haired girls."

Rea, "are you sure? because Jabra is on the news."

Solace, "no paternity is done, I would love both child and mother. Solae a décor."

Rea, "What? No, no, that's little Giselle?"

Solace, "yes."

Rea," where are they at?"

Rea, "Frank! Challis just had 4 quintuplets and he's getting married to the lady's daughter that made me and Solace clothes for years in Ohio."

Frank, "Alright then."

Rea, "that girl in the park is her daughter Giselle."

Frank, "what she's going to do, she brought herself back to life, Jabra."

Rea, "Not a damn thing, anyway."

Solace, "Challis and Mac just rescued her from some fool that had kidnapped her."

Rea, "he now knows how she feels about that and she hopes Challis beat the hell out of him."

Solace, "Challis and Mac shot him in the elbow and FBI was closing in."

Rea, "he's going to get his kidnapping ass beat up in prison, they cannot stand men that kidnap women and children."

Solace, "Jabra and Teresa kidnapped Challis and Giselle's infants the day before but Challis had put on them all jewelry with GPS."

Rea screams in happiness, "faking death bitch."

Solace, they tried to mix his kids up, trying to make them think these other 4 babies were theirs."

Rea, "How did Challis know the difference between his kids?"

Solace, it's because he had taken lots of pictures of their kids, he knew his boys had a birth mark on their right ankle, big just like his."

Rea, "Now you know, don't nobody have that, but Challis is unique."

Solace, "he knew that his daughters first of all have sandy blonde mix hair and green blue hazel eyes."

Rea screams, jumps up and down.

Frank, "what's wrong with you?"

Rea, "We got some girls all very beautiful, 2 ham hocks, our grandsons huge, they weighed 17lbs at birth, 21 inches in height and husky."

Rea, "How many weeks?"

Solace, "24 and 3 days now."

Rea, "Jabra is going to bust hell wide open, just look at my nephew coming out on the other side and Giselle is gorgeous, she got manners and was raised right."

Solace, "where did Jabra faked her death?"

Rea, "I am so excited, this really is Christmas my love we'll be there, doesn't Challis have all those rooms there?"

Solace, "come on its plenty bedrooms."

Rea, "do you like her for him?"

Frank, "yes, I genuinely do."

Rea, "she was always so sweet, proper and mannered to us, her parents, I got to come, how long where they going to live?"

Frank, "With us, for a year."

Rea, "see this is real when Challis wants to come home when he discovered that trick, he stayed away from us. I remember I saw Challis I was like why have you not been around, he told me things are not just how I would want them to be, to include my family but know this I'll call you and he always has. I looked at my boy, he looked so defeated, and I ran off so he couldn't see me cry. That hurt me; she is just where she belongs."

Solace, "Challis is happy but sad, he's so concerned about Giselle and their children, because Giselle has a serious concussion, torn rotary cup, tear bicep and butted in the head by a gun."

Rea, "it's just what those fools do when you're being nice but letting them know you're taken and still gone. Lord, let me get where all of will be able to be together like we should be when one of us is celebrating or in trouble."

Solace, "Rea, I love you."

Rea, "I love you to, Sade and Don are still over in Africa, I cannot wait till she can see and hear.

Any way on our way, she screams again, hangs up and dances and 3 hours goes by and Challis isn't back with the kids or Giselle.

Mike's wife, Cindy, "Baby I'm here."

Mike told her to come let them go and eat. Cindy speaks to everybody, they speak back, and another hour goes by. Karen said to him to everybody, she is Jamison's II wife; everyone speaks and leaves but came back in a couple of hours. They are all are sitting around watching TV and music is on low.

Rea and Frank, "we are here!"

Solace runs and hugs her sister. Jamison Senior hugs his sis in-law then shakes Frank's hand.

Rea, "Where are our babies?"

China, "Hello."

Challis, "Hi, we're still doing test, can you help us?"

China, "What?"

Challis, "it's another bag that says night please, goes in the closet and bring and 4 more bottles and we're in the maternity side, in the office."

She hangs up.

Solace, "What are you doing?"

China, "Challis needs him to get some stuff because they are still testing."

Solace, "This long? hope everything is alright?"

China, "He didn't say anything, let me go but let me grab my sister."

Solace, "he just bought me all kind of stuff."

Rea, "China, how is she?"

China, "she peeped in on her, but it is taking longer because she is injured, she cannot be under a MRI machine long."

Rea, "I wonder if they don't sedate her."

China, "She isn't going to let them do that and she has to nurse."

Rea, "She can't do all that."

China goes in an hour; the babies are all bathed, fed and asleep. Challis strolls in and Rea screaming quietly; "Let me see, let me see."

Challis, "They're asleep"

Rea, "they're all so cute and all that hair, boy you got some good-looking kids. I'm so proud of you."

They hug Challis, picks up Challis II.

Cindy, "Hi my fullback nephew, Rea, what's his name?"

Rea, "Challis II."

Karen, "he's nice, handsome and too cute."

Challis puts him to bed then he gets up.

Caviar called, Frank look at that boy, big hands and huge feet.

Rea, "they are so handsome."

Challis, "China, help me so I'll go and shower."

She washes her hands, goes and picks up her sister's daughter Solace. Rea saw her open her pretty eyes.

Rea, "Hello!"

Solace cries, she gives her to her grandmother, mama sugar and she stops crying.

Rea, "I like that."

China, "they still hate you."

Rea, "they're going to love me."

China gets up, picks Solace and she cries.

Rea, "with your beautiful self, these kids are gorgeous magazine movie like."

Challis, "give her to me."

She stops crying.

Rea, "well, I don't know what to tell you but keep trying."

China, "yes, they're just funny acting."

Challis mom asked for Solace and lays her grand-daughter Solace on her lap and rocks her then pats her on her shoulder. Rea told her they're use to her; she sings to them and they fall back to sleep.

Rea, "They just wanted their Sugar, they smell so good."

Challis showers, washes and dries his hair, apply oil, cologne, deodorant and dresses up. He comes out, takes his daughters, and puts them both in bed.

Challis, "I'll be right back."

Mommy, "where are you going?"

Challis told her that this is too long for her. While he is gone, the nurses and transportation unit bring Giselle back, she is knocked out and asleep but has been bathed and changed.

Cindy, "the Lion Queen, she's on everything, she is really pretty."

Karen, "yes, she's very pretty."

China, "put her in bed."

The men lift her.

China takes off her boot slippers, Jamison Senior offered to call Challis because he'll be out looking all over for her, he dials Challis number. His Dad, they just brought Giselle and she was asleep when they brought her.

Challis, "ok thanks I'll be up, I'm in records and billing."

Dad, "what's wrong?"

Challis, "they've not switched billing, they got bae still paying for everything. I'm here so they'll redistribute all her money back."

His dad accepted and hung up.

Mommy, "what's going on?"

Dad, "they still haven't switched the billing."

Mommy, "they'll change that."

Mike, "they better, before Challis bust a gasket."

Mac, "he's right."

Some time goes by and Challis is back.

Dad, "have you handled it?"

Challis, "yes."

Dad, "The best view of in the world."

Rea, "you know it."

Challis saw his auntie, so he goes to hug her.

Challis, "I'm so glad you're here oh and Uncle Frankie.

Challis, "Frank", then after he shakes and hugs him, his stomach growls, "man I am starving."

Mommy, "what do you want to eat?"

Challis, "Thick crust pizza salad meaty Italian subs."

Mac offered to order.

Challis, "cool!"

Rea, "Kind."

Challis, Dr. Shaunae with Nurse Vicky comes in.

Dr. Shaunae, "we just need to get their vitals."

Challis turns on one light and they start with the babies and none of them woke up. They weighed the girls,

Dr. Shaunae, "1lb more each."

Challis, "what is there weight at now?"

Dr. Shaunae, "6 lbs."

His mom and Auntie Rea clap, "Yeah."

Dr. Shaunae, "What of Giselle's vitals?"

Challis, "she said her head is killing her and her neck hurts so badly."

Dr. Shaunae feels her.

Dr. Shaunae, "Her head is warm."

Nurse Vickie took her temperature.

Nurse Vickie, "104 doctors."

Dr. Shaunae, "blood pressure?" She puts the cuff on.

Nurse Vickie, "166/100 Dr. Shaunae."

Challis sees her falling, he grabs her, and she faints. Rea, that's just how she did in that park.

Mommy, "she's just exhausted."

Dr. Shaunae writes to nurses then goes and checks Giselle, she feels her skull, Giselle wakes.

Dr. Shaunae, "Right that is where it's swollen Inflammation. I have to give you something for that and let me see."

She calls to find out labs on.

Dr. Shaunae, "I'm starting her on 1000 VCU's and vitamin D lab tech deficient and she is anemic iron. Nurse Vickie will be back with the low dose of Ibuprofen, vitamin D and Iron supplement."

Giselle, "Dr. Shaunae" I have never been anemic."

Dr. Shaunae, "when you have babies, they pull down your iron levels, and you were very malnourished when you had them and too much underweight and if your numbers do not improve your babies will be on Similar and back in the nursery till you get better. Think, if you also pass out you could harm or worst your preemies."

Giselle, "I don't understand that just because I have never done drugs, alcohol or smoked."

Dr. Shaunae, "when did you lose your parents?"

Giselle, "6 months ago."

Dr. Shaunae sits on the bed, "not as everyone else but as your doctor, I observed your fainting at the park because of loss of oxygen, then you probably did not fall asleep on the boat because it drenched you. If so, why didn't the water awake you? You were comatose then you got hit in the head with the butt of a gun."

SEASONS OF LIFE AND THE ALTAR CALL OF CHRIST

Giselle said, "I don't know about that Dr."

Dr. Shaunae, "do you remember what was around you, anyone, or thing at the park?"

Giselle, "I did not fall to sleep in the park, I had too much work to do."

Dr. Shaunae, "then you're kidnapping?"

Giselle said, "I remember nothing after I was getting off the elevator."

Dr. Shaunae, "neurologists Dade will be into see you tonight, my obligation is to you and your children."

Dad, "she needs to see she's lion queen."

Dr. Shaunae, "ok, Nurses will be in with meds and what have you eaten?"

Giselle, "soup and crackers."

Dr. Shaunae, "you should eat protein (chicken, boiled eggs), salad, fruit, veggie, smoothies and nuts and to eat when others eat and eat much."

She accepted and said she'll hydrate as well.

A nurse comes in with meds and food, China put it on a tray. The nurse gives Giselle her meds and water and they start Iv's.

Challis asks Mike to play it which he gladly does. Giselle looks at her and China, then they both see China, Giselle says nothing, just turns and cries and pushes her tray away more cover over her and she hugs her children closer to her; moved to a private room."

Challis, "Why?"

Giselle, I'm going under."

China, "For how long?"

Giselle, "Until I hear from God and I'm healed from God."

Challis, "you can hear from him right here, he can heal you from right here."

Mommy, "she couldn't." Giselle, "I need my dad."

She cries and they all hear.

China, "don't cry, I'll feed and take care of my boo boo's all night as long as it takes."

Giselle, "take my place until I can be better, or I am going to lose my children, don't give them cow's milk."

China, "I won't let them, no worries."

She sobs more.

Challis, "no I got them and stop crying."

China, "how do you like your new sheets and comforter? Challis bought you all."

Giselle, "I wanted to be alone

Rea, "she's right, no she can't too many of us."

Giselle, "our children are accompanying me with China."

Challis, "no, none of our kids are going."

Giselle, "it's not up to you, I'm the custodial parent tell him."

Mac, "Challis, she has them here you're not married."

Challis, "we're getting married."

China, "Where?"

Mac, "stay out of it, go baby."

Giselle presses a button for another room and Nurses come in, she tells them to take her and her babies to the maternity ward floor. The Nurses left and starts putting the babies in their hospital basinets.

"Dr. Shaunae wants to do a scope on them."

Giselle, "ok."

They leave with them and China follows, then she comes back.

Giselle, as she changes into other bed, "I believe in God and this is not descent and in order, this is about my Lord, my kids and me having a pure blessing that we need that only He can give me from my father Christ."

Challis, "is it decency and in order that I love you and our children, that I want to spend the rest of my life with you all to protect you, to provide for you."

Giselle, "Challis, I'm not leaving you but let's be clear and true, I am not having my children on cow's milk that's number 1and I will not kill one or all my children and lose them, number 2, go home let me do what I have to do and no I'm not getting married in the hospital."

Challis, "why does it matter where we get married as long as we do."

Giselle, "I want to be taken to my room, see that's the problem, 6-months right."

Challis said he proposed Giselle yell as she leaves.

Challis, "wait, I called you and your father."

She cries, "when?"

Challis, "Monday."

Giselle, "that's all that mattered to me."

China kissed her husband, "do you want any of this stuff? Challis bought you all."

Giselle, "leave it."

China, "it's a nice stuff."

Lawyer Salmon appears and rushes in, "Giselle, I'm so sorry, I just got the word. When security contacted me, I was over in Dubai settling some of your abroad affairs from your father's instructions before the New Year comes in, then suddenly, a team of 10 lawyers with different ethnicity and dressed to the nine come in he finishes Attorney Salmon, uh, we hurried as quickly as we could I and your fathers care council for you has all arrived."

Giselle, "Lord God, thank you,"

Mr. Salmon just comes without a knock, "I need to shut everything down immediately."

CHAPTER 10

Isolation

Mrs. Sowell comes in as a very sophisticated classic movie actress but a little older and walks over, "the facility is ready for you to shut down; we will move you immediately. All these people are unacceptable, and we know we have intercepted your children."

Challis, "can they do that?"

Mac, "It's in his will and they go word for word from his estate and she's the custodial parent, you aren't married."

Mrs. Sowell kept looking around, "we have a team of doctors, nurses and specialists that your father handpicked for circumstances just as this at a disclosed private hospital out of town. No one there but us and you."

Giselle said, "thank you Lord, we're from the house that Caviar Simonies the IV built, we always have everything I need, always."

Mrs. Sowell, "The 2 lions are controlled by a satellite GPS monitored imbedded within you that triggers your security, that pen points where you are at all times. It activates the Navy by a signal from the two to the security panel your father formed for you. Now let's be clear."

Giselle talked about her bracelet and necklace, which her father gave her.

Mrs. Sowell, "yes and your princess right ring finger and toe ring, he did as well."

Challis, "where the hell have you all been?"

Mrs. Sowell puts on her glasses and looks Challis up and down, "He must be Mr. Calms-ways.

Challis, "Where are they taking my family to?"

Giselle, "Mrs. Sowell, please tell him."

Mrs. Sowell, "The White House, the President of the United States of America is Giselle's Uncle, her father's brother. He's expecting her and her children. He has sent us Air Force One."

China, "this is what am talking about."

Mac, "be quiet!"

Mrs. Sowell, "will Mrs. China be accompanying Giselle?"

China, "yes, ma'am."

Giselle, "I'm ready to go Challis, we will return in 3 weeks."

Challis, "No, am coming with you, I'm their father."

Giselle, "I won't be able to speak, and I have to, when I return, I'll be well and our children will be, you'll see."

Challis," it's not just about you, but it's about our children and me. Three weeks is a long time they will not remember me, they would have grown, I would have missed them."

Giselle, "God help me, I don't know what we're going to do, this is not how I want to be but well, I will not lose my children. I have to make peace and wellness at the altar call of Christians. There is no other way, God he does not understand."

Giselle passes out and China runs screams for the Dr. Shaunae comes and checks her, "we have to take her right now", and other staff came and rushed her to surgery.

Challis runs behind them. Solace, "Ethel, why are you giving your baby boy a hard time?"

Mrs. Sowell said, "I'm not Butter, and her children are my obligation."

Giselle had to get surgery; she had some inner bleeding going on some hours ago. Specialty doctors came, Dr. LaHu, a neurologist entered, she's in a semi-coma, and breathing on her own, time goes by.

Challis, "mom, she is just afraid."

Mommy, "she did not plan this but there is no other way, she has to shut down, when you all go, you cannot interact with her."

Challis, "I'm sure."

Giselle wakes; he goes over and kisses her.

China, "stop scaring me."

Giselle, "quiet please, I have little time."

Challis, "God told me to marry you today."

Mrs. Ethel Sowell, "the President has arrived."

President Waters comes in, "well, what a true Christmas for me to see you, and what do you need my only niece?" President Waters sees his huge nephews and tells them he loves them.

President Waters, "you all I know have not seen me since you were a child."

He kisses Giselle on the forehead.

Giselle, "Thank you."

President Waters, "I heard you want to get married today."

Giselle, "yes sir"

President Waters, "ok. Ethel, take care of everything."

He left after 2 hours.

China, "why are we leaving so soon?"

Giselle, "God woke me just to tell you that me our babies will go into a deep sleep and He told me to tell you till next Christmas, and Challis don't be afraid we're going to be all new when we return."

Challis, three deaths are coming soon in the New Year."

China, "Who?"

Giselle, "it's none of them, God told me to tell one of you but not me that 3 unexpected births will be."

China, "not me, we're done."

Giselle, "God does what he wants to do."

China, "I know but just not this to me."

Giselle, "anyway, he has given you a task as well, Cha, you are to build us a home with only God's fullness of earth and God said He will tell you where for us, He also told me to tell you to get our house in order. Mrs. Sowell, the Lord told me to trust God with all my heart and to give Challis the power of attorney over us all and all our cash and assets and that he is to take us home with him."

Mrs. Sowell, "where will that be?"

Giselle asks her to come and she does.

Giselle hugs her; "we will be fine wherever he sees fit."

Ethel took a breath and kissed Giselle on the cheek, "ok."

Challis, "the Lord is our and we shall not want. Study yourself to show yourself approved and it will be up to the Lord's measure as to you, now, we will awake by Christmas coming. He also said, be accountable over a few things, no cow's milk and take good care of us please. Giselle, I will, though as we sleep at The Alter Call of Christ, He will direct you as to what to do. He also said your spirit is to be right as one with the onetime speeds."

Mrs. Sowell, "everything is finished."

Time goes by and they marry.

Mrs. Sowell, "Challis, family council with you at the head now we will remain but now as you and Giselle's entire family council."

Challis, "I promise you that when you and our kids awake baby, we're going to have a real wedding and our home is going to be finished."

Challis, God helps them. us

Dad, "come on home son."

Challis cries.

Ethel, "the same medical team will assist you at home."

As time goes by, Challis kisses his wife and kids.

Giselle, "when they awake, they will be all brand new."

By midnight, Giselle and their babies are in a deep unawake able sleep.

Challis, "Dad, this is a lot.

Dad pats him, "we're all going to be alright."

With the help of Giselle's Uncle, the President, he flew all of them home, China and Mac go home, and months goes by, they still feed them by I V's and all is still alive and asleep. The staff, doctors and nurse are all around the clock, Rea and Frank have moved in to help then the Physical therapist, Sony, rings the doorbell.

Challis runs and gets the door, "hello"

Sony, "HI, I'm from the agency."

Challis, come on in."

He hands him her folder; he reads and sees she has great credentials.

Challis, "it will be my wife."

Sony, "it will be fine as well as him."

Challis, "I'm fine, my policy though, are you married?"

Sony, "yes, never mind."

Challis, "please say."

Sony, "all is well."

Challis, "Nurse Jamia, please fill my wife's new physical therapist in."

Nurse Jamia, "let me show you."

Mommy, "who was that?"

Challis, "it's the Physical therapist."

"I got to run."

"Where are you going to?"

Challis, "Dad, are you ready?

Dad, as he puts down his coffee, "yes, let me grab my jacket."

Challis Grand Daddy walks in.

Challis, "hey."

Mommy, "hey, how are you doing daddy?"

She hugs him.

Paul IV, "where are those pretty babies and wife?"

Challis, "come with me and see."

Constance comes in, "hello!"

Solace, "yes mama."

Rea, "daddy when did you get here?"

Paul IV, "This morning."

Rea, "Mama, God is good."

Constance, "I'm here to see for myself God's family, his bride, children and creation."

Rea, "Come on, can't keep nothing from you."

Couple of hours pass and Challis, his dad, granddaddy and his brothers all meet at an enormous piece of land with the Hudson River trees directly in back and huge right amid downtown.

Challis "Mike this is huge all these acres."

Dad, "it's beautiful,"

Grand Daddy Pope, "it's good for fishing, I better jump on it."

Challis, "I already purchased it this morning."

Dad, "here the house will be?"

Challis, "I want the water to be seen on every side of us."

Jamison Senior, "it's massive and secluded; you can almost miss it if you aren't looking."

Challis, "that's what I like, all business Private schools in the loop, I like this and the breath of God at the helm of the treetop, I feel this is us."

Jamison II, "Challis, I like the works."

Dad, "how much did you pay?"

Challis, "guess."

Dad, "30 million."

Mike, "40 million."

Grand daddy, "20 million."

Jamison, "100 million,"

Challis, "as far as you can see and not see, we own all the mountains at the hem of God's Breath for 1dollar. The land went into an auction and I was ready to battle. No one showed but an auctioneer and his staff and the rest is history. Here's is our deed."

Mike, "Hell no!"

Their dad takes it and reads.

Dad, "What God has for us is just for us."

Challis, "This is where our home is going to be."

Mike, "Yes, you, your wife and children, the Lord is with you all I know."

Hugs his little bro.

"Man, this is sensational."

They hug each other.

Challis, "Wake up here with my wife, our children, as soon as I woke up I prayed and the Lord brought me here in the wee hours of this morning as the sun came in, fresh morning dew fell and when we were home, it rains."

The fence guy, security guy came.

Challis, "I want a security both at each entry."

Kenneth, "ok but sir, in the outskirts, wild horses roam free."

Challis, "I'll need a map guy."

Challis pulls out a pen and looks at his purchase.

Challis, "ok, we're here and we're 127,000 miles out, so we own the free range. I want to put over their wire fence, barbed wire, set alarm triggers to main gate security unit, all horseback and mountain bike patrol all along 24 hours."

Kenneth, I'll do it and my team will start in the morning."

The rain really pours, and they all rushed to Challis car. His brothers go to theirs.

His Grand Daddy acknowledged his work.

Challis, "it's God's doing."

Month passes by, spring has come, and Easter has risen. His mom, auntie, and grandmother have cooked up half of the stores.

Mommy, "let me get on my shoes" as she takes off her apron.

Rea, "we all better get going."

Challis, "I'm not going."

Mommy, "you are, God said He's with the one."

Challis, "I don't want to leave my family."

Dad, "what do you have a staff for?"

Mommy, "one dollar for Gods hems of breath, boy, you better know Jesus' truth, do as He has told you."

Challis went to throw on a Jacket and his mom reminded him of his tie. He goes to his family, and he kisses each of them then he looked at his wife and could she be healing. He was happy but he miss them all tremendously; he thought as he gazed that his children were growing right in front of his eyes; he went and put on a suit and tie. As they were about to pull off, China and Mac pulled up.

China, "hi, we came to stay with my sister a couple of days."

Challis welcomed them and they all left.

Sony whispers in Giselle's ear, "Mrs. Calm-way is pretty but old and I'm here to tell you that when you wake, you'll be divorced and all 4 of your kids will call me mommy."

Suddenly, Nurse Jamia and Nurse Kimmie both walk in the room and say hello.

Nurse Kimmie, "let's get you dolled up for Easter, your husband has left specific instructions and laid you and you all are children out some beautiful spring clothing."

Sony, "can she hear?"

Nurse Jamia, "of course."

Dr. Hymen and Dr. Renesys comes in, both say hello.

Mrs. Calm-Way, "how are you, hope you're doing well?"

They check on her.

Sony leaves and looks around the house, goes into Challis other room and takes off her panties and leaves them under his pillow.

Nurse Jamia notices the door ajar of Challis other room and she goes in and startles Sony!

Nurse Jamia, "what are you doing in Mr. Calms-Way room, we are not allowed in there?

Sony, "I was just seeing, isn't Mrs. Calms-Way moving in here?"

Nurse Jamia, "yes Mr. Challis."

Sony, "it's big enough to do her physical therapy right in here," and she walks out.

Nurse Jamia turns off the light and shut the door, and "this bitch is trying to get herself served shit, Mr. Challis is totally in love with his wife and children, she better know, the only bitch working here and not married, pretending."

Nurse Jamia, "Hey Nurse Kimmie, why was your girl in boss's bedroom?"

Nurse Kimmie, 'he's not married and prowling, but she will see that the man is sold."

Nurse Jamia, "I'm surprised he went to church."

Nurse Kimmie, "he needs that she went last night and was in the spirit, she and Daryl and even prayed for Mrs. Calms-Way and their babies."

Nurse Jamia, "they're just growing, and she prays for them every day also and it's a lot well. Let me get my work done."

Nurse Kimmie, "and you know mama packed each of us some vittles."

Nurse Jamia, "we know she, her sister and granny can throw-down."

Nurse Kimmie, "I'm hiding mine; Daryl isn't eating nothing but what I cooked. They laugh, they have all missed Praise time."

Challis was tired from helping with the babies, but he would not miss church for the world. He pulls up and

Parks his car in the first spot he can find, which was way in the back of the lot. He jumps out of the car rushing to make it to church breathing hard every step of the way. He arrived just as the ushers all filed in one by one. An usher grabbed him and brought him to the front. Challis didn't mind sitting up front, but he would be incognito plus he wanted to hurry back home with his family. He noticed several women smiling at him, but he remained focus with his mind on lock. Bishop Connors came right in at the pulpit and all stood, "let's pray! Our father art in heaven hallowed be thy name, Lord we come to you this morning with every intention of being led by you Lord. We appreciate you Lord God, there is such a time as this as I ask you to allow your word to come in and singe every-one of our hearts. God, there is something I know that you wish to say, use me, defile my flesh, pull the Veil back, go my God, we all step back in Jesus mighty name, amen. He speaks to the people, now this day that my God has made, the Lord has been moving me in a but certain way now and there's nothing like a pastor being fed up and sick of his own flock. Now I'm not talking about a lot of you but I'm sure you know who you are."

"First scripture I'll use a couple of times today, most stand, "if you can't stand for the word of God then for all of you whom I know did not wake yourselves up this morning, get up for my Lord."

They all do and he asks them to open **Genesis 2:24** "That is why a man leaves his father and mother and is united to his wife, and they become one flesh."

Romans 12:10, please say amen! Most of the church body does then he says amen.

He reads, "Now Be devoted to one another, and asks, you all read that!" most congregations say yes then they say, "In Love, Honor one another above yourselves."

Bishop said they are going to read today till they're tired. He told them to lean on their neighbors. He asks them to read again and they all do, he asks them to be seated.

They all sit.

Bishop, "my sermon today is '**the line in the sand**' now, our church of 30,000 peace be still. Lord there is so much mess going on up in here, we got marriages that for over 40 years falling to the waste side, we got young daughters that have grown up in this church from birth tearing apart marriages that have been the pillar of our church. We got little boys that grew up in this church going with husbands of the church, now I know that a whole le lot of you know, yes, I threw several people out, now if you don't know who they are then you don't need to know, if it bothers you then the doors are open to leave when-ever either of you choose."

Bishop, John 2:15 **King James Bible,** "And when he had made a scourge of small cords, he drove them all out of the temple, and the sheep, and the oxen; and poured out the changers' money, and overthrew the tables, see this is not my church, but I am the shepherd of it just like a lot of men are supposed to be. Now, some but not all are the head of their households."

"How is it that me and my wife could lie down and have all our 5 kids and maintain myself and them and just one simple Simon came in my office talking about how he wanted me to be the first to know? I truly don't know why but I let him talk, he said he was leaving his wife cause she was extinct now, and I told him cause I'm a little slow, I know his wife, she is a pillar here and she don't look like no dinosaur to me, I told the nigga to elaborate some more."

The congregation laugh and he went on and all about how he was ready to live and all his wife want to do is clean, cook, tutor their 4 kids and take care of their home and I asked him did she take care of him.

"She stills irons all my shirts and I ask him what the problem was because I did not understand. He told me she was out of style. I asked him to make it plain, and he told me that all week, she wears jeans every day, work out gear and tennis shoes and he said she says it's easier to care for their kids and do her in home Day care business. I asked him, was the business lucrative? He said yes, she clears around $350,000 a year now going on 5 years, I ask him, and does her business interfere with other things? he said no, by time I get home from my law practice around 6 or 7, dinner is set. My wife then has one maxi or other type comfy dress and my family is waiting for me and he said, "I am so sick of the same old same" I told him well since you're the life of the party spice it up, now these kids he's talking about, they all are cramping his style. He told me between him and me he detested being a parent anymore, living with his children."

Now I say all this to say **Ephesians 2:20-22** "Built on the foundation of the apostles and prophets, with Christ **Jesus** himself as the chief cornerstone. [21]In him **the** entire building is joined and rises to become a holy temple **in the** LORD. [22]And in him you too are being built together to become a dwelling in which God lives by his Spirit,". Now this kind of ignorance is what I'm talking about, save Christian posers cause you can't say you're living this life as a Christian life style, this type of nonsense is not of God nor is it that young souls come up in here and seasons souls want to ridicule them before they have even joined. When I started up in the church, a lot of things I wasn't done with like cussing, drinking, I'll tell my wife stand up baby, she stands and then sits back down. She just kept telling me, "come as you are, it'll vacate slowly because you're willing and that is true, as we serve God, some things from the world should be changed from you. I want every last one of you of Gods flock to know this, that the devil is a liar cause I'm not running no daycare up in here or pity parties, you aren't going to just come up in here and I know with your new, what they say baby, you two doing communion together and your wife sitting right up in there and your children, let's be clear, let the church say amen, the entire body says amen.

Bishop, "Bless God!" At the same time the devil is running the table on most of you and the world is also with all your stair step children, all clean descent and in order, no, and you oh don't try me cause I have not always been up in the pulpit. I'm not having it, now, I know I cannot tell you how to live or what to do but it's apparent that we all should work on getting to heaven down here, he steps out the pool pit and walks down and says, "don't you want to go to Heaven."

His congregation says yes, many crying and standing, "Men, man up now, the women cause you are not innocent swingers, sleeping with each other's neighbors bringing extra partners between the sheets, yes I said it, that is not of God and you think I was watching the news the other night and this woman had been married for over 20 years but she faked her death to receive I think it was 50 million, his wife 100 million, I guess her partner said they had been together throughout her marriage plus she and her husband with several other women and, she said how they had become accustomed to a certain particular life style and then I looked that next morning and both were dead and I see they had also kidnapped this other particular women's quadruplets. I know you all saw it; it's been all over the news 24/7. Yes, they found her and her lover. The wife of the man in their cells in fatal positions were dead, and they were each in a cell alone, they are marveled, they don't even know how it happened but listen to me,

Philippians 2:10-11 New King James Version (NKJV) "that at the name of Jesus every knee should bow, of those in heaven, and of those on earth, and of those under the earth, ¹¹ and *that* every tongue should confess that Jesus Christ *is* Lord, to the glory of God the Father,". Now say amen to that the entire church does.

Then this man that died, he had kidnapped this same woman the day before the same woman whose quant's that were born on Christmas got kidnapped by the 2 so called lovers and he was in jail also and that's the same man they found dead also in his cell the same morning. I told you about earlier, they found the two so called partners then prior to all that the same woman, the quant's mom, she is the Lion Queen almost all say fell out in the park. I saw too and look, God sent them lions to protect her, now they saying they had a trigger to come from her father by a satellite he put in a bracelet or ring before he got killed. Now, I don't care what you say, or they and he is dead, and her mother is also, see, God takes care of his own.

Then she was on the ship, she drove to have a service for her parents, they all say, "yes" and the navy seals off, the navy ship rescued her. I think she got out there and got turned around, but Jesus says in **Matthew 6:26** "Look at the birds of the air; they do not sow or reap or store away in barns, and yet your heavenly Father feeds them. Are you not much more valuable than they?"

People shout all over,

Bishop, "See, God is asking you a question?"

People shout more.

"Stand, if our Lord and Savior can take care of the birds believes me, he can take care of you."

Church gets happier, some start shouting, running and throwing money on the pulpit. Bishop, "Hallelujah! Don't make me shout up in here. See, I say this all to say if your marriages are going flat, pray about them. Take your wife to the spa, all ladies love the spa, most of the men in here are millionaires, if you aren't then come see me and hire your wife a trainer, you all work out together, go home. Wives get those demons out of your beds, your homes move, I'm telling you God is about.

1 Corinthians 14:40 "But everything should be done **in** a fitting **and** orderly way,".

Bishop, "God expects us to live decent and in order, that's it, my wife some-times get on my last nerve, she yells and says I don't care."

The congregation all burst out laughing.

Bishop, "and she doesn't just, because she is aging, I am too. Does not mean you should go out and get somebody young you all think new and improved."

Bishop calls them fools!

His wife yells, "No."

Bishop, "She don't want me to call you fools, any way your wife's self-worth and your husband's self-worth is not no mere cars or mere stuff. Stupid life, love, truth and happiness, I think."

Bishop, "but oh, well, I call you all like I see them now, some of you will get, mad and leave the church, fine, I do not care, ushers show them the doors and they do but if you want to live decent s and in order, this is the church for you, yes, we are all trying, no one's perfect but the edified body of Christ but sit, sit he motions his hands. Please listen to me, I care how all of you are living as your Shepherd."

They all sit.

Bishop, "there comes a time!"

Proverbs 23:5 "Cast but a glance at riches, and they are gone, for they will surely sprout wings and fly off to the sky like an eagle that you all this day choose."

Joshua 24:14-15 "Now fear the LORD and serve him with all faithfulness. Throw away the Gods your ancestors worshiped beyond the Euphrates River and in Egypt and serve the LORD. [15]But if serving the LORD seems undesirable to you, people then **choose** for yourselves this day that you will serve, whether the God your ancestors served beyond the Euphrates, or the gods of the Amorites, in whose land **you** are living."

But as for me and my household, as your Bishop, people run, jump and scream all around, we **will serve** the LORD. Up

"Keep thy heart with all diligence; for out of it are the issues of life." Savior, his worthy people crying got to put the line in the sand and leave your old natures behind. Come on because God is not playing, I don't want to die before my time, no, but see, you got to try. They all sit, and he says, listen to me, just try to live right, people start crying and shouting they're sorry and for the Lord to forgive them.

Bishop Connors tells them that neither he nor his wife is perfect. My wife left me now, not recently this was when we first started our church and she got sick and tired of people talking about us and church not paying us. I quit my job for God, she quit her job too and told me, "if you aren't working, I am not either."

The church body all laugh.

Bishop continued, she then took our kids, and I thought she's going to leave me. I came back and a little hood still in me I said forget her, I called her and told her I'm getting a new wife with new improved kids, she hung up on me and changed her number.

They all burst out laughing.

Bishop laughs a little too, "she was serious."

I was always complaining about my wife and see the devil is real to every one of those men that told me to divorce my wife. Today they are all on either their 2nd marriage or not with their wives. God told me I was the head and not the tail to go get my wife and I said to my God, "she changed her number and I don't like her anymore."

The congregation laughs.

Bishop continued, "and God said nothing. I said, why did you give me her."

They all laugh.

See, I was acting like Adam, I said I don't want her, she can't hold a tune my, mamma can't stand, and his mom yells I love her now but you, they all laugh.

Bishop, "now that's my mama but see women stick together, I asked my mom when she was gone what are you cooking I'm hungry and she said, you got a wife and she slam the phone down on me, she changed her number too."

And they all laugh.

"He says no, she didn't but she would not feed me or talk to me for a while, I was mad and my God's Church had not paid me one cent and I told my God I built that church still he said nothing. I said, all your church people are miss treating me, I'm giving them my last still he said nothing, and I was still preaching all over like a storm."

James 2:17 "In the same way, faith by itself, if it is not accompanied by action, is **dead.**"

I had to fly to California to get her and all our 4 kids and fly all us back. I told my God you sticking it to me, he still said nothing, I told my Him if she don't come then my car back tire blew flat on the interstate in the pouring rain while I was on my way to the airport so I had to fix it then I barely I made it to the airport delayed. I was just like; look at my Jesus, I say, "Lord, you know she left me."

They all laughed a bit.

Bishop continued, "So I arrived there at her sister's house, she hated me and she said your ex-wife, my baby sister and my nieces and nephews are out on a date with a real man, her new husband and their new daddy and she shut the door. I was about to lose it, but her husband opened the door and he said, your wife and kids are in the back yard.

They were having a barbecue, all swimming, just doing it up. My kids all run to see their daddy, they so love me and his kids all yell, yes, we do, and his congregation laughed a bit. I get over to my wife, she's playing cards and laughing, she asks, what took you so long? You know after 5 days we were ready to come home, I told her neither of us got a job to do till Sunday and we were staying 5 more days, she said ok and I said bless God cause it would not have been pretty for my kids but look I went to the store with my wife's brother-in-law Keith and this little white lady says to me, you look like you deserve a gift and I said definitely. She then tried to hand me a lottery ticket, and I refused, her daughter said please take it so me and her can go, I went on and took it. I put the lottery ticket, and she said you won, take your family home, build up your church and put your house in order, if you don't do as God has said you will not live. Now I know it's a lot of things I wasn't supposed to do, I know, but I took that lottery ticket and yes I did."

They laugh.

I put it right in my pocket and when I got back; I gave the lottery ticket to my wife; she said we've been gone 5 days now and you're playing the lottery. They all burst out laughing, he says, I told her what happened and her sister said, let me write these numbers down cause you may win so we all fly home that night, I came to this land as we drove home and I stopped and I heard God say just as clear "you abide in me"

King James Bible

"If ye abide in me, and my words abide in you, ye shall ask what ye will, and I shall do it unto you". And I told my wife and kids to get out the car and we walked the property in the depth of night and it was pitch black, just light from our phones and we prayed and we asked God for our church of 30,000 to be there and help all over the world. That same night, my wife said, let me show you that house I want, so we went. Our kids were all sleeping in the car by now and nothing was there, we walked the grounds and prayed and asked God, we touched and agreed together. We went home, put our children to bed, and I went out on the porch under the light from the moon seemed on high, I just did not want to sleep so I started writing. I, Jesus and the midnight air of God. "Prodigal father", next morning my wife typed it up just on a whim, she had a friend in College that had a publishing company and in three days they wired into our account 1 million dollars first installment then my wife takes her 123 cake mix, send to Oprah to boom in1day, fresh out the gate over a million per orders. Some of you got her cake box, many in the congregation say yes, Bishop continues, then my sister-in-law and her husband called us 4 days later and her sister said we all won the lottery. I said we ain't all won nothing and they all burst out laughing, Bishop said, but we gave them a couple million, the lottery won his wife 777 million after taxes and I have tried my best to find that little old lady. I told my God, "please, let me bless her", he said no need, I already have and count your blessings and feed my souls and she was the angel Gabrielle. All the churches shout again, Bishop shout a little.

The wife of their youngest brother, and the father of her quadruples. The women are navy seal ladies, and the children are too. They have all been in a deep, deep sleep from God for several months.

Bishop, "Now let's pray, I'm calling them because some of us are going to have to go in on a fast and prayer for them because Christmas will be here before we know it."

Bishop, "His wife told them to also pray for Challis; that's her youngest son's name. She told me he has been really caring to them and, in New York."

His wife, "No he moved them home for a year."

Bishop said, "Now we take care of our own."

His wife said, "she's in a baby, no, a deep sleep from God, she said she told them all before it happened."

Bishop, "God did that and here they are today, still asleep for months, they are to awake on Christmas and the wedding is here,"

He thought they were already married.

His wife told him, "yes, but they got married while they were all in the hospital."

Bishop, "they need a nice big church wedding right here, Challis has taken care of them, he is a Billionaire, movie creator, producer, won the Oscars 4 times and he had enough sense to get his family in order before he takes them into their home."

Bishop continued, "see, I can work with that, men go home, and tummy tucks your wives."

"They were young when you got most of them, and the men were bald, we're old and no man weaves."

The congregation burst out laughing. All that glue stuff now comes and just to music plays.

"This is the last call, get your house in order, come!"

Thousands of people came down for prayer, other pastors are waiting.

Bishop, "draw a line in the sand."

Some persons did, but those who loved God only depended on God.

"Tell her husband and his family that God has told me to tell you all that he's putting us to sleep for a while."

"He asks, how many of you are going to fast?"

They all raised their hands.

Now he told them they are going to do a partial fast till Christmas and just on Wednesdays, from 6am till 6pm (completely fast).

He told them the lobby is filled with plenty of info on how fasting works, and on the church's website and our bulletin.

Every Sunday, 25 minutes to go, the doors of the church are open.

Time goes by and the alter call and prayer are finished.

Challis even went up unnoticed. He was glad Bishop did not notice him.

He asks them to sit down and calls for offering, he calls the ushers to come and he tells them that one basket is for offering, while the other baskets is for the offering to Challis' family.

His wife, "We got some stuff, we've got to support our own, and the Burles."

Each row went and paid their tithes and offering, while Challis did his on the website and gave a million. Some did the same, others put theirs in baskets for tithes and offering.

As time goes by.

Bishop tells his wife, "Come on up baby," "now I know some of you want to call or just drop by Solaces and Jamison's house."

"Don't, nor try to call her cause she doesn't like me half the time."

Congregation laughs.

Bishop, "she and my wife, and a lot of you know her, his wife and her sister Rea."

They all ran together.

"One time I got home, Solace and Rea put me out because they were praying."

They all burst out laughing.

"Like I don't know how to pray," they all smiled.

Bishop, "Now she has been our Congress representative in the Congress."

His wife, "For over 30 years, up on the hill."

He, "ok bow your heads and let's dismiss!"

"God rests with us, keep us and thank you God for your mercies, Amen!

Bishop asked them to wait, because his baby wants to say something!

"She said everyone who wants to help with The Calm-Ways and the Burles Family Funeral."

They all say Amen.

Bishop, "The panel should meet with me in 20 minutes over there, we will be there for about 2 hours!"

Tonya, "Chef Bob and Chef Dave subs, chips, drinks and a couple hundred."

Tonya goes, and the congregation came out with over a hundred men and women are going to the meeting. As Calm-Ways reach home, they all went in.

CHAPTER 11

New News

Challis runs upstairs, Sony has not heard them enter, but before Challis enters, she pinches his wife real hard. She already had to pinch each one of their kids.

Sony, "Oh hello, just finishing up."

Challis goes and kisses his wife and, "I miss you baby and love you."

Then he noticed they were all frowning.

He asks how long they've been like that as he keeps looking at them.

Sony, "I noticed it when I came in but no motion."

Challis intercoms the nurses, Nurse Jamia, and Nurse Kimmie come in.

Challis, "why are they still no smiles?"

Nurse Jamia told him that when they bathed them, they were all smiling as usual.

Nurse Kimmie added she was just up here before Sony and they were all smiling as usual. Challis, "ok."

Sony, "I'll be praying for Mrs. Calm-Way and your children."

Challis, "thanks."

And he goes and showers and moves his wife and kids downstairs to a bedroom.

He then makes sure they are all alright, and he goes to wash his hands, sits down, and have dinner. He gets up, brings his kids out of the nursery and reset the feeding tubes and changed. He bathed his wife again.

The room has a bathroom with everything, Nurse Shelia the night nurse and older comes in with 4 health aides.

Becky, Celeste, Doris and Sabrina, they all speak, health aides go and pump her Giselle's breast for baby's feeding, other nurses leave and health aides, who clean up and is doing laundry.

Nurse Sheila checks Mrs. Calm-Way, "no smiles tonight."

She says a prayer, then sits and starts doing crochet as she monitors them.

She turns on preaching on low.

Solace's mom, "what do you need?"

Challis, "nothing but prayer and fasting."

Solace, "Bishop Connors isn't playing."

Challis, "I have always liked him."

He keeps it 100, and that's all true. Solace asked if he saw the news.

Challis, "Not yet."

His dad, "here, front page!"

Challis takes and reads, "Jabra, Teresa and Clarence dead? They're all died last night?"

"I have never in my life been this close to God's truth and I'm living it, God is real."

His father, "Yes, he is so real."

"It's been a long time since he has seen such truth. Show your mama the land and she asked what land."

Challis pulls out push records, and he gives to her.

She gets up shouting, "What is it!"

Challis told her it's where he's building their home. She told him to better jump on it and give him his phone back.

Challis told her he has already bought it, and she says that's a lot of **acres.**

His dad asked him to tell her how much he paid, and he asks his mom to guess!

His mum, "20 million."

Challis, "No."

Her mum, "40 million."

Challis gets all the information, brings it back, and gives it to her.

She sees 'sold for $1' and indeed, his mom screams, "Jesus working it all out!"

Challis, "yes he is."

His mom, "what about all the water, the horses, and the heavens."

Challis, "yes, that's just what I'm calling it, "the heavens" how the Lord's breath just rests upon the tops of all the trees."

Challis, "nobody can do us like Jesus."

His mother told him he didn't have to tell her, God is all in this, that is why Bishop said what he said.

Jamarion Senior and all those people joined.

Challis, "All that shit excuse me ain't nothing but death."

He talked about Jabra, Shayla, Rhonda, Glo, Kelly, Monica, Shelby, Teresa, and my stupid ass.

"I thought I was doing something. She had all that shit worked out."

"I could not understand, you say you love me and you're bringing different women to our bed night after night, I was just like fuck it."

His mom, "she was doing all that for some reasons, number one she was gay, and secondly to distract you from knowing who and what she was really and up to."

Challis acknowledged, "yes, planning her death and I know she was paying all those women steadily."

"I still don't know how I made it out; I almost got caught up."

"Cause dad you asked me just as planned."

"Is this how you want to live your life?"

I was like, "dad I just want one of these women to give me a male child.".

His mom, "When?"

This was after she died, but God would not let any of them get pregnant. Plus, Shayla, Rhonda, and Glo all stayed around day in and day out, but I got sick of them."

"They had this stench that stunk to me and his mom told him they've all been like that, but he just started noticing his funky situation."

Challis, "I know something, and I put them all out, sold that property, and moved."

That was the worst deceitful living I ever experienced in my life and yes, I'm ashamed, I allowed the devil to come in, because I was being the tail. I'm married and going on existential trips with 3 women that are not my wife.

His mom tells him to calm down God loves him, yes, he does, you got a second chance to do right by God. See, that is what is so crucial at this moment.

She continued, that day God heard what Giselle said. When you said you were going, she said, "I don't know how I'm going to do this because I cannot talk to you."

Lord, she says, "please help me."

Challis yells and his mom continued, what did He will do?

Giselle gets sick, wakes, "God told me to tell you 'my God is putting us all into a deep sleep Challis.' His dad yells and his mom, "see God is showing you that what he says is how it's going to be, He's letting you know they are lent to you, but they belong to him."

Bishop, "Let's be clear."

Bishop said the word, confirm what Giselle said to you that things have to be decent and in order. Challis, "he heard her."

Bishop and his mom told him that God is not playing, whatever he has planned will be, no one will interfere, he did not care about you how you felt.

His dad said right because they've been sleeping month after season.

Challis, "yes."

And he got all this stuff to do before Christmas.

His dad, "what can I help you with that is right around the corner?" Mac has been helping him, I've been thinking that the entirety of downtown is for sale, the news station, the sports station, the radio station, hotels which used to be so elegant, restaurants, dinner bar, bank, upscale two high-rise apartment buildings to draw people in."

His dad, "What?"

Challis told him that he and Mac are pursuing to buy all, and his dad mentioned.

"I just bought on the same row, the senior building high rise, the Pharmacy Ballroom."

His wife, "What are we going to do with all that?"

Her hubby, "renovate it, upscale it cause it's all boarded up, sell our home and move in the entire top floor. His wife said she like that right downtown."

Challis tells them that everything is then a text from Mac came in and it reads, "We just purchased it all and we bought the mall, barbershop, beauty shop, bowling alley, ice skate rink, men's shinning shoe back" his dad said, "you did right."

Challis told them they got the Wells school now owned by Orphan's and Microsoft through 12, and they have intertwined with Macca College.

His mom, "Yes, that campus they renovated and scraped B. C's high-end store."

"It's a waiting list to go there, 10,000 per month."

Challis, "Yes, I peeped them ROTC, and I spoke to my wife's head attorney Solomon Samson and he sent me a certified letter and I read it."

As far as us having sons and daughters, Giselle's dad suggests that his works be maintained so that her children will have an ownership legacy.

His dad, "yes."

Challis continued, "Now as far as we know, the house and dress shop is cool. But when she gave me power of attorney, those decisions fell to me, so I have looked it all over and her daddy was heavy and I'm going to tell her we are keeping it all as it is."

"All of her mother and father's businesses have maintained a consistent flow of steady profit, and there are all modernized, and he owned all free no debt."

His dad," I think it's essential that all their works be not in vain."

His mom, "yes, she was not even running them."

Challis, "Yes, I know, and Attorney Solomon Samson is down."

He knew her dad, he told me her father made it his business to own everything that she looked at as she walked to school. That means something.

His dad, "Yes, it does black little girl, your daughter walking, she looking around knows inside my daddy owns all this, we own all this to your children also walking downtown and knows my daddy owns all this we own all this."

His mom, "tell me about it."

His dad, "Your kids need to see what her parents have accomplished to have a high expectation of self-worth."

Challis, "Growing up, going to school, looking at a bank, barbershop, apartments, houses, beauty shop that my father and mother own was saying something to me, now you mom a Congress representative and my dad mayor."

His mom thanked him and hugged him.

His dad said, "Thanks, it makes a difference cause white kids grow up feeling just that and it prong's them to be owners."

His mom, "Right, look at Giselle, she is smart and business-oriented because they groomed her."

His dad, "They came and gave her all her money and ownership right up front because her dad and mom trusted her, he knew who his daughter is."

Challis, "He also knew her heart."

His mom, "Yes."

Challis, "When I was in college, my Junior year Giselle hit the campus, she was quiet, nice, fine as ever but she joined everything, newspaper honor society, captain swim team, she was also on the cheerleading team, freshmen captain, foreign language club, math scholar, she came in on an academic cheerleading and ballet scholarship, she was in everything and I had a steady girlfriend name Candy but when I saw her, she ran up to me all smiling cause she wanted me to vote for her for student council President, she did not talk long but it was refreshing because she spoke about ethnicity and authenticity of even playing field means college life and voting for a cause she was very up to speed and polished."

"Friday night there was no game, she organized a wear all white for rally, and everybody came dressed in all white, I came also because she could cook."

"She had all these huge crock pots going real hot with her homemade chili dog sauce and huge homemade turkey, chicken franks and chips, pickles, condiments, and huge wooden barrels of freshly squeezed lemonade, plenty plates, cups, utensils. Oh, and she had also to die for cupcakes and cookies of all kinds called summer blossom, made with fresh fruit and big buckets of all kinds of ice cream with sugar graham cracker waffle condense."

The rally was about "our campus has to work for us" she was exposing all kind of wrongs that seeped within our campus, she hung on "equal is proven best" she was talking right and she had every persons ear going on 2 hours even mine and she had heavy weight after heavy weight to speak also and perform with her, she can blow as well.

When it was almost over hovering a flat foot solo and she was oh so rocking us and herself, she can go, and she can dance it was all over.

I with a couple of my teammates went to play ball, we were running back to campus around 10pm and as we shoot between building after building; I noticed a torn jacket on the ground.

I went to bed, the next morning I was jogging to practice classes late, and I saw the jacket again. I thought somebody will retrieve their jacket, then I went to throw my apple in the trash and it still bothers me extremely till today. I lift the big can and I hear someone murmuring.

I looked, and it was Giselle and she was barely hanging on. I jumped in the trash can and I got her out of there. Others came to help, and I told them to call 911. She was all bloody and beat bad, I had to give her CPR, that was so horrible.

She was out of school for a while, but when she returned, she was not the same bubbly. She came to me to thank me for rescuing her; I tried to talk to her, but she was not having it she kept it moving. One day I caught her in the library, she was tutoring people so I signed up to be tutored she was a little ticked and I asked her why she was giving me the cold shoulder; she said she was not; I asked her what's going on; she said nothing, and she left.

Marvin came over and told me he overheard Candy and Della playing a recording all over the airwaves of Giselle's early morning radio show, that I thought she was plain and corny.

His mom, "Did you say that?"

Challis, "Yes, but it was not in that entire context."

His mom, "So what was the context?" \

Challis continued, "I told Candy cause she was sweating me about Giselle and she said she's so plain, so boring just so simplified ugly, I was breaking up with her cause I was digging Giselle, she recorded me and kept the parts she wanted."

I said she is right, so seriously plain and corny but so damn interesting, simplified and so over whelming, naturally gorgeous and so damn popping and I bounced.

Couple of days went by, and cops Boom Rush our game and arrest Candy, Della and Dean, Furnace, assistant Dean Capren and the Torrez quintuplets' biker guys. They did not even go to our college; they were all around, they all had committed together a conspiracy against Giselle because she had discovered that they were selling drugs out of Shelta's house and embezzling immigration student's loan money with assistant Dean Capren.

His mom, "How did you found out all of that? "

Challis, "Because she worked in registration, in billing, and while she is on her lunch break."

"Sub for Dean Furnace's secretary, Mrs. Firestein, who went on maternity leave, and she had Giselle fill in for her part-time."

His mom, "Lord, Giselle has been something else."

Challis continued, "We went out for the rest of my entire last 2 years, there we became very close."

"I wanted Giselle to spend more time with me day and night."

His mom, "And lay-up with you?"

Challis said, "yes and no, I had fallen in love with her she wouldn't and even when I graduated, I wanted her to come here to meet all my family, she was mine and I wanted her to go to Mikes' wedding with me. I was so proud of her, and I needed her to be with me for the summer, but she wouldn't."

She said descent and in order and coming to stay with you for the summer and not stay here as I have told my parents I would apply myself to my studies, so I told her bye.

His mom, "You went back there for your Masters?"

Challis, "Yes, and I had a new girlfriend Honey, and I was happy, at least I thought so till we went to dinner, and I saw Giselle out with Codey Barkers' lame-ass, and I saw him all hugging her, and that infuriated me. So, I ran out the door after her, and Honey came right behind me running. I pushed her and got in between them and said descent. In order pointing at her over and over and her dad had pulled up, she was going home."

"I did not know her mom had just gotten into a car accident the day before, and she cried, and she said please stop. She hugged me and laid her head on my chest and she said, Cha, I care so much about you please stop, and she rubbed my head as she hug me more and she said you are such a wonderful person and I'm so sorry if I hurt you.

Her dad, "are you alright my butter baby?"

And she kisses me, "please forgive me!" "

"Yes sir, I'm coming."

And she ran to her dad and for me a terrible night.

I wanted Giselle so badly and Honey broke up with me same night.

His mom, "Guess so."

Challis continued, "And today she and Cody are happily married with 2 kids going on for 14years." His mom, "All this time you loved her."

Challis, "Yes, she did not return, but she graduated, she stayed home and went to college online to help take care of her mother."

His mom told him that all the time her mother was out she ran her mother's dress shop and she did not miss a beat; it was just like dealing with her mother.

Giselle can sew anything, no pattern needed and precise in cut fit and every part else, eloquence and cook from scratch. She made her mother's fruit jelly; I swore back then her mama made it, but the next time I and your auntie Rea went, she had us come in the big house and visit her mom while she was finishing orders.

I went in the kitchen she was just cutting up all this fruit and cooking her mama's jelly and making homemade biscuits; she fixes some air-fried center-cut pork chops and she drizzled them with homemade gravy then she whipped up some mixed veggies with herb butter from scratch and she pressured cooked all these apples with some-kind of mixture and butter over a bed of this herb and rice

Lord knows I ate a couple of plates, I can't lie, I and Rea were like a kid just eating and eating.

The food was so delicious and fresh.

Challis continued, "yes she can, but I did not see her again till she had stayed at Mac's and China to care for Mac junior, so they could still have their New Year's 1 2 3 party. By then I and hell were married."

His parents laughed, but he continued.

"I did not know that she and China were sisters, till that evening and she stayed in the back with Junior and she did not come out, but we stayed over till the next day. Early in the wee hours of the morning. I saw her clean the hell out of their place and she cooked us a gourmet five-star ass breakfasts from scratch, set the table and left."

China came in and she screamed, she was so happy.

Jabra out of the blue, "So lovely, for you how I cleaned your home, cooked and set the table."

China said, "You are a liar, only my sister does this plus this is all her signature linen, she personally designed off me what she made and also the matching signature place settings."

So, I was mad at Jabra and even then, she went on and on saying nothing, but a wall flower does this and she could not be married.

China was like what difference does that make, your husband went steady with her for 2 years in college.

Jabra, "Well, he's my husband."

China said, "I wonder how."

Jabra was pissed, and she kept drinking, pouring cups of coffee. She kept rolling her eyes at me and says, "This coffee is delicious."

China, "Take a really big drink cause look, a commercial came on showing Giselle's coffee commercial made for China."

China, "There goes my best only sister, and she shares the profits with me, also the one you say is a wallflower."

Night came and Challis noticed red marks on his wife, and then he looked at his babies and they all had them. He got upset; he went and asked each nurse as they came in what happened. As they told him, a new Physical Therapist came.

Challis, "ok." He had a camera installed, cause more and more he had to be gone, because his home was going up plus, he had to order everything for their wedding.

He thought that the hotel he just purchased today would be lavish for their reception, but he thought no we're getting married and going home, plenty of food, drinks, and love.

I just want to be with my kitty booboo and our babies who will be surely walking by then and talking cause Giselle was reading to them all the time and putting on tiny beats for them to listen to different languages and English CD's and the word of God.

It was late, and the crews were working, Challis was talking to his Forman and suddenly Challis sees Sony a walking, he tells his Forman excuse me, he goes, "You're alright?"

She, "Yes, I live a mile down the street, my car broke down."

Challis, "well, I could have your car towed to me friend, what's the problem?"

Sony, "I don't know."

Challis asks for her keys and tells her he will handle it then.

She says, "No, I'll get it tomorrow."

Challis, "Ok then she went on walking and it started to rain."

Challis did not really want to take her, but he had to, so he ran with that ride and she got in. She went on saying thank you, thank you.

She got out, and he went home, the next day it was still raining.

He saw her and dropped her home, he asked her how she got here in the morning.

She, "Oh my friend drops me, but she gets off before me."

Challis, "Ok."

He went over to look at his sons, he got each one out, heated their feeding tubes, hugs and kiss each of his sons and whisper "you are each a strong husband, providing, productive, kind but not compromised man for God."

Then he picks up his daughters and kiss them, "Each one of you are women, feminine, beautiful, loving, kind, productive, strong, nice wife, cooking, cleaning, domestic and for God."

He goes over, kisses his wife, and tells her she is loved by him always and he misses her.

Challis kicked off his shoes and got in the bed with his wife, he snuggles under her and he falls to sleep he awoke to Sonya saying, "That's a shame."

Challis, "What Sonya?"

She, "I did not want to say anything, but I think your wife is faking because I have just now caught her with her eyes open."

Challis, "Next time film it, maybe a reflex and no therapy today, you can go."

She leaves and Challis fixes his side and goes down and its dinner time.

He, "Sonya told me that she had noticed my wife with her eyes open."

His mom, "No way cause if she had her eyes open then why haven't we seen and why hasn't she got up."

His dad, "Right and she surely would get over there to her babies."

Challis, "Right."

His mom, "Betty saw you driving some woman 2 times."

Challis, "Yes Sonya's car broke down, I took her home twice in the rain."

His mom said she thought she was married.

Challis just eating, "Damn if I know."

His dad, "let her husband take her home."

Challis, "right because I do not want any problems, I got enough."

His dad, "I would say amen to that some days ago, how the house is is coming along?"

And Challis is thinking maybe she might just wake up quick, so he decides to camp out in their room two days and night and nothing.

CHAPTER 12

Responsibilities

His mom gets the door and saw Jabra's mother Carol and Jonathan her dad, she says, "hello Solace."

Challis's mom, "Hello Carol and Jonathan what brings you all this way?"

Carol, "We need to speak with Challis."

Solace told them he's up with his wife and children but hold on.

Carol, "I know you detest our daughter, but may we come in."

Solace, "Oh, of course."

And she goes to the intercom, "Challis our ex-in-laws are here."

Challis told her he'll be down, when he came, his mom had sat them in the front room and Challis is pissed, he goes in.

Jonathan Jabra's dad, "Now I know you feel a certain way about Jabra, but regardless she was your wife."

Challis, "yes."

Carol, "we want to bury our daughter back home."

Challis, "Ok."

Jonathan, "We have many expenses to bury her; do you have any insurance on her?"

Challis yelled, "I did when she died the first time."

Carol, "Challis, I know she was not the best of a wife, but in a sense yes she was."

Jonathan, "She loved you, she allowed you to sleep in her bed with all those multiple women." \

Challis, "I have nothing for her."

Jonathan, "You're a father now."

Challis, "Yes, and I'm extremely happy."

Jonathan, "Understand how I feel, you have 2 daughters, correct?"

Challis, "Yes."

Jonathan, "Would you want a man no matter what to treat your 2 daughters as so when most of this you brought on for yourself."

Carol, "And I know Giselle very well, I was her Professor 2years when she was studying for her doctorate."

Challis, "Ok."

Carol continued, "I say that to say that Giselle I know has an extremely huge heart."

Challis, "Yes, my wife I know does, and she also detests injustice like your daughter kidnapping our quintuplets."

Carol, "You lived with her over years now, you know she would not hurt your children"

Challis, "I will pray about it and I'll let you know by tomorrow."

Carol, "Challis, may I please see Giselle and your babies, I know I read and listened to the news that they are in a deep sleep till Christmas."

I have been fasting praying for her, I care about Giselle, you, and your children, but this is my daughter.

Challis asked her to come and Carol takes off her coat and leaves her purse,

His dad asked Jonathan, "Would you like a drink?"

Jonathan, "Scotch on the rocks thanks,"

His dad goes and makes him a drink, they reach the room and Carol says, "Oh my God."

She cries a bit.

Challis, "Are you alright?

She, "Yes, you can just see the Lord resting all upon them."

Challis, "Yes, I feel and see his presence whenever I'm around them."

Carol, "Look at them so pretty, all this sandy brown blonde hair almost to their feet."

Then she prays, looks at their sons, they are huge, so handsome, their little muscles, they got some hair also.

Challis told her he can't wait till they wake up because he'll cut both of their heads almost bald.

Carol, "Challis, I know you're going to be a wonderful father."

He said he'll try.

Carol goes over to Giselle, "Always so beautiful and kind to everyone.
"

She told challis her hair has turned and Challis, "Yes Carol, and her hair is all the way down her back to her knees."

They leave and go down, Jonathan gets up, "You and our daughter should have never been married but as a father, I can't but thank you for how you loved, cared for, and treated her when you were together."

Challis, "I played my part as well, I just pray God to rest on her soul."

Carol, "She wanted no parts of Jesus, my only daughter always difficult but to whom she became I just still can't imagine."

She cries and her husband consoles her, "it's enough to go around, me being on the road all those years did not make a better."

Jamarian Senior, "Let me walk you all out."

They gather their stuff and when they reach outside Challis dad hands Jonathan a check for $40,000.

Jonathan, "I have to pay back."

Jamarion Senior, "No need to say or pay back, just father to father."

They both say thank you and Carol and her husband leave.

Challis was sitting down and going through his phone when his dad walks back in, "What are you doing?

Challis, "About to order some food."

His mom, "Yes, because I am not cooking, I just want to lay right here and watch a good couple of movies."

She curls up on the couch.

Challis asked, "You want me to pop you some popcorn?"

His mom asked, "You want some?"

Challis, "Of course, I'm making a big bowl."

His dad, "plenty butter son."

As Challis enters their huge kitchen, off the living room and front room open space.

His mom, "still what are we eating?"

Challis, "Let's do deep pan crust."

His dad, "Yes, get two and a couple of Italian subs."

His mom told him to get her an Italian salad.

Challis, "Dad, I'm popping popcorn, get several types of meat and veggies, extra cheese and sauce, I am too hungry."

His mom, "Challis put on 2 bags of frozen corn and butter."

He, "Oh yes ma'am, cannot forget the corn."

His dad, "Son I took care of that."

Challis, "I got you."

His dad, "No."

Challis, "Thanks because we're moving the hell on."

His mom, "Challis, I never asked you, but I want to know, why did you ever choose to fall in love and marry Jabra?"

As he cooks, "I would not have ever married her, Giselle broke my heart and I slept with her a couple of times that's all, she was easy, it was but she told me she was pregnant, I got one of those test sticks and she peed on the stick and she was."

His mom, "right."

Challis continued, then she scheduled an appointment and the doctor said she was 6 weeks pregnant. I moved her in with me, she was sick every day then at the third month, we went to the doctor for ultrasound and she said we were having twin boys, then she got into a suppose car accident. It was a lot and then we supposedly miscarried, and she was devastated for days, I was too. Neither of us could eat and the rest is history.

Now I think she probably played me cause the way she acted, she was happy we had no kids, we use to see people with babies so cute she would lie and say, "I can't hold, I have a cold or I got a virus."

I did not want to divorce; I wanted us to work it out but never.

She always had something to do and I stop caring a lot of times. I was happy when she was gone; she was always coming up with some scam or Ponzi schemes.

I'm like what the fuck and she's like, "you don't understand, I want my own shit."

So, I just let her.

Challis said, "I just thought that loving her would change her but she never changed and she truly did not care about me before we married, everything I like to do she like to do if it was not us being seen she was good what a waste."

His mom, "is it boiling?"

Challis, "Yes ma'am." and gets up.

His mom, "Put it on simmer."

Her hubby backed up and said, "We're going to have to pick it up."

Challis, "I'll go."

And he pops the popcorn then put on his shoes.

His mom, "You know what son?"

All things work together for the good of those that love God and all of that you take it and you use it to know that you must be totally in this life with your family and Savior.

His dad, "Yes son, Giselle is a fantastic disciplined woman."

His mom, "Yes she is."

Challis, "I know I want my wife and my kids to wake up, please Lord wake them up."

His mom, "In his time, you just need to keep on being accountable over them and what you supposed to be doing."

As time sailed on and on, Challis and his dad arrived at Toddies Pizzeria and they saw Sonya in there, they had to wait because the place was packed.

Sonya was with a group of thug people, they got their order and bounced. The next couple of days pass and Challis was in and out and their home was coming along, he went home and packed some vittles and ran up to check, Sonya slipped in the kitchen, open his bottles and drop a quick disposable pills in each one and she put the bottles back. Challis grabbed the 3 antibiotic bottles and left.

Nurse Jamia, "Are you finished with their therapy?"

Sonya, "Yes and have you seen Challis?"

Nurse Jamia, "He just left, I'm sure he'll be at their house."

Sonya, "Ok, then just let me go 4 days off!"

Nurse Jamia, "That's cool, I am also, let me go get Mrs. Calm-way together and I am good."

Solace, "Hello Sonya may I speak with you!"

Sonya, "Yes ma'am."

Solace, "Have you gotten your car fixed yet?"

Sonya, "No ma'am, I bought a new one, I junked my old one."

Solace, "ok, how are they coming along."

Sonya, "Oh fine, they're all the same."

Solace, "Challis you saw Giselle up a couple of times."

Sonya, "yes, only twice, I just hope this is all true for Challis."

Solace, "whatever my God has orchestrated it shall come to pass." Sonya, "Amen to that" and she asks, will that be all? Solace, "yes, have a blessed evening," she leaves.

CHAPTER 13

Rape

It was Sonya's ovulation day and yes, she has another car, it is not new but at 11 pm she goes back, and her medication has worked.

She sees Challis in his car, she goes up, "Hi."

Challis, "Hi," then he passes out.

She pushes him over and drives his car, she calls Gomer and tells him to pick up her car that it has stopped, and he does.

She parks in her garage and she puts Challis in a wheelchair and rolls him and pushes him in her bed and takes off all his clothes and she sucks his dick till it is hard then she rides him like a pony, Challis comes twice then she puts more date rape meds and sleep meds and shoots up his vein and goes to town on him again.

Daylight comes and Solace asked Nurse Kimmie, "have you seen Challis?"

Nurse Kimmie, "No ma'am."

Solace thought this is odd, but he is diligently working on their home and so much more.

Challis was still asleep, and Sonya was going to town. She is having a ball.

Jamarian Senior, "Baby, have you seen Challis?"

Solace, "No."

His dad, "He's probably at the site."

His mom, "Right."

It was 2 am; she gets down with Challis then at 3 am she dresses him, drives back his car, and parks a bit up to where workers can't see and she walks and goes over Snakes and then goes, it was 2 days already and.

Solace, "Now this is odd."

His dad, "I'm riding over to the site in the morning, he is working."

Solace, "Ok."

They go to sleep and during the early morning Challis has awoken and one of his workers knocks on his window.

Allen, "Mr. Challis, the chandeliers have arrived."

Challis, "In a daze?"

Allen, "Sir."

Challis, "Oh headache, just put them in one of the trailers."

Allen, "Will do, are you sure you're fine?"

Challis, "Yes, just need some rest."

Allen, "Ok, we got this."

Challis thinks then starts his car and goes home. He goes in and

His mom, "Hello stranger."

Challis, "Hello, I got the worse headache."

His mom, "you want some pain medication?"

And Challis, "I'll try to shower and lay down."

the medication was still wearing on him and he knew nothing that had happened, and he showered and got in the bed with his wife and cuddled her in his arms and went to sleep for 2 days.

Solace, "is he still asleep?"

His dad, "Yes."

Challis woke up hard and he was mad because he had come in his wife, he had never put himself inside of her while she was asleep but he had done that and he did not want his staff to see so he cleaned himself and his wife and changed all their linen and her and cheeked kissed their kids and went down to eat.

Sonya came in and none noticed she smiled but to herself, she thought Challis baby is hugely packing.

She just smiled and went up, Solace is in their media room looking over the house camera footage, and then she sees what she thought and she keeps watching then Challis goes in and fries up ham eggs and a whole can of buttermilk biscuits, he puts butter and jelly on and he still felt crappy.

He thought, "I'm all fucking my wife, and either she or I am pretty fucked up, shit God I need my wife please."

Challis sits down and pushes the remote for smooth tunes, he thought, "maybe I should make love to my wife to wake her up."

God said, "Leave her be."

and Challis, "yes sir, what is wrong with me?"

God please I'm just ready for us to get going",

He says Grace and goes to town then he clicks to some old school tunes, "Walking in the Rain by Oran Juice Jones."

His dad dancing yells crumb cake.

His mom, "what's going on?"

Challis now jamming to, "don't look any further"

Challis still eating, "I 'm just getting ready for me and my peeps to get going",

his dad dancing, "it's coming."

He tries to hand dance with his wife, but she breaks away and continues, "Challis, these past two days you've been missing in action."

Challis, "we're going further"

He is jamming to Dennis Edwards, "Yes I'm not looking any further."

His mom, "Ok, don't be making overnights at any places."

Challis, "Mom, no, I have not been feeling well at all; I believe what God has told me."

His mom continued, or taking no walks and Challis, "Mom, I love my wife and our kids, see?"

He's singing while he eats, "walking in the rain" his dad is jamming to, she asks, Challis why are you singing that?

Challis, "Mom it means nothing, I just like the song, always have."

She, "Well you got the wrong wife, that's you and Jabra, you should have been running up in, and now Sonya likes you. I can tell, fire her."

Challis kept on rocking and his mom, "She wants blueberry bags and Bentleys."

Challis, "Mom I 'm in love and gone."

His mom, "that doesn't mean one thing and if."

Challis cut her short and, "Ok, but I need someone else."

Solace, "What's wrong with you?"

Challis, "Mom, I feel my babies love, their light eye, the love of our kids, and God's love for me, I just feel good."

His mom, "I'm sick of this, both of you come here."

They both do and his dad asked, what you mad at me for? And she took them all into the media room and she sits and turns to all the footage even now of Sonya miss treating Giselle and his babies.

Challis runs fast, almost jumps up at least all the steps, and calls Sonya, she answered, "Yes."

Challis, "Come down."

His mom has called the police.

Sonya, "Ok."

Challis asks her to sit and she does then as the cops come in, he asks, "why the fuck have you been abusing my wife and kids?"

Sonya, "I haven't",

His dad, "we have the footage showing her for days abusing my son's wife and grandbabies on video."

Cop Delmar, "Please show me the way."

He goes and he plays then he retrieves all the footage after Challis's dad dubs it all so they can keep original copies then they come back out.

Cop Delmar, "Ok, you're under arrest."

Sonya, "He's just saying this because we've been sexual these past couple of days."

Challis, "That's a lie."

Sonya, "Ok just wait, I was ovulating these past two days, I'm sure I'm pregnant. We have been together non-stop."

A cop, "That makes no sense here or there, you're on camera" then he leads her out saying, "you have the right to remain silent".

The Cop, "Mr. Challis, you need to come down and press charges."

He hands him a paper then they leave.

Nurse Kimmie, "Hello."

Nurse Jamia, "Yes."

Nurse Kimmie, "Sonya just got arrested."

Nurse Jamia, "For what?"

Nurse Kimmie, "She has been abusing Mrs. Calm-way and their children."

Nurse Jamia, "I knew that bitch was up to something, is Mr. Challis firing us?

Nurse Kimmie, "I do not think so because they got this entire house on camera.".

Nurse Jamia, "Good because he is cool as hell and pays us so well."

Nurse Kimmie, "Get this Sonya said they have been sexually active."

Nurse Jamia, "I don't believe that."

Nurse Kimmie, "I don't either because if so, why the fuck was she still working here, and her damn car been broke?"

Nurse Jamia, "Right."

Nurse Kimmie, "Ok, let me go check my clients," and they hang up.

Challis, "Nurse Kimmie I have to go downtown a while, can you stay over, and I'll pay you $10,000 right now, and can you call in Nurse Shelia early?"

Nurse Kimmie, "I can do it all till you all comeback."

Challis, "Night staff will be here in 3 hours and I'm paying you $10,000 more and all of them each $20,000 for you all taking such good care of my wife and our babies, I truly love them with my life and you all keep your regular payments with a $20 raise".

Nurse Kimmie, "I love my husband, but Mr. Challis don't take this wrong," she hugs him and

Challis hugs her back, "Thank you so much again," then he zooms off.

Nurse Kimmie, "Thank you, Jesus, thank you, Lord. Take your time, I got you all Mrs. Beautiful Calm-way and growing beautiful children."

She finished taking care of them and went to get water, "let me make sure this door is locked," she goes to the security guy Hamilton, "Hello."

Nurse Kimmie, "Hi, just checking."

Hamilton, "We got you secured."

Nurse Kimmie thanks him and runs back up, she thought to herself, "silly me, I see these guards roaming all day safe, yes, wait let me call my hubby."

Jack, "Hello baby."

Nurse Kimmie, "I'll call you when I 'm finished, I'm working over."

Jack, "Ok."

Nurse Kimmie, "And just for this overtime I got paid, guess."

Jack, "Time and half."

Nurse Kimmie, "No, $10,000",

Jack, "You can spend the night."

Nurse Kimmie," You know yes, but bae when I text you, they come back and get me, I don't want to drive that late."

Jack, "Ok baby, its Friday night and we are going.".

Nurse Kimmie, "Where are my kids?"

Jack, "With your mom."

Nurse Kimmie, "Right I forgot, but peace and love."

Jack, "I see you baby".

Nurse Kimmie, "You know right".

They hang up, "My water, this recliner is comfy".

She sat sit and turned on the remote on low, she grabs the Bible on the table and starts to read and time goes by at the Police Station, Challis presses charges and they leave, they go by the house.

Challis, "I want to go to the hospital."

His mom, "why?"

Challis, "I cannot take this headache and something I think has been done to me, Sonya has me feeling violated."

Allen, "Hey Mr. Challis, the other day I drunk one of your antibiotic waters and my sinuses were banging, I tried to shake, and I replaced it."

Challis, "That's cool."

Allen continued, "I wanted you to know though that when I drunk it, thank God my wife had our truck while hers is being fixed to pick me up because all of a sudden I was knocked out, she rushed me to the hospital, they tested the water because I was still drinking it when I got in our truck."

I left you a message that they said, "the date rape drug is a drug that causes temporary loss of memory or inhibition, surreptitiously given to someone to facilitate rape or sexual abuse and also 100 mg of Ambien, a sleep aid my wife called it because I have been out for 2 days also the police pulled that camera footage and they saw a black lady get in the car with you a couple of nights ago on the driver's side and push you over and they saw the same woman bring you back two nights later, a couple of hours before I asked you if you were alright."

Challis, "I knew something has been wrong with me."

Allen gives him a card, "Detective Brower wants you to call him".

Challis, "I will but I'm going to the doctor myself, thanks, man. Hey, take off with pay and an extra $5000."

Allen, "Thank you because my wife is due any day now."

Challis, "See you in 3 weeks with pay."

Allen, "Wow, thanks".

He leaves and his mom, "That dirty bitch."

His dad, "Come, the hospital is right down the street."

They go and Challis gets tested and it was the same results, date rape drug Ambien but at higher dosages.

His dad, "She raped you I bet."

Challis, "No God, don't let her be pregnant by me."

The Cops called him, and they sat down and talked, then they asked does he know anyone, "Sonya."

Cop Bar Brower, "How do you know her?"

Challis, "She worked for me."

Cop Bar asked if he knew where they can speak with her and Challis told them she's in jail for abusing his wife and children.

He continued, "She was their therapist and the police have the corner footage where she kidnapped me."

His mom, "we have footage of her at his home opening his bottles of water."

Challis, "Mom."

She, "I thought they were hers."

Cop Bar, "Ok, we will".

They all leave, and they arrive home, Nurse Sheila is there now and all the health aides,

Challis, "car service can drop you home if it is too late."

Nurse Kimmie, "Thanks but my husband just pulled up, is it alright if I leave my car here till morning?"

Challis, "Sure but you're off."

Nurse Kimmie, "No."

Challis, "Yes, take 3 days with your new pay, thank you."

Nurse Kimmie, "Thanks so much, my husband can follow me."

She shakes Challis's hand and he gives her a check for $20,000, she almost screams and, "I'm hugging you again," and she does and leaves.

Jack, "Come on baby."

Nurse Kimmie, "Follow me, I'm off for the next 3 days with pay."

Her husband, "Oh hell yes, come on."

Nurse Kimmie, "Hey, I want our kids home."

Jack, "Let them stay, I'll snag them in the morning" and his wife accepted, and they left.

Jack Kimmie's husband is a Doctor that is renowned in lots of circuits. Morning came and Challis had the doctors thoroughly check his wife and kids.

Auntie Rea, "I'm back family."

Challis, "Hello, I forgot you left."

They hugged each other.

Rea, "Solace told me now you've been raped."

Challis, "Yes."

She continued, "Boy, you're going to have a detail going everywhere with you."

Challis, "I'm pissed."

She, "I guess so, which one was it?"

Challis told her it's Sonya.

Rea, "She looks sneaky, all on camera?"

Challis no just her beating and pinching my wife and kids.

Rea, "She's going to bust hell wide open and they should kill her if they just wait on God."

Challis, "Yes, my wife told me she had been in love with me," and she asked how.

Challis, "I had been in love with her all through our college days."

Rea, "Ok, you all went to college together, now that makes sense."

Challis, "We dated 2 years straight, but I broke it off."

Rea, "She wouldn't give you none" and

Challis, "Right, I regret that but years later I saw her, and she did not bother me with my wife, she lived her life."

Rea, "I bet you wish you had still been with her."

Challis, "And yes I love her, and I always have."

Rea, "You all are going to have enough kids and don't need anybody else raping you to get some."

Challis, "Yes and I want at least 4 more babies with my wife."

Rea shakes her head and, "Nephew 2, let the women breath."

Challis, "They probably will be just like we had our 4."

Rea, "You know what you're probably right cause by Christmas all your 4 are going to be walking, talking, potty trained."

Watch God is going to move them right out the way for their sibling's parents in a Shoe.

Challis, "That's fine with me."

Rea, "What are you eating Solace?"

She, "I'm eating pizza, salad, and corn from last night."

Rea, "Let me take off my shoes and wash my hands because I am famished."

Challis, "he was hungry too."

Rea called out, "Hey Sam and his dad answered, hey sis-in-law."

Rea, "I can't even leave you all, the devil is busy but all morning I've been going around here with my anointed oil, Bishop will be over here at 6 pm, him and first lady."

Challis, "Yes ma'am, I'm not going anywhere, I still don't feel so good."

His mom, "Boy wash your hands and eat something, women are been raped for years, suck it up."

Rea burst out laughing and his mom, "Challis told me he feels violated."

Challis, "I do for one, the other night when I came in, it made me cuddle with my wife at night and talk to her, but I woke and I'm all in her."

Rea, "You damn raped her."

His mom, "Challis I knew you sleeping with her was not a good idea."

Challis, "I did not know, I just cleaned us both up and threw out everything."

His mom, "You don't know what to do, you could have washed that stuff."

His dad, "Well, it's all over."

Challis, "no it isn't, I got to wait a couple more weeks to see if she is pregnant."

While Rea ate with her shoes off, she asked, "who? Your wife or your rapist?"

Challis, "Both, that would be something for my wife and kids to wake up to a kid or kids, not me and my babies."

Rea, "You would want your baby by your rapist?"

Challis, "Yes because she is going to jail most of her life, she will probably be old when she gets out."

Rea, "They would be around the same age, Giselle will probably have a field day about that."

Challis, "It's not my fault."

His mom, "Yes, it is."

I told you days ago to fire her but you, "Oh no, mom, I'm on it."

Good thing you are here, she probably would have kept you for several more days, but she knew you had to get back.

Rea, "She is crazy, though psychos are our type."

She still slams and continues eating.

Challis, "all my crew knows I was raped now",

Rea, "So what? You pay their salaries?"

His dad said, "You better man your ass up and go the fuck on my crew",

Mike comes in and, "Hello family, my beautiful mother and auntie."

He kisses both, "I heard, and I ran over here, Sonya is wanted in California and Detroit for the same shit."

Challis, "You can really pick them."

Jamarion II, "Family, yes your boy Is in the house, baby brother what are we going to do with you?"

Challis still eating, "If you know how I'm just trying to take care of my family and people keep fucking with us."

Rea, "You cannot fight this battle on your own, you're going to have to fast and give it to the Lord. You have got to build up your armor not in you but in God."

Challis, "I'm going to talk to Bishop about that because this is all fucked up."

He gets up cleans his stuff up and runs upstairs and gets in bed with his wife.

Mike, "Challis is used to being how he wants to be, he's going to have to tighten his shit up."

Mac said, "And you daddy, buying up almost all of downtown, Challis also about every hotel downtown."

Their dad, "So?"

Mike continued, "I'm just saying people talking about the auctioneer up the time of the auction just for Challis."

Their dad, "None of that shit matters, he has the deed."

Jamarian 11 said, "but dad he paid $1" and

His mom, "So people negotiate that way all the time."

Mike, "he doesn't know he owns the river acreage and the outer corridor acres and as much property as he owns."

He could have a city in a city so if he thinks he and his wife and 4 kids are going to go ride off in the sunset he better pack up and move to Heaven.

His mom, "Why can't they? Downtown was going to hell and back and nobody was coming in they're just mad because they all know that Challis is going to revive this city and bounce."

His dad, "No, he is not he is planning on raising his family here till he becomes president."

Rea, "Now that is what I'm talking about."

His mom added that this is just like Noah in the Bible, everybody was busy doing nothing, but Challis is woke come here.

Everybody want to hate, give me a break, it's been like this.

Everybody was Jealous of Challis when he was a kid, nobody did mind when he was living all foul, making movies, writing novels but now they want to say something because he's trying to live right.

God gave Challis that land and he has orchestrated this or have all of you forgot God is not rattled or shaken, he has said, and it shall all be done in Challis and his wife and children.

Mike, "Right, I'm just saying about my baby brother, he needs to be careful and mindful."

His dad, "Mindful of his ass, they are going to have a beautiful life in God not man but the Lord. Let's pray for them because I know the Lord has not brought them this far to leave them."

His mom, "Jesus help my child and his family please."

Challis comes back down to get something to drink.

CHAPTER 14

Hello Daddy

Mike, "Look."

His mom, "what?"

Challis Jr and Caviar come down the steps, they all look in amazement.

Challis and their dad, "Hi!"

Dad, "Rea, I told you."

Challis, "Who are you?"

His sons, "We're sons but men from the house of Challis Calm-ways Senior."

His mom asked, who told you that?

His sons both point to their dad, Rea, "All that hair, all down their backs, so handsome, is your mommy up?"

His sons, "No ma'am."

They go to her, "God wants you to hold each one of our hands."

Rea, "Why?"

Challis Jr, "You have been praying for a special healing and you've been faithful to serve our Savior."

Rea puts down her drink and she takes their hands. They bow their heads and say a prayer in tongues and Rea's eyes go back in her head and then they come back and let go over her hands and step back and say "you're healed" and Auntie Rea raises both her arms up over her head and says, "thank you Jesus" then she bends over and touch her toes.

"Lord you've been so good."

Solace, "Hallelujah"

Rea crying, "Since I slipped on that ice last year you all know I've been so stiff in pain and thank you Jesus I have not been able to bend", she bends forward again touching her toes.

Challis goes and hugs his Auntie, they all do, she cries, "God is real and, in these children, and their mother, Challis you better treat them all right I've been in so much pain".

she weeps and cries and, "Lord you've been so faithful to me."

Challis Jr, "Dad, we are also here to give our dad a message from our Savior."

Challis, "What."

his sons, "Our Savior says to you, don't be amazed that he is proud of you and you are doing a good work in our Lord and Savior and he said for you being such a good steward you can cut our hair and we can spend a short time with you but also our God says if you do not indulge your mind in him and gird up your state of being then we will sleep longer."

Challis, "God, I promise you I will."

His sons say Psalms 24 "The earth is the Lord's and the fullness thereof, the world and they that dwell therein."

God heard you, he said use what he's given to achieve for the latter days will be better than your formative days.

Challis, "Glory to God."

He jumps and, "Thank you, God."

His sons say, "for the Lord reigns forever amen".

Challis filled up went and hugged them and kissed them both, they smiled and said, "We love you our dad".

Challis cries and, "yes I am your dad and let's get to it",

Rea, "They're just 9 months",

His mom, "God said he can."

Nurse Jamia, "Jesus."

They all laugh,

"They scared you.

Nurse Jamia, "Yes, all the rest are asleep still."

His sons, "Hi and thank you Nurse Jamia for being so nice to us."

They touch her stomach and bow and pray and, "All your prayers have been answered."

They hug her.

She, "I feel so warm inside."

She cries and Challis jr., "2 daughters and 1 son you're pregnant for right now, and for your goodness our Lord says this time next year." she covers her mouth, and, in her stomach, she feels a sharp kick and an inner body tremor she says, "I feel them all" as she cries, she hugs them and says, "thank you, God" and she says, "excuse me, I must call my husband".

Challis hugs her and, "You're fine, you can go home but have your husband pick you up, you're too excited."

Nurse Jamia crying, "Yes, he will."

Then Challis, "Sons come."

His sons, "May we please use the restroom?"

Challis, "Yes right in here."

They do and they take off their pampers and both go and pee in the stalls and wash their hands. Their family all claps.

Challis, "Way to go."

Nurse Jamia, "The underwear, t shirts and shorts", she goes and gets them, their dad puts it on them, and he puts a sheet on them and cuts their hair super low but faded. It looked really sporty with each part and he washes and condition both their hair and then he puts them both in the shower and clothes them."

Challis, "Are you hungry?"

His sons, "Yes sir, soup please and straw."

They see 2 little basketballs and they pick up one each and both shoot and make their shot from far off and their family goes wild then both boys fist bump each other and shoot again as their dad looked on at them and went and poured their soup. His mom made cream pea soup and put in cups with straws, Challis asked them to come and eat.

Mike, "That they play like they're big."

His dad, "Yes they do, both boys."

Their dad puts them in a booster seats he purchased a while back and he gives them wheat crackers and they both hug their dad; Challis gets himself some also. They all say a prayer and eat, all watched how his sons talk among themselves and laughed and fist-bumped again, they just smiled and eat.

Mike, "Well you're all cool" as his mom hit him."

Solace, "No cursing, God is here don't you all feel him?"

All say, "Yes."

Jamarian II, "How do you all know how to shoot?"

His nephews, "We shoot in heaven."

Challis, "What else do you all do?"

His sons, "We sit a lot at the right hand of God."

Mama Sugar, "What does he look like?"

Her grandsons, "We don't know but Paw Paw and Jesus sit with us, he is tall and strong with long hair like ours, he's our color and he teaches us a lot of things."

His dad, "Why?"

His grandsons, "Because Jesus says when we finally return, we will have the skills and knowledge attained but we will not remember but our mommy will."

Challis Senior, "Do you hear everything?"

They, "Yes sir."

Their dad, "Good, why didn't you all wake when Sonya was hurting you all?"

Challis II, "Dad we knew but we did not feel."

Their dad, "So?" they said, "when you all smile, Caviar we're happy and when we were frowning, we were sad for Miss Sonya's Soul".

Auntie Rea, "Do you all see your mother and sisters?"

Challis II said every day.

Their dad said, "What Caviar, our mom's sins and burdens are all gone and she is her age but God has taken, every single imperfection of appearance in and out of her are gone, she will look like free and be healed inside out".

Rea, "She's going to be new, what about your sisters? How are they both."

The boys, "Learning, dancing, flipping, and singing. They're always with our mom and grandmother."

Their dad, "Who are you all with?"

Challis II, "They stay with Paw Paw and he taught them different games."

Their dad, "Has he got to my wife his sons every day?"

They, "We have to go back now."

Challis, "Wait let me get a picture of my little men."

Challis sits on the ground and he cries.

His sons both, "Don't cry dad, we're men and Christmas are coming daddy," his family both happy and sad laughs.

Challis wipes his eyes and snaps lots of pictures and his mom said, "let me take you all one together then they both fall to sleep, and Challis grabs them and carries them both up.

Nurse Jamia puts them back on diapers and their IV's, Nurse Sheila has arrived and

Rea crying a little, "I knew they were going to be so ahead."

His mom, "Not missing a beat."

Mike, "They are very intellectual and tall, I love my little nephews, all cool."

His dad, "And they got teeth, yes they do and smart."

Jamarion II, "this is a lot for us I know and for Challis."

Rea, "Well he knows now that his work is not in Vain and they both look just like Challis."

His mom, "Yes they do, I love their haircuts."

Mike, "They had too much hair when they got home, Challis is probably going to have to cut their hair twice a week."

Their dad said that he's up to it.

Rea, "Yes he is, now when are you all going to be able to test the rapist?"

Solace, "Probably in 8 weeks."

Rea, "God is not going to let her carry no child of Challis, he never let even Jabra get pregnant. This child slept with him one time and 4 kids."

His dad, "Yes."

Rea continued, "I still cannot believe all of them died, we cannot play with the Lord's anointed ones."

8 weeks passed and the test has been taken, the doctor came out and gives Challis the paper and he read, "99.9% you are not the father."

Challis, "Thank you God."

They all walk across the street, a test has been conducted on Giselle and the doctor said she is not pregnant.

His mom, "Thank you Lord."

Challis, "No worries because when my wife gets home."

His mom, "Now Challis."

She hits him and when they got home

Mac, "What's wrong with you?"

China, "Nothing."

She cries.

Mac, "These are our children" and

China, "And I'm already six months."

Mac, "It's God's doing and we're moving to Virginia."

China, "We're going to have 5 kids," as she cries.

Mac, "I'm ecstatic our own daughters and another cool ass son, yeah this is alright, what else is there and you look so beautiful."

China, "Thank you and finally I have huge breast I pray I get to keep them, ouch! baby they're just kicking me to death, let's go home please, yes and order in I'm so tired plus I got to order our kids some stuff and we got to get up early and swim for 45 minutes oh and did you tell our boys?"

Mac, "Yes and they're both ecstatic for our family, they're going to be the bomb big brothers."

Challis, "Hey captain, how's life?"

Mac, "Extra special."

Challis, "Where is China?"

Mac, "We're pregnant."

Challis, "What! Congratulations?"

Mac, "Thanks, we're having triplets, 2 girls and 1 boy."

Challis, "Man that's alright."

Mac, "We're due in 3 months but we're going to move there in 2 weeks. I'm building us a house, something on that land I purchased across adjacent from you and your family."

He continued, "I'm tired of here, I want nice and slow this time around."

Challis, "And you got daughters."

He, "Yes I don't want to have to fuck nobody up but let me go we're walking home."

Challis, "I'll be praying for you all."

They hang up.

Mac, "Baby if your breast doesn't last why not just get you some double DD's God your gift."

China screams yes and

Mac, "What?"

China, "God just told me your gift", she squeezes her boobs, mine all mine but still I'm getting a tummy tuck, but I'll still work out."

Mac, "There it is."

He picks her up and carried her home,

China, "This time around I'm better than before."

Mac, "You were great then."

China, "I know but I'll be damned if our kids are not going to be right up with Giselle's and I'll start taking some foreign language classes, you know we both already speak fluently Spanish."

Mac, "Ok mommy I see you."

Challis, "Mom guess who's the 3 baby carriers? His mom asked who?"

Challis, "It's China and Mac, they're moving here in two weeks and they are having 2 girls and 1 boy."

Rea laughed, "they're going to have 5 kids, 2 grown that's alright, China was like we done."

Solace yelled, "But like I say God has his own plans."

Rea, "Ok let's go in this store right here, I'm cooking."

Solace, "what are we going to have?"

Rea, "I'm going to fry a couple different kinds of fish, peel some potatoes make some fries and a nice Cole slaw."

Challis, "Yes that sounds good", they enter the grocery store and

Rea grabs a cart and, "Baby let's have a couple deviled eggs, and I'm making a nice rice and some mixed greens with turnips, we can eat off that and a pan of cornbread. I'm baking some chicken also, let me get some stuff for chicken salad."

Challis, "We're going to need some of this malt vinegar."

Rea, "We can do cod for the fish and chips and I can just fry."

They got some beautiful orange roughie.

She, "Excuse me."

The meat guy, "yes ma'am."

She continued, "I would like 10lbs each of cod, haddock, whiting and give me 8 of the sea bass also please, oh and 6 of the long salmon fillets, what is that?",

The meat guy said, "crab salad."

Rea, "Oh yes, give me 10 lbs. of that".

Solace, "You got some of those keep fresh bags?"

She, "Yes, let me grab 6 cucumbers and 3 bags of onions, Challis go grab me a cart."

He, "Yes ma'am."

His mom, "What do you want?"

He said some stuff, he runs and grabs 2 carts and he leaves them and goes to other deli and gets himself chicken lunch meat, pepperonis, hard salami, capicola, roast beef, corn beef, bruschetta, brown sugar ham and provolone cheese and jalapeno cheese.

He called Solace and told her to grab him 3 heads of lettuce, 8 beefy tomatoes, 2 bags purple onions red wine vinegar, couple boxes of crackers,

She, "is that all?

He, "Slice pickles and 2 jars of those fat pickles and miracle whip mustard Italian dressing."

They hang up.

She, "Oh, yeah, let me grab some paper plates yes can I have 10 rib eyes and 10 porter house with potatoes and a couple bags of salad and dressing, banana peppers, and some of these different rubs, did you just make up these packs of seasoned breast and pork loins?"

The meat guy, "Yes, all freshly made today."

He, "Ok, let me get 6 packets of these 8 chops each."

The meat guy, "We have all that in the case, I could individually wrap you up 2 per package or whatever."

Challis, "Ok, give 24 of the seasoned breast with the bone and 20 without and 30 of the center cuts seasoned and 30 not and packaged and 20lb of ground Sirloin and 20 of those full pond Sirloin patties 2 to a packet."

Meat guy, "if you have any more shopping, I can get all together and be ready in 20 minutes",

Challis, "Ok, I do oh and 20 of the pickle eggs."

The meat guy, "Yes sir."

CHAPTER 15

The Past Returns

He, "Yes, Now I need, 15 grain huge hamburger bun yes and I need some yogurt and granola and frozen fruit and individual oat meal oh yes bacon 2 – 5lb thick oh yes and my bread right here ok wheat ooh yeah 25 grains the better."

Glo, "Hi handsome."

Challis, "Oh hey."

Glo, "I heard your wife died, really?"

Challis, "Yeah, I'm remarried now."

Glo, "yeah, I heard."

He, "I ran into Rhonda with quintuplets, how would she know".

Glo, "I do not know but anyway you still look awesome to me."

Challis, "Thanks."

Glo, "I live here now, here is my card."

Challis, "Look this is different, take care of yourself."

His mom, "Who was that?"

He kept on ordering things, yes peanut butter and straw berry jelly and 2 big can of these mixed nuts.

He, "Mom nobody."

She, "He shouldn't tell her that."

He, "Glo ok, I told her this was different, take care."

The meat guy, "Sir, your meats.".

He asked if he got all that , "yes my indoor grill is still in your garage."
Challis, "They're set."
He reaches in his wallet and
"Here for you."
The meat guy, "We cannot accept tips but thank you."

Challis asked him for cottage cheese pineapples, olive oil yes, the both of them and asked his mom, you got 10 dozen eggs?

She, "Yes, I thought I would boil you 4 dozen."

Rea, "Are you all ready? I have shopped so long, they have a Chinese place in here, I got us pepper steak, fried hard veggie, chicken, orange chicken, green bean mushroom, chicken white rice, fried rice, noodles, 20 crab Raegan, 12 chicken egg rolls, these paper plate, these utensils and lemonade and big bottle of soy sauce and hard noodles and I'm going to the line."

I'll cook tomorrow, that all sounds delicious to me.

They all go to the aisle and look at daddy, he has two buckets of chicken and guess he got sides.

They pay and load the car, gets home and the security guys bring in all, they put up all together and wash hands.

Challis grabs his food, jets upstairs and sees his family, jumps in the shower and turns out on the game and gets tray and sat in bed eating with his wife.

Nurse Kimmie said, "I can grab that, thank you" and he falls to sleep, and all go fast to sleep.

It was a busy morning, Bishop Connors and First Lady says, "thank you son, it looks gorgeous".

His dad told them that the new faces they're seeing are asked who the new faces he sees their new staff and cleaning crew, what's wrong with them?

His mom, "We need better my family, a lot and you all need a break on me and meet our chefs John and Vernon." and asked, how's you all?

They, "Doing well ma'am."

She, "That's alright, ok, the menu is located on the chalk board for today and rest of the week."

Vernon, "we brought a lot of our groceries that we need, cool dinner is at 5pm, servers will be here at 4pm, 2 on kitchen, 4 out here and 3 clean-up, 2 garbage away."

Challis, "Cool, let's get ready to do it, laundry is down here, Temper and Zelda you all have a break room to the right and it's a lounge with TV, radio rest room, fridge, microwave, full kitchen and you all enter from the side door, security will let you in and you can park over there as well."

Tempera Zelda thanked him and said they will start now and

Challis, "Yes thank you, regulars after today will be 7 till 3pm."

They went down and he, "Now oh this door locks, you all can intercom me if you need me or someone, you both have my number",

They, "Ok yes thank you," and they go.

Challis, "Now fella's all the glass is done twice a week thanks" and he told the cleaning crew that all carpets should be taken up.

Nurse Jamia, "They will need to clean all up, I brought my family down here already, in here, the lady's carpet is getting cleaned and entirely ok."

They all go and he, "Now it's an entire living area, right out those glass doors you all can just leave open the second kitchen outdoor, full furnished patio also."

Kelly, "This is nice."

They all go out to the outer yard and

Tim, "You can look, we're done."

Kelly, "In one week."

Tim, "my guys got you."

John, "Which floors are to be buffed?"

Challis, "The foyer corridor and all the back areas and dining area around."

Rea, "What is all going on, coffee right here?"

Challis, "More than transformed, we got chefs and everything now."

His dad, "When he leaves, we sale we're going to keep a Chef, nice couple times a week and cleaning crew."

He continued, "Now Squeal and Aquarian do well baby but look at this glass and wood the floors, I like that we're not able to do all this because you're writing a book and I'm selling our apple butter, I got two stores already and our pancake mix Speedy hops and So blue birdie wants to have consistently for their breakfast customer's productivity, I got to redo the pharmacy, get our building you got to be up on the hill more. I want to just go and be up there writing about the hill, a murder mystery I'm thinking about but we got to get going, right I'm designing some clothes too, I want a 40 and over business line and I'm sure you have all my drawings and fabrics by Christmas to give to Giselle, I don't know but I swam 4 laps this morning living is happening loveable he kiss his wife".

She, "Yes, it is," and he goes.

Rea, "What are you all talking about our new improved life?" tell me and they chat on.

His dad asked, what about trees all on the outer core of the drive, little ones, no look that truck has been there, yes, all along with night lights that come on.

"Get Bob my electrician right here!"

Bob, "I'm on it, the gate will be up and going from the front box and house, and now there's someone at the back gate and front, Bill Don Kevin or Burt."

His dad yelled, "Tighten this shit up, I feel it."

Challis, "Dad, Glo came up to me at the store, she has moved here, and I know the rest is coming. I don't know what I'm to do, I got to tell my wife about all that shit, I went and got tested early this morning for what? to make sure we're cool, no std's. I can't be, I got restraining orders on all of them."

His dad, "There isn't nothing like scorned women, they better go on before they end up like Jabra and Teresa. God is here and he is not playing nor are we."

Challis goes and his phone keeps dinging, he looks then, "What the fuck."

Mike, "What's going on here?

"I had to show, who is that Bill? ID, that's how but not for you all it's going to be what it is."

Challis, "Don't say shit."

He shows, "Glo and Renea's ass I filed for restraining orders this morning."

Mike, "Pay them off."

He, "No, I'm telling my wife everything and use these to get them out of town. I got a restraining order on all of them."

His mom comes running and, "Look right here."

Mike, "Hi mom."

She, "Hi, look dead in fetal position."

Challis, "I don't wish anybody death, that's between them and God."

Mike, "Is that your rapist?"

He, "Yes, let me go and pray, this is too much Mike, let me read that what is going on with our Savior God but do what you please, I am not fucking around with nobody but my wife". Some time goes by and frank said, "baby I'm here, damn you look good" and

Rea kissed her hubby and she does the splits.

She, "Hot Tamales, you're going to have to put that back on because later Bishop is on his way, the boys awoke and touched me and God healed me, yes he did in here, in this is our room".

Frank, "Come on baby later ok?"

She, "I'm holding you to , and thank you God time flies".

All are dressed even with their feeding tubes done, they unhook, and all are dressed and beautiful and handsome,

The doorman, "Bishop Connors and First Lady Collate."

Challis, "Come in, I'm so glad you came" and Bishop said, "this place is gorgeous, hello Solace."

She, "Right in here."

Bishop, "Before we eat may we pray and see your wife and kids" and Challis thanked him and led him in.

Bishop continued, "Now I got anointed oil."

First Lady Collate exclaimed, "wow Jesus! Lord have mercy, the beauty on them all and your sons. They look 3 years old or 4."

Challis, "It's just 11 months and 2 days, she asked, your wife, was her hair this beautiful, blonde and red?"

Challis, "High lights but now her brows looks gorgeous, her skin glistens, they all do."

Bishop said, "baby that's God, now let's bow, all come in of family only Lord life is here I did not know what to believe but Lord you are always true Jesus he cries this is your beauty and your desire, forgive for galling Lord we just are so marveled in you but Lord we pray that when they rise on your birth Lord let them be healed and in their right smart intellectual minds, let their limbs be as they had not went into these deep sleeps, Lord let no harm come to them or this close family that is caring for them.

Lord this is so wonderful Lord for their lives you took lives we don't know why but God as a pastor of yours I wish to know so that I can explain to your sheep Lord this is a marvel of no kind I have ever seen but as soon as I saw them I felt like I was at the burning bush and had to remove my shoes. God whatsoever it is that you want each of us to do let us know true and clear God and all these people that set out to harm them, warn them Lord so they won't die. Lord I just can't get over you; this is more than I ever thought but why?

When you are so magnificent. Lord with this oil, I apply in Jesus mighty name bless you, Father Christ your daughter, bless your children of God, each bless you children of God and you father of God's wife and children. Let no man no woman takes him or them under, I plead the blood all here, all over this house in Jesus mighty name amen."

All say amen and the women and Challis cry a bit.

Jamarion II, "we are here you all, just missed prayer, wash your hands everyone to the left or right" They all go.

Bishop, "Challis, I want to start counseling you, once a week at the church, what is your time like?"

Challis, "May I send for your car service to here so you can counsel me in my father's office?

Bishop, "Ok, may I ask why?"

Challis, "It just seems like when I go out alone, I pass women and they like me, today two, I don't know how they sent me all these vulgar pictures."

Bishop, "Ok but son you're going to have to fight this battle with the weapons of warfare and the blood of God, he is your true weapons for this warfare, you got to give it to him. I'm leaving you with some scriptures to read on and write as to how they related to you."

Challis, "Thanks, I need all that", they go and say grace and eat as Mike and Cindy his wife comes in and Jamari an IIand his wife Karen."

Bishop Connors, "This here is delicious."

Solace, "Thank you, glad you like it."

First Lady Collate, "so Challis, when will you begin planning the Wedding?"

Because we have to get it on the church calendar.

Challis, "Well does Christmas fall on a Sunday this year?

Rea, "Yes it does, Bishop will there be a night eve service?

Bishop, "You know the more I think about it, yes because the entire Sunday service can be dedicated to your wedding."

Challis, "People from all around the world will come, I just do not want to make it a spectacle. I want it to be personable, I have not been with my wife and children a day recently but as far as all know this has to be sentimental.

Bishop, "I believe that this situation and all these deaths has cast the Lord in people's hearts in a way that I have not seen in a long time."

First Lady Collate, "You know that's true, my calendar is booked up with so many women rather single or married that are truly trying more than ever to get closer to God, I think it is crucial that we get out here this season women and get out of our suburbs and mansions and hit the streets."

Rea, "Amen to that because I was at the salon before I came back and I could hardly get my hair done for trying to listen to what mostly all these young women with money not happy with their lifestyle but they keep going because there in hope to be married it's the dandiest thing."

First Lady Collate, "Elaborate please".

Rea, "A lot of them from what I heard have not learned how to prepare to be married", in the Bible it states Proverbs 18:22 King James Version (KJV)

[22] "Whoso findeth a wife findeth a good thing, and obtaineth favor of the Lord". But if you have not learned how to apply yourself as a good thing how do they think they will be found.

First Lady, "That is good really good."

Solace, "Because when we were growing up, we had our mother who started us out in example church, either keep your legs close so no one can see up your dress or cross your legs pull you dress down."

Rea, "Because we would get popped with our mom's ruler our father also would be furious if our brothers would not wait and open our door or walk outside of us our daddy did not play, and this is I believe at this time God is pulling all of us back to the basics of what a man and a woman was truly to be."

First Lady, "I already got my shoes off these greens don't make me run around this table, Hallelujah God is good me and she fist bumps her husband was just talking about this on the drive over".

Bishop said, Galatians 6:7, "Be not deceived; God is not mocked: for whatsoever a man soweth, that shall he also reap".

See this is what at this time what you ladies have said as well as what is really going on this here is truly the crust of life to commit to God on his accords not man or women's but his God feels a certain way about a man and a woman and what I feel is that he is showing an example more than ever with Challis and Giselle because for years men and women have fornicated but in the word of God it states **1 Corinthians 6:18-20**[18] "Flee from sexual immorality. All other sins a person commits are outside the body, but whoever sins sexually, sins against their own body. [19]Do you not know that your bodies are temples of the Holy Spirit, who is **in** you, whom you have received from God? You are not your own; [20]you were bought at a price". Therefore, honor God with your bodies. This is a time more than ever to guard your bodies as a living sacrifice **Romans 12:1 King James Version (KJV).** 12 "I beseech you therefore, brethren, by the mercies of God, that ye present your bodies a living sacrifice, holy, acceptable unto God, which is your reasonable service". People are calling us day and night they cannot believe that people that in the usual way to them have been some say crucified. Jarmian Senior all that's going on Revelations 3:16 **King James Bible**

"So then because thou art lukewarm, and neither cold nor hot, I will spue thee out of my mouth". The Lord is spewing it either his way now or till death plain and simple the line in the sand.

CHAPTER 16

Dead or Alive

Houseman Barminco, "Excuse me Sir Challis, telephone."
Challis, "Thank you, excuse me," he goes, and he gets in the kitchen

"Hello!"

Challis, "Yes." this is Jabra's father, Challis, "Yes what can I help you with?"

Jabra's father Jonathan, "We got into a terrible car accident."

Challis, "Sorry to hear that",

Jonathan continued, "And we have no way to start to bring our daughter here and have her funeral, I will be mailing back the money because you are going to have to do it there is no one else".

Challis, "I'm married."

Her dad, "Ask God about it, I have to go no matter she was your first wife until you do right by her you cannot go on," and he hangs up.

Challis is pissed and he comes back mad.

His mom, "What's wrong?

And he, "Jonathan, they got into an accident and they are not going to be able to bury their daughter right now."

His mom asked, and they want you to?

Challis, "I buried her the first time and I'm not taking myself through that again, Bishop do you think that I am out of line with God?"

Bishop Challis, "You're going to have to ask God that son."

Challis, "I'm tired of this, why does everything keep coming back to her when she has wronged me."

Bishop, "That's it, I get it now you may not want to hear it but am I your Bishop."

Challis, "Yes."

Bishop, "Ok well I'm going to tell you straight."

Galatians 6:1 "Brethren, if a man be overtaken in a fault, ye which are spiritual, restore such a one in the spirit of meekness; considering thyself, lest thou also be tempted. **2**Bear ye one another burdens, and so fulfill the law of Christ. **3**For if a man thinks himself to be something, when he is nothing, he deceived himself. **4**But let every man prove his own work, and then shall he have rejoicing in himself alone, and not in another. **5**For every man shall bear his own burden."

Bishop, "now I'm also a lawyer, and let's be clear and you can go check at the county, but ok Jabra died the day after you two were married."

Challis, "Yes and they paid when she died first out her insurance to her sister."

Bishop, "Well I promise you this, may not be tomorrow but mark my word you're going to get a call from the insurance company to pay back every last bit of that of that money."

Challis, "My wife's uncle the President married us and signed our license and had our attorney file them."

Bishop, "Son I know the law and you and Gisselle's marriage is void."

Mike said, "I had a most-wanted case like that, the person faked their death, we caught them after 4 years and we took his wives, property she had acquired with her new husband because his name surfaced back on her property and he was caught smuggling 25,000 kilos of cocaine and the law is civil forfeiture involves a dispute between law enforcement and property such as a pile of cash or a house or a horse, such that the thing is suspected of being involved in a crime. So, baby brother, you're still liable for her means. Let me call our lawyer."

He gets up and his phone rings.

Challis, "Hello",

Attorney Salomon, "Challis I was calling you because I just got back a cease and void as to you and Gisselle's marriage, the Insurance company filed it yesterday because an Attorney Reed had filed a rift the day before that Jabra first entered prison and that brought her back as your legal wife".

Challis asked, do I still have power of attorney over my family?

Mr. Salomon, "Yes, Giselle signed you both, signed no one can take them from you but Christmas really you will have to marry, and that marriage will be legal".

Challis, "Thank you".

Attorney Samuel Salomon, "I just got papers today also that you have to move Jabra by Thursday and you owe back the insurance company 50 million dollars they did not give out the other 50 million I don't know why what you want me to do about Jabra."

Challis, "Send her to 4309 Laramie lane Chicago Illinois, I don't remember the address, that's her father's church I'll call them."

Attorney Salomon, "The money."

Challis, "Pay it out of mine".

Attorney Salomon, " I got it ok."

They hang up.

Challis goes and puts on his jacket, his mom asked, where are you going?

Challis, "I just need some air," and he leaves.

All have left and Challis has been gone till 3 am his mom sees him come in and she says nothing. Morning comes quick and Challis left for their house to work with his crew.

Solace, "Nurse Kimmie do you know where Challis went?

Nurse Kimmie, "No ma'am."

His dad, "Baby he's got to work out his own Salvation."

Challis goes over to the deli in the grocery and got him a huge deli sandwich made with all the fixings then up walks.

Bishop, "Well, hello son!"

Challis, "Oh hello."

Bishop asked, well what have you got there?

Challis, "the works, you want one I can treat you".

Bishop, "yes, now I never turn down any food", Challis asked the deli guy for another works sandwich, chips, and drink.

Bishop, Pepsi, and barbecue chips, son you on your break?

Challis, "waters also please, and something like that."

Bishop, "Well how about a counseling session right now, it's some outdoor tables"

Challis, "Sure, do you eat pickled eggs?"

Bishop, "Oh yeah."

Challis, "Can I have 6 no 10 some for later?"

Both sit and pull out their sanitizer and they say grace and a prayer and begin to eat. It's a nice, warm, sunny, mild breezy day.

Challis, "why is God punishing me? I buried my fake death wife once Jabra"

Bishop, "He's not but see God is about what is in 1Corinthisans 14:40
King James Bible

"Let all things be done decently and in order."

He continued, "You're going to have to forgive Jabra so you can bury her and get on with you and Giselle's and your children's life but I believe that God wants you to learn something from this and he wants you to have closure. This is surely tasty thanks".

Challis, "you're welcome, she left me, I did not leave her and I'm mad as hell. Why won't God let me get on with our life? She faked her death; she kidnapped our kids".

Bishop, "I hear you but none of that matters to God, what matters now yes, he loves you, cares how you feel but he loved Jabra also".

Challis, "I just want the love of my life to awake, my true to the core of me and our babies, please God I'm trying."

Bishop, "Challis as your pastor Bishop Connors, do you have your Bible?"

He, "Yes sir."

Bishop continues, "Ok son here is a paper with all the scriptures I have prepared earlier today. I just felt for your concerns within your life-related in God, we're going to take our time to eat, enjoy fellowship, and read each one all to entirety then discuss at the end."

He, "Yes, sir I'm ready."

Bishop spoke on, " Now as to what your concerns are, this is about what matters and what does not nor the matter per say that your wife faked her death after a couple of years, it does not matter that she kidnapped your quintuplet's, it does not matter that your wife had her lawyer Attorney file a writ and the Judge ruled a writ of execution that was issued after your wife Jabra the plaintiff won the judgment, it does not matter that judgment voided your marriage to Giselle it does not matter that you feel that life has thrown you a sucker punch and you were not looking or prepared, it does not matter that you are disappointed, it does not matter that you are extremely hurt, it does not matter that you feel like why me?

It does matter that you've given your life and you're all to God, it does not matter that you think she was the defrauder, son what matters is that Genesis 2:24.

Therefore, shall a man leave his father and his mother, and shall cleave unto his wife: and they shall be one flesh."

He continued, "It matters that Romans 14:11- For it is written, *As* I live, saith the Lord, every knee shall bow to me, and every tongue shall confess to God, it matters that Corinthians **3:9** KJV: For we are laborer's together with God: ye are God's husbandry, [ye are] God's building. It matters that 2 Corinthians 6:1-4[1]As God's co-workers we urge you not to receive God's grace in vain. ²For he says, "In the time of my favor I heard you, and in the day of salvation I helped you." I tell you, now is the time of God's favor, now is the day of salvation. ³We put no stumbling block in anyone's path so that our ministry will not be discredited. ⁴Rather, as servants of God we commend ourselves in every way: in great endurance; in troubles, hardships and distresses it matters that Matthew 5:11 Context. 8 Blessed are the pure in heart: for they shall see God. 9 Blessed are the peacemakers: for they shall be called the children of God. 10 Blessed are they which are persecuted for righteousness' sake: for theirs is the kingdom of heaven matters" that

Matthew 10:22-23

Though God is capable of the kind of physical salvation or deliverance that He indicates He will give to His people in Psalm 91, His general advice to His people is to "flee, get out, get away from the trouble." Even though God could protect one in the midst of trouble, He still gives this general advice. David authored Psalm 3 (where he said he felt safe surrounded by ten thousand people) while fleeing. So, this in no way denigrates God, and it in no way makes for a "cowardly Christian" when he flees persecution and possibly certain death. We have to understand that God places responsibilities on us. As we take His advice to flee, He will "open up the mountain" before us, so we can follow the path that He makes clear for us. It matters that Peter 1 King James Version (KJV)

1 "Peter, an apostle of Jesus Christ, to the strangers scattered throughout Pontus, Galatia, Cappadocia, Asia, and Bithynia,

² Elect according to the foreknowledge of God the Father, through sanctification of the Spirit, unto obedience and sprinkling of the blood of Jesus Christ: Grace unto you, and peace, be multiplied.

³ Blessed be the God and Father of our Lord Jesus Christ, which according to his abundant mercy hath begotten us again unto a lively hope by the resurrection of Jesus Christ from the dead,

⁴ To an inheritance incorruptible, and undefiled, and that fadeth not away, reserved in heaven for you,

⁵ Who are kept by the power of God through faith unto salvation ready to be revealed in the last time. It matters that Romans 8:36-37 King James Version (KJV)

³⁶ As it is written, For, thy sake we are killed all the day long; we are accounted as sheep for the slaughter.

³⁷ Nay, in all these things we are more than conquerors through him that loved us". It matters that <u>1 Corinthians 6:9</u> "Or do you not know that wrongdoers will not inherit the kingdom of God? Do not be deceived: Neither the sexually immoral nor idolaters nor adulterers nor men who have sex with men". It matters that ² Corinthians 4: 7-8 "But we have this treasure in earthen vessels, that the excellence of the power may be of God and not of us. ⁸ *We are* hard-pressed on every side, yet not crushed; *we are* perplexed, but not in despair"; It matters that 1 Peter 4:12-13 ¹² "Beloved, do not think it strange concerning the fiery trial which is to try you, as though some strange thing happened to you; ¹³ but rejoice to the extent that you partake of Christ's sufferings, that when His glory is revealed, you may also be glad with exceeding joy". It matters that Romans 14:4 ⁴ "Who are you to judge another's servant? To his own master he stands or falls. Indeed, he will be made to stand, for God can make him stand". It matters that John 15: 9-11 "As the Father loved Me, I also have loved you; abide in My love.¹⁰ If you keep My commandments, you will abide in My love, just as I have kept My Father's commandments and abide in His love.¹¹ "These things I have spoken to you, that My joy may remain in you, and *that* your joy may be full". It matters that 1 Peter 1: 2-13 ² " elect, according to the foreknowledge of God the Father, in sanctification of the Spirit, for obedience and sprinkling of the blood of Jesus Christ:

Grace to you and peace be multiplied. A Heavenly Inheritance

³ "Blessed *be* the God and Father of our Lord Jesus Christ, who according to His abundant mercy has begotten us again to a living hope through the resurrection of Jesus Christ from the dead, ⁴ to an inheritance [b]incorruptible and undefiled and that does not fade away, reserved in heaven for you, ⁵ who are kept by the power of God through faith for a salvation ready to be revealed in the last time.

⁶ In this you greatly rejoice, though now for a little while, if need be, you have been [c]grieved by various trials, ⁷ that the genuineness of your faith, *being* much more precious than gold that perishes, though it is

tested by fire, may be found to praise, honor, and glory at the revelation of Jesus Christ, ⁸ whom having not ⁽ᵈ⁾seen you love. Though now you do not see *Him,* yet believing, you rejoice with joy inexpressible and full of glory, ⁹ receiving the end of your faith the salvation of *your* souls.

¹⁰ Of this salvation the prophets have inquired and searched carefully, who prophesied of the grace *that would come* to you, ¹¹ searching what, or what manner of time, the Spirit of Christ who was in them was indicating when He testified beforehand the sufferings of Christ and the glories that would follow. ¹² To them it was revealed that not to themselves, but to ⁽ᵉ⁾ us they were ministering the things which now have been reported to you through those who have preached the gospel to you by the Holy Spirit sent from heaven—things which angels desire to look into".

Living Before God Our Father

¹³ "Therefore gird up the loins of your mind, be sober, and rest *your* hope fully upon the grace that is to be brought to you at the revelation of Jesus Christ"; It matters that Philippians 4Home

Bishop continued, "The reason that I had you read with me all these scriptures is because it does not matter that Jonathan and Carol her parents got into a wreck, it matters that you are her husband under God and you need to put her away right so that you and your children and Giselle can go on with your lives and get married right under God."

He continued, "in Acts 2, The Pentecost fully came all with one accord in one place, no matter what people think that you are right not to no that's wrong if you are a new man."

2 Corinthians 5:17 King James Bible

"Therefore if any man *be* in Christ, *he is* a new creature: old things are passed away; behold, all things are become new."

He asks, "Now what are we going to do Challis?"

He, "I' m going to bury my wife Jabra to the best of my ability, my only requests though she had no regard to God is will you commensurate her funeral please?"

Bishop Connors, "I would not have it any other way."

Time goes by and it's Six pm, Challis returns home and its dinner time, he goes in and checks his future wife and children, he showers, dries and oils, puts on Nike t-shirt then wears Nike footie socks and his Nike flips cologne and goes back down, sits and says his grace.

His mother, "Nice to see you, Challis."

As he fixes his plate, he, "Mom I have been going through something."

She said he could give them a heads up and showed him the mail that came, he could see his mother open.

His dad, "Even from the dead she's causing hell, you're going to have to take care of this immediately and Jonathan wants you to call him back."

Challis told them he's going to Chicago to bury his wife on Thursday that Bishop told him he would do the commensuration for her funeral.

His mom, "The Attorney Salomon called also and asked, so what? Is the counsel going to take back your real family?

Challis, "No, he said nothing as long as we get married immediately, she wakes up."

His mom, "See when you lay down with trash you come up with a mess just like this."

Challis's eyes are wide awake like they never have been and he's going to explain this all to Giselle tonight before he read the Bible to her.

His mom said, "that's what you better do because you do not want to spring this on her at Christmas, I'm going to bed it's one thing after another."

He, "No don't say, that I'm going on."

His mom, "Let's do it!"

She sits back down, "This is your messy fight."

She grabs a paper and asked him to read a particular one, he does.

His mom, "Yes I called her mother and I asked her, and she said yes at 17 due to serious fibroids that Jabra did not want to get levered so she went signed her mother's name and got her uterus removed."

Challis asked her, "How was I to know?

His mom, "This is all on you, blind leading the blind, so busy wanting lusty nasty not love, look what has happened and if you do not put this all behind you I guarantee you that your family upstairs you won't have any of them, mark my word I'm going to bed."

She kisses her husband and goes.

The days and nights go by and then it's Thursday and before they know it Challis has sent a car for Bishop and First Lady; both are going, and Challis lets them in, and China comes from the back.

Mac, "We got here at 5 am, your security let us in."

His mom, "I know."

Mac, "I'm going, and China said she's going to stay here at the door, during their wake, I'm going to peep in on my boys."

Challis, "cool also who's Gracie?"

Gracie, "Hello."

China, "Come in, this is Giselle's and her mom's prodigy, and our youngest son Maximillian drive him crazy love interest forever."

Gracie, "No," as she smiles and laughs.

Mac, "Yes she's Giselle Junior."

Challis, "Ok, alright then she's ours."

Gracie thanked them and his mom, "we'll all nice to know and you are Indian like you're beautiful."

China, "She is."

Gracie, "Yes I'm African American also thank you."

His mom, "And all good because China looks like she's going to go any day now."

Challis, "Hey sis, you're all glowing."

He goes and hugs her, and he hugs Gracie, "I am Challis."

Gracie, "Cool my Chisels lady G's husband."

China, "Yes that's what she calls Giselle."

Gracie, "I just came from shy town a couple of months ago visiting my girl Judge Turkey and her baby girl my goddaughter Sassy, so here's her card."

"If you all have any problems just Mention my name, she'll help plus I'll send her a text."

His mom takes the card and Challis said it sounds good, he was looking ok and they all chuckle before they know it.

Rea, "I'm here."

Frank, "Me too".

Challis hugs his auntie Rea "You all go on," she screams, "look at you."

China, "Yes our trips."

Rea, "Girl you look good."

An hour passed and all were on the plane. The pilot has informed them all it will take an hour and a half; Challis is pretty quiet before they know it, they are off the plane and at Jabra's father's church. They all go in, Jonathan and her mom thanks them for this, all the men shake hands, and the women all hug each other. Challis looked around at the Church "New Faith Memorial Baptist Church".

Challis, "Hello Mrs. Sowell, what are you doing here?"

Attorney Salomon, "We were on our way to the Chicago Police Department; Mrs. Sowell puts on her glasses and asks, do you know? As she reads from the paper on her leather clipboard a Turquois Sadia Garnier? Let me see, age 30 I have a picture."

She digs in her bag pulls out and shows a picture of a nice-looking red hair with turquoise eyes. Challis takes the picture and his mom comes by him.

He, "Yes, why Attorney Salomon?"

And now four more of Challis family lawyers come and said they got a call couple of hours ago from the Chicago Police department a horrific smell was attracting the neighborhood, dogs at 1313 Dole vie Lane Condo D and they discover the mother Turquois had been dead round couple months and her daughter.

Mrs. Sowell, "She's returned from a trip overseas with neighbors this past Friday and she was let in the home by her neighbor unknowing mother was dead but she was left in the home unattended till now, the little girl said her mother was hiding her from JayBird and Treasure they asked her why she did not go for help she said because she was not aloud, I think she may have been trained to wait for her mother the little girl gave the officers this paper."

She gives to Challis, "That she was to call in case of trouble."

Challis, "This is my number and Gracie's."

His mom pulls a card and gives him, and Challis told them that this is her Turkey and sassy.

His parents, "OMG!"

Attorney Vaughn hand paper to Mrs. Sowell, she reads and hands it to Challis and he takes and reads.

Mrs. Sowell, "We have your DNA on the file from when the quads were born."

Challis, "He forgot so what now?" His mom just walks away when she saw the paper.

Mrs. Sowell continued, "You're her father, her solely only living family other than Gracie and you know she's too young and she can be released to you."

Challis asked how much time before the funeral starts and Pastor Jonathan said 3 hours.

Mrs. Sowell, "I figured, as so I have already had Mrs. Mustier to shop for her."

Mrs. Mustier goes and whispers in Mrs. Sowell's ear, "All is finished, and I'll go stay with her."

Mrs. Sowell introduced her to Challis, and she puts out her hand, "Hi."

They shake Challis, "Hello, we'll let us go we got 3 hours."

Jamarion Senior called his wife and she said she's coming and cries a bit, "If it ain't one thing it's another."

Mike, "Hey where are you all going?"

His father, "just come on, we'll be back."

Jamarion III asked where and his dad, "Just come on."

In about 30 minutes, they arrive at the police station.

Mrs. Jenny, "Very good"

Mrs. Sowell, "This is Sapphire's father, Mr. Challis Calms-way."

Mrs. Jenny, "Ok, ID please, will you be taking custody?".

Challis, "Yes."

Mrs. Sowell, "Well ok, the father will be taking custody, is Judge Brenner in Officer?"

Mrs. Battles, "Yes sign here and here and I need to copy ID."

Challis gets out and Sapphire cries, "My mommy does not allow me to be with no men but Captain Berry and his wife Bunny and Judge, then my best friend Jasmine Paw and parents Marie."

She puts up her legs and hides her face, Challis goes over, squats down, "I'm your Dad"

Sapphire, "You're Calms-Way?"

Challis, "Yes and this is your grand-mother Sugar and your grand-father and Mike your uncle, Jamarion II your uncle."

Jam who are you? She points to Mrs. Sowell, she sits on the chair arm, "Your fairy Godmother."

Sapphire, "Like in Cinderella?"

Mrs. Sowell, "Yes."

Sapphire, "That's cool."

Officer, "You all can go right next door and Judge Parsons will do your change of custody, just take this paper it's already on the docket."

Sapphire, "Mrs. Jenny I have to tell my mommy I'm leaving please."

Challis, "I'm sorry, do know your mother was hurt or not at home?"

Sapphire, "She's asleep but she could not wake her mommy up so she told a fib that her mommy was at work and just went to sleep so she would not get in trouble."

Challis, "Like your dad, your mom is still asleep."

Sapphire, "Is my mommy ever waking up because I was really quiet so she could sleep because my mommy works a lot to take care of us, am I in trouble?"

Challis, "No and I'm sorry but she is never waking up."

She cried more, "Who's going to take care of me? Our flowers?"

Challis, "Me and I'll plant you as many flowers as you like."

Mrs. Sowell picks her up and she, "come on, let it all out. Do you have a shower here?".

The court officer said the Chief is out that she could bathe her in there and change her.

Sapphire, "I'm dirty."

Mrs. Sowell told her, "Yes."

And asked them to go and calls Mrs. Mustier, she comes almost still running with a dress bag and backpack bag.

His mom right next door, "Let me go help, Lady Coletta."

All the men go over to the court and all Challis Family Attorneys.

Mike, "Cha we need in how much?"

Jamarion II and their dad yell.

Challis, "We will see!"

His dad, "This too shall pass."

Challis, "I know she's just a baby, my baby girl also."

Attorney Salomon came in and out he goes ahead, and four other attorneys follow.

Mike, "Shit they're on it."

Challis, "It's all kinds of shit and asked to be excused."

Bishop, "You're alright son, it matters but it doesn't matter. We got to finish what we came here to do."

Challis, "I'm going to bury my daughter's mother."

Jamiron Senior, "Not here, allow your daughter to be able to visit her mother's grave."

Challis, "Yeah, I'll tell our council to ship her and bury her stone, I'll take my daughter to plant a couple of sunflowers."

Mike asked why and Challis told him that's her mother's favorite flower and he's sure it's hers.

Mike, "Mrs. Sowell is thorough."

Their dad, "Yes. Challis said he did not know anything, and they were on it and his dad said that's what he's talking about, action. some time goes by and Sapphire's hair is all done and curly zig-zag ponytails, 2 Rhinestone ponytail holders and strap two-tone white Sapphire colored saddle shoes leather and 2 pieces pleated bottom white dress, set thin charm necklace with her mother's picture, ankle bracelet, charm bracelet, and two-tone saddle purse and her nails and toes are Sapphire shimmer."

They all arrive at court and Mike, "Oh, wow, don't you look pretty."

Sapphire, "Thank you, Uncle Mike."

Sugar, "Come on baby!"

She holds her arms out and Sapphire takes sits by her then Jamarion II, "well now mom got 3." Attorney Salomon, "You'll just come up, state that you're taking custody and that you wish to do what with mother."

Challis told her to transfer her to Virginia so their daughter will be able to visit her grave, no ceremony buried information of her dead parents and her daughter listed. Attorney Salomon accepted and his dad said she's young and has a beautiful spirit as Giselle has, she'll be just fine, and she will be able to live a normal life.

Mrs. Sowell, "Excuse me, all her preschool records and medical ask for in tow as we leave."

Challis, "Ok."

And thanked Mrs. Sowell and she said it's her job and she goes.

Attorney Judge Parson, "I would not normally do this to a person so close to us, but it feels only right to me."

Sapphire breaks free from her Sugar and runs up to the podium.

Challis, "Judge Parsons, she's fine, I'm sitting where her mother just was elected to take over my district."

Sassy, "Hi."

Sapphire, "Hi, Judge Parsons we won, why are you in my mommy's seat, get up please with her gavel."

Mrs. Sowell goes, and Judge Parson said she is fine, gets up, and sits.

Sassy, "Here he gets out a turquoise wood set gavel with gold plaque puts in an engraved case, takes out gavel and goes down."

Mrs. Sowell goes up and he hands her a case, which she takes up with her. A lot of the court workers are teary-eyed and Judge Parsons asks challis for the docket, Challis gives the paper to Attorney Salomon, he hands it to Judge Parsons "Gail now come on, we got to get through this for Sassy" Gail brings in the file, opens it and she takes the paper from Judge Parsons.

He then signs, "My stamp, Sassy may I have my stamper?"

She gets it and she give it to Mrs. Sowell; she leans over to give him; he takes comes back and stamp papers.

Gail, "The father needs to sign here and here."

Challis goes over to the table and signs and Attorney Salomon signs underneath as representative counsel.

Judge Parsons, "Where will Sassy be moving?"

Attorney Salmon, "7777 Tudor Drive West, Virginia Huntington 25709."

Attorney Salomon hands Gail a card, "We need the mother transferred to address on the card and cost will be covered by the father."

The Judge, "Gail to release them. Gail runs and grabs other papers and runs back and had Challis sign them."

The Judge, "That's it."

Gail, "Yes."

The Judge continued, "If you don't mind I'm her mother's Godfather and we must be in her entire life and sometimes I and my wife and grown children would like to send her things, visit with Sassy, and allow her to be with us sometimes."

Challis, "I don't mind but give us a year for us to get mentally healthy." and

The Judge said he would not have it any other way, but this court department are in love with Sassy and their Turkey. He sheds a tear and says it has done a job on them and he prays he'll be good to her.

Challis, "He will."

Sassy, "We watched her, and her mother grow up here and never look back, Turquoise was set to go places, it's a real tragedy. v Gail cries and covers her mouth and asks, will this be all sir?"

The Judge, "Yes, file right now his copy and she says oh and takes it out and hands it to Challis." The Judge, "And you can go."

Gail, "Can we?"

The Judge, "The staff here wants to see Sassy off."

Gail runs back then comes back with a turquoise Gold African sash and a black robe on a hanger in a see-through bag, she gives it to Mrs. Mustier, and she said, "I'll take that then".

The Judge, "Ok, it's time to go Sassy." She cries.

Mrs. Sowell, "I thought you were a Judge."

Sassy, "I am."

Mrs. Sowell, "Ok then you cannot be crying."

Sassy wipes her eyes, "I'm not, see?"

Then she comes down and Mrs. Sowell carries the case down then almost twenty thousand court workers come in.

Someone's, "I'm Dan and we raised this fund to pay off her mother's student loans, we also received 5 million dollars in CDs in this certificate of deposit from a silent donor for our forever Turquoise and Sassy we filed it and all the Judges signed off and we bestow it to you now for our girls but we all think it'll be all better served in the future for Sassy's College and Life. Trust we know you're well off, but we all want to do this for our very own."

Attorney Salomon takes the check for half a million dollars and a 5-million-dollar certificate of deposit in Sassy's name and the staff gets in two long lines.

Sassy, "Can I take my mommy's walk?"

Dan, "Come on baby."

Sassy goes and waves the staff, crying, but she stops, "Daddy that's me and my mommy, see." Mary a court worker looks at Sassy, "we're naming the court after our own a.k.our Judge Turkey Sassy Turquois Sadia Garnier, the 5th Circuit Court".

Sassy, "let me see."

She picks her up and she looks, and some time goes by. The wake is actually just ending, and Sassy sees Jabra, she hides behind her dad, "don't let Jay Bird see me, Treasure wants to sell me."

Mrs. Sowell grabs her and takes her out.

Sugar, "I can't destroy this child's life, my granddaughter's life and her mother's this is just wrong". Challis, "Mom."

Jamarion Senior, "I got her." and he goes.

Bishop, "Challis let's talk outside a moment."

They go and Bishop, "You cannot stop for what you came here to do."

Challis, "I know closure but I'm not going to lie, I read everything again early this morning and it's hard all of this like a rambling fire has me all to blame".

Bishop, "How?"

Challis, "Turquoise was never was down, I found out later she owed my wife Jabra some money and that's how she coheres her but as soon as I got word of it, I confronted my wife and I gave Turquoise 15,000 for a new start and I gave her 5000 for her to pay Jabra but still I was a bastard I just went along, felt I had it going on and you know the worst thing that every-day I have to look at my daughter and know that I played a major part in her mother's killing."

Bishop, "let God pray and as long as you keep him first and her and you and all whom belongs to you and talk to her first she'll be fine and you all will come on out on the other side."

Challis, "I don't think I can do this; I keep thinking of my remembrance of her mother."

Bishop, "Only you can end this."

Challis, "I got 3 daughters of my own that I love genuinely with all my heart, I'm a monster." He breaks down,

Bishop, "let's walk."

They are about to leave, when his dad demanded, "where are you going Challis?"

Challis, "we'll be back in 15 minutes," and left with Bishop.

After they had left, Pastor Jonathan walks in, "where is Challis?"

Jamarion Senior, "they went to get some air, they'll be back."

Mike, "damn, this is terrible."

Jamarion II, "trashing people's lives trying to do the right thing."

Mike, "I know Giselle is great, but my niece needs to know her own damn mother, back then Challis called me to take her to the airport, and I did, her mother told me that I'm judging her."

"That day I just thought you aren't going, shit, but you were going, damn, she knows it, she said that she knows you dealt with me and there is something in me that's gone, making me the way I am," he stops talking, looking intently at the other man, "these two bitches got off so fucking easily."

Jamison Senior, "I'm sure they beat her to death like that because she would not tell where her daughter was."

Jamison III, "I heard she went behind her dad, 'daddy don't let Jay Bird see me,' this shit is all on Challis ass, he kept that Squeezer with unlimited amounts of cash to do to people what-ever she wanted to."

"I remember I and baby drop in on that nigga, we were in New York for New Year, the next day I remembered he has my extra remote key to our speed boat and we went over there, something told me to leave my baby in the car."

"In a minute I knew where his keys were, I go in and see this nigga with a heirloom of naked women, they were walking around the house naked, and I went to him in bed sleeping with Jabra's ugly ass, she was all hugged up with manly looking Teresa and him with 4 more and he thinks he is going to sail off in the sunset, right?"

"Surprise? Fuck no! He played a major part and I hate to say it, I pray not, but when we get home, he has to come take his three gorgeous daughters Solace, Solae a, and Sapphire."

Their dad comes in; they're about to start and then Challis and Bishop comes in with baby, their mom and her husband.

Mac jogs up to them, "hey Mike, you made it back."

"yes, Mac where is my brother?"

Mac, "Somewhere, he was right here."

Bishop and Challis sits down, and Jabra's dad motions them to come up front, and they do.

Mrs. Sowell comes in, "they've have closed the casket."

Sugar, "she is sleeping, let me take her."

She then sits her right by her, then Mrs. Sowell hands her a throw, and Sugar kisses her on the forehead, "help me take off her coat, she's burning up."

Mike pulls her coat off the first side then the other, and then Sapphire wakes up. "Your Sugar got you,"

Her grandmother, "I'm scared and I'm sleepy uncle Mike."

Her granddaddy, "we all right here to protect you, you can sleep, we are not going anywhere without you."

"Thank you, Pappi," to her granddad, and she goes back to sleep.

Sugar really looks at her, "she's as gorgeous as her baby sisters."

Jamarion II "yes her tone, her eyes are really pretty."

Sugar, "and all this two-tone hair."

Mike, "I 'm really going to make it my business for I and my wife to spend a lot of quality time with her."

Jamarion II, " mine also too."

Sugar, "you're not going to be able to just center her out like that."

Mike, "mom we are not slighting our other nieces, but she's special."

And then, Challis and Mac comes sit down.

Pastor Jonathon Bird Stein III, "ok, thank you all for coming; please be seated. It is my pleasure at a time like this to call on Bishop Neil's Connors IV who will be doing the Eulogy, now I know that we are all very sad but I and my wife at this time have prayed up sorrow for the Lord is here, but I know that if there was ever a time for our baby daughter, her mother is holding on but happy."

"But certainly, she would tear up reading the eulogy so Bishop Neil's Connors IV said he would read it, because I know she cannot stand up here but it's alright cause as praying parents we got this letter. Joy is here in our baby girl's last words to our hearts, thank you our Savior."

He gives the letter to Bishop Neil's Connors IV and he said thank you and said all heads bow and they do then, "let's pray, Father God come forth."

They all repeat and Bishop, "Lord there is a job to do here and we know who needs this, each and every one of us bless you God, I pray you our Savior, come let the King come, in." Psalms 24:8

<u>King James Bible</u>

Who *is* this King of glory? The LORD strong and mighty, the LORD mighty in battle."

Bishop, "come in the King of all Kings."

They cascade in the Holy Spirit for a minute, Bishop.

"Amen. I've looked a little at this letter and can you all musicians play real low as I read?"

"I will get right to it, this letter was dated and mailed the day before our daughter passed away in Jay Bird," he stops to put on his glasses, "it reads daddy and mommy, although I'm here, I' m in a way glad. I know to you it's not the best situation, but in a way, it is what I prayed for, in a sense, mommy I just did not know how to stop several days ago.

I understand how gruesome I had allowed myself to become, don't cry mommy don't regret, daddy I'm right, where I should be. Mommy you told me that I had a demon inside me all these years and every time I talked to you or you saw me you would rebuke me and I say the hell with Jesus, Fuck your Savior.

Then you would slap the words you thought defying God out of my mouth, then you would snatch me up with a skillet or gun in your hand.

I just wanted to talk to you and you would force me to kneel down, you would plead the blood of Jesus over me and throw oil on me, you would rebuke me and then pray the Lord's prayer.

I'm kneeling now mommy in heaven. Our Father who art in heaven, hallowed be thy name. Thy kingdom comes. Thy will be done on earth as it is in heaven. Give us this day our daily bread, and forgive us our trespasses, as we forgive those who trespass against us, and lead us not into temptation, but deliver us from evil. For thine is the kingdom, and the power, and the glory, forever and ever Amen.

Mommy, over the years, for me I did not understand, but now every-thing you told me, the great calamity, the love of God and how God is here, it all came true. It's clear and I believe it as the day rises in me. I'm WOKE now and mommy you said the last time I saw you, you said aren't you tired? You didn't hit me or hold a gun to me.

Because you were sure I always brought you something expensive, you would throw it out in the yard and you would say, "all I can give you is to choose life," I love you mommy, I told you so many times. You said I should tell the Lord my heart's desire, you said when I was a baby you would ask God to protect me and keep me as I got older, you would say it over and over again, you would recite it every time to me .

Psalms 23 "The LORD is my shepherd; I shall not want. He maketh me to lie down in green pastures: he leadeth me beside the still waters.

He restoreth my soul: he leadeth me in the paths of righteousness for his name's sake.

Yea, though I walk through the valley of the shadow of death, I will fear no evil: for thou art with me; thy rod and thy staff they comfort me.

Thou preparest a table before me in the presence of mine enemies: thou anoint my head with oil; my cup runneth over.

Surely goodness and mercy shall follow me all the days of my life: and I will dwell, my mommy, your Jay Bird in the house of the Lord forever."

Mommy, yes ma'am, yes ma'am, yes sir, daddy, yes sir, your song, tell God I am all about it.

I did my choices, I won't keep you, but I need you to know that I know; your birthday is tomorrow, and God has smiled on me, he has been good, so good just to me.

It's 15 minutes till midnight and my birthday gift to you the only one you ever asked of me this day, mommy this hour that the Lord has made this moment, I fought your Lord as long as I could, but days ago he came to me and he told me he loved me to choose life, and he told me that he died on the cross way back then in Calvary just for my sins, he told me everything else in my way was sinking sand, and mommy I accepted, I repented.

I know I'm to blame for my evil, but now I choose life for me. I couldn't let on to Teresa that God was rising in me, remember mommy every birthday, every holiday before my trespasses I needed you to know that the last time we were together we ate and watched TV, both of us fell to sleep in you and daddy's bed like when I was your little Jay Bird, you were the and is the best thing that ever happened to me, no matter what, I'm proud that you were and are my mommy.

Just I and daddy being on the road was the best time ever in a long time for me, I know your song I always acted like I didn't. I just been singing it all day, I couldn't eat or drink, God told me I'd never thirst again, and I haven't, everything looks so beautiful to me in here.

It's so nice and warm in here, some people shout Jesus and singing it that God is yes, he is, I just keep hearing that rich fragrant song you use to sing in our home early every Sunday morning.

I wake to that strong big breakfast smell as you cooked us all the best huge big breakfast while playing James Cleveland, and mommy I told God to bless you and daddy with peace. He said it's finished because mommy I told him that you both have been the best parents.

There are no windows in here, but I swear, I keep seeing this light and I see that I'm in a cell, but now I' m free, and this hour, this minute, God's joy and strength has risen in here and overtaken me, I see it, the Salvation of Christ.

I keep seeing it mommy, and he told me that it's in a narrow place, but he said when I get there; you hear that mommy? I'm going to heaven right now, in a few minutes. I feel my hands are holding on to the right hand of God and Glory to God, not us, to God be the Glory and may the Lord be Blessed.

I woke up this morning feeling so good. God is good, He is this minute so Gorgeous, he is the light and the strength of my life, mommy he is my own, and so happy birthday mommy, millions of kisses, my inequities, misery and strife is gone.

I have repeated over and over again, mommy over all the things that I've done to you in life and also to you daddy, I don't have a lot of paper, but I had to get the most important things down.

I asked God if I could surrender to him here, and he told me that although all the things I've done, that none of it has made Him forsake me, He said, "I am The Lord," He told me mommy that mere life is temporal but the Salvation of the Lord of Christ in me is eternal in me.

Just me mommy people scream out Jabra all the time in the world, in here he chooses me, just me, I feel so good. I just keep feeling God's breath upon me. He said I'm going to a better place, then He told me that He never left me.

In short of his words, people cry out, they almost can't sustain Jay Bird's mommy.

Our other house song is all in my ear, God is my all in all, I'm singing it in here with angels filled choir, God told me to tell you that by the time you receive this declaration I will be dead in Glory, and mommy, daddy I'm not scared, and I ask God to bring us back where all our sin started, and he did and I asked Him if Teresa can die today also, because she will break out and harm Turquoises daughter, Sassy, and sell her.

I asked God if he would please cover Sassy Turquoise with the blood of Jesus and He told me abide my house, my servitude, no worries, I told God I did what he told me to do. Which was to give what I have to all as He has given to me? So, I wired the entire of my money, which is 45 million in CD's to Illinois courthouse and they had it wired, I know by now to you mommy and daddy, to our church.

That's why Teresa is planning to kidnap Cha Town and Giselle's beautiful babies. Mommy, daddy you have to see them they all look like picture perfect and tell my husband that I'm so sorry, he was the best I could have ever prayed for and I know he really loved me, and I'm so very sorry Cha Town thinks I did not love him, but God knows I beg to differ, he was always other than God, you mommy and daddy, the best thing that ever happen to me.

I'm just so grateful that I got to see his babies and Giselle and Cha Town don't know, but in many night dreams I would hear him call out her name a lot, but my response no matter how horrid was because of the inadequacy that embarked in me, that's why I consumed our home with so many others, so I could drown out her name.

He did not know but I did, I told Cha Town that I brought all the smorgas board in because I knew it was only a matter of time before he finds me out, he thought I was sleeping on New Year's eve but I was not, I saw Butter and in time she's the real deal, and look right now, but I'm the happiest for him cause I don't hurt any more.

Mommy and daddy, I love you so much. I'm so sorry for all the hurt I caused you. The other 5 million I asked my Lord if could send it to the Government nonprofit, and God said everything is in his hand and I had it put into Sapphire's Trust fund in CD's under her mother Turquoise name.

I'm just trying to write all my wrongdoings; trying to make a few rights, please accept, you and daddy should take a long-extended vacation, you don't have to wait on me no more.

Last time, I was there out front where the sun cascades our home, I planted you a purple rose bush, God told me he plants, and you water, so keep its beauty.

I want you to remember me not as one of the rest, I know you will try to pull it or send the CD's back.

The hem of God's garment; Mathew 9:20 **King James Bible**

'And, behold, a woman, which was diseased with an issue of blood twelve years, came behind *Him*, and touched the hem of His garment,' but first mommy please ask God because I told him, and he said it's yours and my daddy's and whatever he gives me is mine to take.

Ok love to you Queen of my heart, the best of me, the solely hem of Gods garment, my love to you; you reign supreme at the right side of Jesus Christ, God told me that, daddy is the only hero I know besides God.

I love you all, and I have to give this declaration letter to this nice Warden, he is dressed in all white and he looks so nice, he said he would make sure it gets to you today, which is your birthday.

I don't know how, and hey mommy, daddy, God said when you see me again, I'll be all brand new. I'm laying down now, mommy; right in here is so nice and warm.

I have such a beautiful fur comforter; God gave it to me, I'm sleepy, hey mommy, Gabriel just came, he's so huge, I yelled to Teresa just now to see if she could see big old Gabriel, his wings fill my cell, he's all muscles, and so gorgeous.

Mommy he's about 10 feet tall, and he's almost touching the ceiling. It's now 10 till midnight, so Happy Birthday mommy, I have the nicest comforter, all white, and smells so good and comfy, mommy also tell daddy to preach that out of **Deuteronomy 22:5**

Verse Concepts

"A woman shall not wear man's clothing, nor shall a man put on a woman's clothing; for whoever does these things is an abomination to the LORD your God.

See gay on the DL is nothing but a legion; a demon fornication lairs, shakers fornicates, adulterers swingers, all are sins of the devil. I keep rebuking being gay, a swinger, a lair adulterer by the blood of Jesus. God told me that He is my light, my shining armor in all my darkness, he is my all and all, that Violin music just keeps playing, 'my God, the Lords all in white,' Jesus it's so nice and soft to my heart, Gabriel said he will stay with me, and God said, "hey, no pain," he is never short of his words. Happy Birthday mommy.

Bishop, "You all can help her mom get up she can hardly stand, a couple parishioners and ushers help her out, as people stood up to go out."

"come on James, I think it is a Christian thing, but there is always one back slider some, we all have but back sliders complaining, but you see, no matter how rich or poor, how strong you or me have been in the faith or in the Word of God, things will always get better in God, all of us is on a clock, a time table."

Bishop, "where is that hour glass? Deacons bring it,"

A deacon brings it and places it in front of him. He flips it upside down and the sand slowly pours into the second part of the glass.

"See how that is doing? That's how all of us are, this running sand is like our time, and when it finishes out, no flipping around for it to start from the beginning."

"And when its each of our time, we will either cross over or fall in sin, when this happens, some say where is our faith? It always has to be a channel in God. See God knew Jay Bird was in trouble he never left her nothing is too hard for God. Where is your faith? Is the answer God? If it isn't, tell me about it. Some of you, you feel that your money makes you feel strong, it's funny. some of you, your bills are due, tell the Lord about it, or let us say you got a habit, you are hooked, and you don't know how to break free. Where is your faith in God? Can I get a witness? Jay Bird was down, she knew where to cash in. Proverbs 22:6.

Bring up a child in the way she should go, it doesn't matter when you choose it, what matters is what you do, and to all you parents that are out here, at your willing time, tell God about it, and bring your children no matter what age to God, troublesome teenagers, college students going to jail, you people run around screaming, saying that you are sick of buying your Kids the latest Jordan's, iPhones or PlayStation 4 or 5, most expensive cars, party stuffs. These things are not going to get them into Heaven, tell the Lord about anything that is making you not to turn to him, is it lust? Are you hooked to Porn? Drinking? Gambling? Cheating? Adultery? Do not be afraid to tell God about it so you can't get yourself clean, tell God about it, everyone should stand up and praise God.

Bishop comes down, "Some of you can sit if you want." "Jay Bird made her place, she had her ticket, the Question is; do you all have yours? See her parents did the work, she said her mama had a gun to her head and she went gangster on her, but she got in, she knew when all was gone. Some of you think you got money, and that makes you feel superior, you see what she did? Because none of you or me can pay our way in, you all heard me read her letter, Jay Bird said its path is narrow, and not anyone can come in, choir please sing 'whatever reason there might be', thank you Jesus, I was alone on my way straight to hell, shouting and singing. Jesus is the best thing that ever happen to me, God bless her soul, I know what her mama and Jay bird heard seen, but there has never been a time in my life like this, James Cleveland come on change the words if anyone should ever write my life story for whatever reason, there should be several people screaming, Jesus is the best thing that ever happened to me, if anyone after I'm gone should ever write my life story, this Jesus is the best thing that ever happened to me. First Lady Collate takes Sassy from Sugar and stands up shouting, now hundreds have gathered outside of door.

Deacon opens the door, "I'm sorry it's a funeral."

Hundreds of people just walk on in through the other door, Bishop Connors stopped to look at Pastor Jonathan, who waved that it was alright. The funeral then continued, the church was now singing, 'he is the best thing that ever happen to me,' Sugar shouts, her husband cries a bit, and Mac, and the pallbearers all come up as the choir sings James Cleveland song, 'on the banks of Jordan.'

Bishop, "God has smiled on me, he has been good to me."

"Looking at Pastor Jonathan who comes up and whispered something to him at the altar."

"Jay Bird made her choices, it's not too late for some of you to get your affairs together, come on this day and choose who you are going to serve."

Over 300 people came down at different times throwing wigs money condoms guns on the altar, as they chose to give their life to God.

"Please Lord, help me to hold out until my changes come, as you all go, smoking will fade, lust will go, gambling will stop, say it one more time."

Bishop, "his wife brings him an oil."

First Lady Collete goes over to Sugar, "you got oil Sugar?".

Sugar, "yes."

Bishop, "ok, come help several other pastors in the audience."

Sassy wakes up then and starts to sing and shout, she goes right up to her Sugar and Bishop.

"Even the baby knows she is been brought up right to come serve the Lord,"

Bishop, "help me to hold her, In the Father, Son and the Holy Ghost," to each deacon.

"God has been good to me."

SEASONS OF LIFE AND THE ALTAR CALL OF CHRIST

Then the choir starts singing. Pastor Jonathan comes up the altar, and the music becomes low.

Bishop, "let us all bow our heads, no moving, 'Apostle Granites, please lead us in prayer!"

Apostle Granites, "God, you are our father, at a time like this, we all repent of our sins, the ones we know and the ones that we may not know, but God we come this day of abundance that we pour out our heart to bless you God we all want to go to heaven Lord, we are all in need of you, but Lord you know the best."

They all say, "Amen!"

"Bishop, but tomorrow Sunday, we will be on the next street block."

Bishop, "ok, for you all here, your new church will be in the street over there."

A lady in the crowd asked, "will Pastor Jonathan be their Pastor?"

"Yes lady."

"What about you Bishop? Now that we are going to be sister churches,"

Bishop, "we just opened newly, our revival week begins this Sunday, I'm inviting your Pastor and his wife, they can stay with me and my First Lady."

First Lady Collete smiles, "you hear that baby? We got an invitation."

"Our pleasure."

"Ok, its praying time, all bow, no moving, no playing, it's serious time." And they all did as he said.

The ushers and deacons all put oil on joiners, "the Father, the Son and the Holy Ghost.

In 45 minutes, after all prayer, many came out, and said that this is their church."

"Now Pastor Jonathan his been good to me, come on sons and daughters of God and hug Pastor Jonathan."

Several people came out, "we have seen you pastor and first lady doing the work in the community."

Bishop and Pastor Jonathan shouts, "Hallelujah! Glory to God, not us, to God in Glory, May the Lord Bless you all real good."

He starts dancing and shouting one more time, that the lord may bless you real good, he sings, the choir sings and plays, people join on to sing, 'may the lord bless you real good,' Bishop dances, people do the same, and sings and shout. Even Challis, his daughter, is dancing and shouting, he looks at her she claps. His brothers, some who haven't been to church, dad and Mac are dancing.

Bishop, "this is alright send the blessing."

Sassy gets on the piano, send the blessing,' in the mic and plays.

Her family is floored. Bishop and the whole church sing and shout, and after some time, they all say their goodbye and leave. After all have been dropped off; Bishop and First Lady went home with Jay

Bird's parents.

CHAPTER 17

JayBird meets the Family

"Challis now you have to meet some people." Her dad, Challis sits, Sassy, "daddy I'm hungry."

Her father, "She hardly ate anything at the funeral, pass me the sandwich soup. Give me the soup crackers please, and ice water." They give them to her. "I'll go shower and check my family."

"Ok that is good,"

Her father, "I already got on my night clothes where am I sleeping Sugar?".

"She has a total room set up in the adjacent living space, I had all other things moved up to the attic, and got her the whole room set up."

Her father, "that's good," "she'll be right there with you all."

Challis had all her stuffs brought from her home.

Challis, "let me go to her nurse, Jasmine." "Hi my daughter Sapphire, will be under your care, also three extra hands were hired for her."

Jasmine, "how old is she?"

Challis, "she is 4 years old."

Jasmine, "ok."

Challis goes checks on her, kisses her, and then goes into the shower. She comes back out and sees Sapphire sitting in the hall with her new nanny, Charlotte Premise, a middle aged but good looking lady that is a retired professor, teaching nursing. She had just wanted something else in her life that meant something, because she is married with 5 grown children, and she has 4 elementary school, and junior high grandchildren, that live on the base in Germany with her eldest daughter, and her husband.

Mrs. Premise, "this is the Commissioner of the Police Department, she will be sharing the job with Karina Vilsack, who is married to the Chief of Police Mr. Vilsack, and is a retired ice skater, and is also a writer and married with a son, and daughter. Neither of them will do weekends, well, night falls, morning springs, and what a morning."

Sugar, "Who is that?"

Security Bose intercoms, "It's Mrs. Sowell and Mrs. Mustier." "Challis, go wake your father up, tell him that Mrs. Sowell and Mrs. Mustier are here."

Sugar, "okay."

Challis said. "let them in."

Sugar intercoms, "fine, place them in the kitchen," Sugar released the intercom.

Her dad, "I just took my shower; I'll go down in 5 minutes."

"Challis waited for him, and they both go down. Both ladies are drinking coffee, given to them by Chef Trey when they came into the kitchen, Sugar was surprised that her new Chef Trey Phillips, that Challis had got her, had already prepared hot coffee and breakfast.

Mrs. Sowell, "as I have already told your mother, we met with Oprah and her staff late last night."

Mrs. Mustier stands up, "these are the papers."

Her father sits down and Challis does the same.

Mrs. Sowell, "we read all her records, and they will allow Sassy to attend summer school to bring her up to speed for all day pre-kindergarten."

Mrs. Mustier, "but if she test high she'll be put automatically in kindergarten, and as we discovered Sassy's mother just had started training her for ice skating and she plays piano."

Mrs. Sowell, "In her belongings we discovered her diary and schedule, and from there on we discovered that her hopes were for Sassy to be an ice skater one day in the Olympics at the age of 16."

Mrs. Mustier, "I am a 2 time gold medalist in ice skating, same as Giselle."

Mrs. Sowell, "and already we saw and heard she is a gifted pianist and the school can continue to train her as well as me, at 6 we would like for her to begin with her mother's notes to learn violin, she can read now, the school will start at 5 to teach her how to read music."

Challis, "she's 4."

Her father, "so Mrs. Sowell, may I be frank?"

Sowell, "yes."

"Sassy has already being prepared I see no reason why you should not continue to do that as well, as Giselle started at this age for all her athletics and learning."

Challis, "I think it is awesome, I'll look over all this."

Mrs. Sowell and Mrs. Mustier gets up and say thank you. "wait, she is now going to be Giselle's daughter, and she will always be, this is what her mother has been training her for, as well as in wait for, and I'm sure that it is what Giselle will expect. No twirling thumbs."

Challis, "I'm sure."

Mrs. Mustier, "I also read that her mother was putting her in The Winter pageant this year, I hold a doctorate in psychology and education and I live here around the corner from her school, and I believe it is my job to be what Mrs. Sowell has been to Giselle to all your daughters, let me do my job, language learning now in this kind of upbringing will heal her heart and strengthen her mind, body and soul."

"Mrs. Mustier, good day the clock is ticking." Her father sees them out, and he comes back and says His grace.

"What the hell is wrong with you? "Sugar asked.

Challis, "she just got here, so you are going to be at work all day, and she needs to be doing her own work, not sitting here twirling her thumbs."

"I agree with your mother on this," her father said.

"Look at this, she will be gone from 7am till 4pm Monday to Friday," Challis said.

"What else does she have to do? I guess you did not hear Giselle," her father reiterated.

"I did. I know I got to teach her how to swim and ride a bike," Challis said.

Then Sassy comes down the steps, bathed by nurse Jamia, and dressed in a terry cloth, sweat suite with suede slipper boots on with three big long zig zag pony tails.

"Good morning," she said.

Challis gets up and picks her up, kissing her fore head. Sassy hugs her dad and he puts her down, she goes to Sugar and hug her and said, "I ice skate every morning and play piano at Judges House are you taking me to her?"

"Come here," Sugar said to her, she does, and he kisses and hug her, "no, asks your daddy."

"You like ice skating and playing the piano? "Challis asked her.

"I love it," Sassy replied ,"I and my mommy do it every morning."

"What about Pre-kindergarten?" Challis asked.

"Oh yes," Sassy said, "I'm enrolled this summer at Calvary, I'm in Pre-Kindergarten, it's fun, are we going?"

"Not today, but come eat breakfast," Challis said to her.

"Challis wait," Sugar said, "there are two phone books there."

Challis gets them put them in the chair, and motions for her to sit ,she sits, and said her grace out loud.

They all smiled, and then she said, "I'm hungry."

"What do you want?" Challis asked her.

"Grapes, banana, brown-sugar, maple, oat meal, 1 wheat toast and orange juice thank you," Sassy said.

Chef Trey had already made everything and brings it on cue to her.

"Thanks Chef Trey, it's a little hot." Challis said.

"Right, you put the banana in my oatmeal, yummy that's just how my mommy makes it, you're the best, thanks." Sassy said.

"You are very welcome." Chef Trey said.

"Where is baby."

"Let me," Challis said and blows, "who is that?"

"You know daddy Lady Butter, our helper that made me my princess fall costume, she is upstairs sleeping, I asked her where my baby sister was? She would not wake up," Sassy said.

"You talking about Gracie?" Sugar asked.

"Yes ma'am, she is my God mommy baby sister." Security DJ intercoms, "There is a Gracie here,"

"Show her in," Challis said.

Gracie came in all teary eye, and Sassy runs and jumps up in her arms, then she hits Gracie, "baby G sister why didn't you come for me?" Challis gets up.

"Stop I did not know, I just found out, I drove there last night, I went to Judge Parsons he told me everything, and that you were here." Sassy hits her and said,

"I hate you, I hate you, I told the police, and they dialed your number over and over again." Her dad grabs her, Gracie is crying, "I'm so sorry, my phone got broken and I still have not had the chance to replace it till yesterday," she pulls it out of her pocket, "See, it's gold, I had black before."

Sassy really cries harder, "Oh my God!

This is all so terrible." Gracie cries.

"Child sit down," Sugar said to her, she sits down, and says, "I'm so sorry, God please, my Lady," she sits, "let her stay awake now, for I do not know what to do."

"You don't have to worry about her, I'm her father and I'm going to take great care of her," Challis said.

"How old are you?" Sugar asked.

Gracie says 19.

"You are just a baby yourself," his dad said.

"Won't you be graduating college this year?" Sugar asked.

Gracie replied, "I did last week."

"Where are your parents," his dad asked.

Gracie replied, "my father is dead, and my mother that's a another whole story, my grandma raised me since I was born."

she cries a little, "till she died during my freshman in high school graduation year, so Madame and my Lady B helped me get emancipated so I could take over my grandma's estate, and I dropped out of high school and I won a scholarship and enrolled into college, and the rest is history."

"Damn!" Chef Trey said.

"Where are you staying?" Sugar asked, she cries more, and says," I have a place in Ohio to live, but since all this has happened to my Lady B and Turquoise, it's harder."

"Are your stores still functioning?" Sugar asked.

'Yes ma'am, I have a staff, but what I'm doing now is after my show I will be channeling online," Gracie said. "also, oh."

She gets her out, checks it and gives it to Challis, "this is my 2 years salary my Lady B gave me, she is not operating right now and Roma only needs Alayna she hired fulltime and Lynn special occasions right now."

"Well, you are too busy to help her any way," Sugar said.

"No, you keep this, it's cool and I'm sure she will need you when she awakes." Challis said.

Sassy gets down and gets up in Gracie's lap, "I'm so sorry."

They hug each other. Gracie says, "I'm so sorry. I love you."

"I love you too." Sassy said, hugging and kissing her.

"You hungry?" Challis asks Gracie. "Yes sir, please, but may I go?"

"Yes," Challis replied.

After she eats, Gracie puts her down.

"No, stay," Sassy cries.

"I'm just going to see our Lady B, I need to talk to her," Gracie says.

"Come on, let go of her, Sassy, she is not going any-where," Challis said, "you got clothes?"

"They are in my car." Gracie replies.

"You drove here?"

"Yes sir, straight from Chicago."

Gracie runs up the steps.

"Everything is on warm, I just got her a little of everything, and I'm going shopping for lunch dinner." Chef Trey said.

"Cool, but go check our stash first." The Chef said cool and leaves the room.

"I'm calling China, I want to know more about this." Sugar said.

Two hours pass by, and they go on the patio, Gracie is reading the bible to Sassy, so she can go to sleep. Sugar sits her husband and son down.

"Mom," Challis says.

"Listen," Sugar said, "guess who her mother is."

Her husband shakes his head.

"Ok, our Governor, Clark's wife, Constance, is her mother." Sugar said.

"Isn't she white?" Challis asked.

"No she goes for white, and China said she disowned Gracie as a baby because she was too dark," Sugar replied, "Jamarion Senior who is now her husband is white, and their sons are a little older than her, China said that she had an affair when her husband was away in Saudi Arabia, and she covered it up. Her mother came to the hospital and intercepted Gracie and Constance's real mother, China said she is a dark black Indian, and her father was white, she said that her grandma and her dad are Seminoles Indian, and they both really loved Gracie. She said her dad died of 4th stage cancer when she was a toddler."

The Security intercom beeps, "There is a Mrs. Constance here to see Gracie."

Challis, "Show her in.".

They all go in to see her.

Mrs. Constance, "I'm very sorry, I need to speak with Gracie for a moment."

Challis, "I will get her," he intercoms her.

Gracie comes down, "Nurse Jasmine is watching Sassy because she is playing with her dolls, and dressing them, and watching the Moses cartoon in your room."

Challis, "That's cool."

Gracie, "I will be gone in 3 days."

Constance, "Ok come I want you to tell me some things, did you graduate?"

Gracie, "Yes ma'am, do you have your list?"

Constance, "Right here, didn't you get my messages?"

Gracie, "No ma'am, not till two days ago."

Constance , "Walk me to the door, look it over." requested, and gives her a paper,

Gracie looks it over, "I will have all this finished by next week."

Constance, "Do you have your travel and sewing machine with you,"

Gracie, "Always."

Constance, "Ok stop being all over the place you're a business owner now, act like it, and look how dark you're getting for Miss. Teen, you won another ball game Miss. USA, stay out of the sun."

Gracie, "I'll be traveling in a day or two."

His mom, "Make your hair, wear no make-up, also do you have my VIP's for your fashion show?" "I'm about to cuss this."

Challis, "Mom please."

Gracie, "Constance wait, there is something in my bag, now these are people in the front row, and of course you will be in the same row with Yves Saint, Lauren, Michael Kohrs, Oprah, Michelle Obama and Melania Jay," going to grab her bag,

"Paris here I come!" Constance exclaimed.

She kisses Gracie on each cheek and then leaves.

Gracie comes back to the room, "I'm so sorry, I apologize, she won't be back again. May I please shower and change?"

"Yes," his mom said, "the room with the glass door knob, you can have that room for the next few days."

"Oh no. I'm going to a hotel, I just think I…" Gracie said, his mom cuts her off, "no I think it'll be good if you stay here as long as you like."

Gracie, "I don't want to intrude,"

Challis, "You are not intruding,"

"But I have to grab…"

Challis, "Tell the security what you need and they will get it for you."

Gracie, "I wanted to know if I can move my car around back."

Challis, "They can put it in a garage."

Gracie, "Thank you, I just don't want to bother anybody."

Jamarion Senior, "You are not bothering anyone, consider yourself home."

Gracie cries a little, "thank you all so much. I just had a blow out on the road and I had to change my tire, please excuse my appearance."

Sugar, "You are fine. What's wrong?"

Gracie, "I'm alright, may I please be excused?"

Sugar, "Yes."

Challis, "Where are your keys? I'll tell them."

Grace, "Just put in 7777 as its pass code."

Challis, "Cool, they will bring up your bags."

Gracie, "Thank you all so much."

They all say no problem. Time goes by,

Jamarion Senior, "Baby, what's wrong with you."

Solace, "Yes I' am tempted to bust this bitches bubble."

Challis, "Mom, stay out of it."

Solace, "This child is a lovely young lady, she is the reason why we are all cleaning and helping take care of your kids and Giselle, I'm ready to go there."

Jamarion Senior, "Baby it's not your fight."

"She was so respectful to her and she then tells her to stay out of the sun? That child is absolutely beautiful, her eyes, her color are beautiful, and her shape is beautiful too."

Jamarion Senior, "She is pretty, hell, she won Miss. Teen already."

Challis, "And to get in for Miss. USA? that is not no walk in the park. She is extraordinarily beautiful."

Solace, "And sweet as she can be, she can come here anytime."

An hour passes by.

Grace, "May I please take Sassy ice skating, and to get hers and my hair done, we will also get a manicure and a Pedicure, plus a little shopping at the next county over."

Challis, "Yes, but security will drive you, and stay with you, and why next county?"

Gracie, "It will just be better."

Challis, "Ok, when will you be back?"

Gracie, "It's noon now, we will be back by 6pm." Glancing at the wall clock,

Challis, "Cool, they will be with you all day."

An hour goes by after they had left with the security guys, Bronze and Opine.

Solace, "She is trying her best to appease to her mother."

Jamarion senior, "Hell yeah."

Solace, "I will have a good talk with her."

Challis, "Mom."

Solace, "She is not ugly and I want her to know that."

Jamarion Senior, "She should know, she won Mrs. Teen."

Solace , "Wait I recorded that for Sassy, take a look at her."

Jamarion Senior, "Out of all of them, she looks like an Indian."

Solace, "China said that her dad was a Seminoles Indian."

Jamarion Senior, "It was terrible the way that woman talked to her, I'll be damned."

Solace, "And she's a high achiever, those sons she got I bet are not worth a dime."

Challis, "I know them, they are pretty straight."

Security intercom beeps, "Mrs. Constance is here,"

Solace, "Let her in."

Constance walks in, "I need to order two more tickets."

Solace, "She is not here."

Constance, "Has she left?"

Solace, "She'll be back later, and I'll tell her."

Constance, "I left her two messages."

Solace, "thank you."

They wait for her to leave.

"She got one more time, she is just trying to use her."

Jamarion Senior, "I bet you none of her high mighty friends know who she really is."

Challis, "Nope, Never."

Mike walks in, 'What's the Governor's wife doing here?"

Jamarion Senior, "It's a long story, what can we do for you?"

Two days goes by.

Solace, "Gracie, do you want to leave today?"

Gracie, "I better, I'll be back next weekend," as she leaves.

Four days go by.

Sassy, "May I call my baby sis?"

Challis, "Yes, just push 1 on the phone," watches her as she does this.

Gracie, "Hello my princess."

Sassy, "When are you coming back?"

Gracie, "In one more day."

Sassy, "When you come back, can we go ice skating?"

Gracie, "Of course, plus we are going to ask for permission to use the kitchen."

Sassy, "For what?"

Gracie, "To bake some cookies, Yeah, yeah!"

Gracie, "And Caramel apples."

"Yes, with lots of nuts, and what about our secret blankets?"

Gloria, "We are going to work on all those, but I just colored the fur."

Sassy, "I wanted to help."

Gracie, "You will get to do a lot, we still have to do flowers, ribbons, and your dresses for the pageant."

Sassy, "Yeah yeah! I miss you."

Gracie, "I miss you too. Did you ask your dad about the pageant?"

"Today,"

Gracie, "Okay, my only shining star baby," as Sassy dances all around, "I love you my baby sis."

Gracie, "I love you too, be good, kisses."

Sassy kisses and they hang up.

Sassy, "Daddy can I talk to you?"

Challis, "Yes, but that would be while you eat your dinner."

"Daddy I want to be in the winter pageant, my baby sis said she would help me, and be my umh… uhm,"

Solace , "Chaperon."

Sassy, "Yes ma'am."

Challis, "When is it?"

Solace, "November 4th."

Challis, "Yes, you can do it."

Sassy, "Can I call my baby sis back?"

Challis, "I'll text her."

Sassy, "I want to do it."

"After you eat, now eat,"

Sassy, "Yes sir."

Solace, "What are you going to do in the pageant?"

Sassy, "play the piano, I really want to ice skate, but my baby sis said I should do what I'm best at now, so daddy, I want an all-white fur piano my size with a microphone, because I'm going to be singing to my baby sis."

Challis, "Okay, I will get right on that."

Solace, "What are you going to wear?" Solace asked her.

Sassy, "My baby sis said that she is going to make me a real fur cape, and dress to match with rhinestones, and I will need another dress, that will be the satin flower dress with umh… bow sleeve matching coat."

"I'm finished; may I go watch cartoons and color?"

Sassy, "Yes, but tell your nurse to bath you; then you can watch cartoons," as she kisses all of them and goes out of the room.

Solace, "I am so happy."

Jamarion Senior, "Why?"

Solace, "Girls stuffs. I love it, I have just been praying for all us and Gracie."

Challis, "She's perfect for Maximillian Junior."

Solace, "She is so lovely, you both heard China and Mac, she's ours."

Jamarion, "Yes, they did."

A day goes by. It's Friday and there is no Gracie.

Sassy, "She said she would be here."

Challis, "She will, I called her this morning."

Sassy, "I will wait for her."

Challis, "No, take your bath and go to bed."

"I'll bath her, come on baby."

They both leave the room.

Jamarion Senior, "I don't think she would stand her up."

Night falls and Saturday comes, there is still no Gracie.

Maximillian, "Hey Uncle Challis!"

Challis, "Nephew Maximillian."

Nephew Maximillian, "Hey is Gracie there?"

Challis, "No."

Maximilian, "They are out?"

Challis, "She is not back, that's not like her; didn't she have plans with Sassy?"

Challis, "Yes, they have been talking all week about it."

"I'm going, I'm flying to Columbus, Ohio to see, because my baby don't do this."

Challis, "No deal, keep me in the loop."

Maximillian, "You know that I will," and they hang up.

Solace, "What?"

Challis, "He said that he is flying to Ohio."

Solace, "Something isn't right,"

CHAPTER 18

Where is Gracie

The day goes and night falls, there is no Gracie. Sunday morning China calls.

Challis, "I'll call her back."

His mom doesn't say anything to him.

"Hello," as he hears China screaming and crying.

"What?"

Mac, "We're in Columbus, at the hospital, Maxie found Gracie beat up in the alley in the back of her delivery truck port, but she's alive."

Challis, "We will be there, what hospital?"

Mac, "Ohio University Hospital, Campus North."

Within hours, Challis, his parents and Sassy arrived at the hospital, Maxie is really upset and saying, "she doesn't deserve this soon, as soon as she wakes up, and I'm marrying her."

Mac, "Calm down"

Challis, "Who did it?"

Mac, "They sprayed all her back."

Doctor Pepper comes in, "You can't leave,"

Gracie, "I'm fine."

China, "No you are not."

Gracie, "I can't stay here."

Maxie, "You're going to be here Gracie, I'm here with you"

Doctor Pepper, "She needs to be under supervised care,"

Three days go by, and Gracie is out, but she went home with Challis's family because they already have staff. 4 days go by, Maximillian has not left her side.

Security intercom beeps, "Mrs. Constance is here."

Solace, "Let her in," Solace said.

She comes in, they were all up having breakfast.

"I'm sorry to intrude so early; I just need to speak with…" Solace cuts her off, "Nurse Kelly Ann, please tell Gracie to come down, she has a visitor."

A couple of minutes go by.

Gracie, "Hi, I have all your stuffs, can you bring it?"

Maxie, "yes," and goes to get them.

Constance, "I did not come for that, how are you?"

"Oh, fine and you?"

Constance, "Not good."

Maxie brings out a store rolling hanger with 10 wardrobe bags and with other bags hung on it.

Gracie, "I will open them," as she goes to open it.

Constance, "Please I'm sure."

Gracie, "No ma'am, take one look, open it Maxie."

He does, it's a slate blue suede tight dress, with a turtle neck collar button, to match side deep slit, and a slate suede boot toe out stilettos to match, and a fox fluffy shawl.

Solace, "That's beautiful."

Gracie, "Thank you."

Constance, "I love it, but can we go somewhere and talk?"

Solace, "You can go in the library."

Constance, "Thank you."

Maxie tries to go with them, "oh no, please I'll be fine, can you load this please?"

He said ok and they go into library. It's nice; there are loads of books, two long purple suede couches, tables and lamps.

Gracie, "You still have a week, the hat wrap shades I…"

Constance, "Hush, sit let me look at you."

She sits down.

Constance, "No, over here, Gracie I went to your studio, and Lynn told me that you were attacked."

"Who did this to you?

Who?"

Gracie, "please do not worry!"

Constance, "I told Clark and our boys and Skokie that you are my baby girl."

Gracie cries, "You did not have to do that."

Constance cries, "Yes I had to, it's been a long time, you were such a beautiful baby, but we were barely making it. I was married and my mother… I 'm so sorry I want you to come home with me, we're your family."

Jamarion Senior, "I be damned."

Gracie, "I'm alright here, your party have a…"

Constance interrupts, "you hush now, you've always been so sweet to me. I've been the worst mother to you."

Solace, "Isn't that the truth?"

Constance, "And I pray God and you will forgive me, you're the best thing that ever happened to my life, I love you, thank you for all your years of kindness."

"It's alright," Gracie said to Constance as she stands.

Constance, "No, it isn't. I was weak and pathetic. I'll never forget. I've been sitting in that alley where they found you all day, and every night, believe this, Ill find out who did this to you, never will I rest."

"I remember when I had my accident, I know everybody told you not to come, but you came any way and you said nothing, you bathed me, and took care of me, prayed for me, read the word of God to me, cooked and fed me, you even cleaned me up. Nobody will do this to my daughter. I had Clark to hire a team of several high rank investigators to find out who did this careless crime to you also I'm willing to pay for you a new set up, here is too far and no family there, and Giselle is here, you've been through enough, Gracie, please let me take care of you, look at me."

Gracie does, and her mom, "You are my daughter, my baby girl, you are my everything."

Gracie really cries, and they hug and kiss each other.

Gracie, "Yes ma'am."

They both come out. "I'll be in the car, and thank you to you all."

Gracie, "Maxie, I'm going."

Maxie, "Hell no."

She cries, "She is still my mother, I'm so sorry everyone. I appreciate all you have done for me."

Gracie, "You are family, let her go," as comes over, cries and hugs Solace, they both cry.

Solace, "We're right here, we are your family."

Gracie kisses her, "Thank you."

She goes and hugs Challis and his dad.

Gracie, "Sassy don't cry my baby sis."

"Come here!"

He picks her up and walks with her and Maxie with his bag,

"Thank you."

They all say bye.

Challis, "Let me talk to you."

They both go outside. Time passes, they are all on the sun porch watching the game, and Sassy has on her language tutorial beats and coloring.

Solace, "What a day!"

Challis, "I told Maxie that that's her mother."

Solace, "I hated to see her go."

Challis, "She'll be back, we're her family too, but she needs this time with her own mother."

Solace, "Her bogie ass woke up, she is not playing."

"Believe this, she is going to get to the end of what happened in that alley."

Challis, "That blew me away."

Jamarion Senior, "I knew she was crazy coming in here not minding us."

Solace, "But her fake ass came to her mother instinct, Gracie is fantastic."

Challis, "Yes she is."

"She's got everything to be proud of her for."

Jamarion Senior, "Gracie is a beautiful spirited person."

Challis, "Yes she is, in and out."

Challis, "Maxie said that he asked her to marry him and she said no, not like this, he got angry and threw the ring. I got it, and then he said he is going to find out by himself who did that to her," showing them the ring.

Solace, "Let me see, gorgeous, I love how the basket sets down, 8 karats," examining the ring.

Challis, "It's very nicely made, I have to call Mac, he said that he's going to bust up in there at the Governor's Mansion if she is not back by Monday."

Jamarion Senior, "He better leave that alone before he loses her."

Solace, "Kids come in all types of horrific circumstances, and still love their mothers till death."

Jamarion Senior, "Yes, she deserves her to be good to her, they say in hell you open your eyes, Luke 16:23."

Solace, "Jesus got that lovely daughter come over here, hurt, clean and play with this child and teach her."

Challis, "She is really good to all of them, she has been checking on them, and helping bath them, and she always got a place with us, she's is a baby, just 19, she don't need to live by herself in a city alone."

Jamarion Senior, "She can stay right here as long as she wants."

Solace, "She is of no use, either she orders us all kinds of stuff or she makes me a floor length tweed dress, and cape boots. She's going places."

Challis, "Oh! I got to go," standing up to leave, come on my daughter."

Solace, "We are going to bible study at 6pm."

Challis, "Yes, I got to change, come Sassy, let's go change."

Sassy, "Yes sir."

Two hours pass, and they are all at the church.

CHAPTER 19

Principles to Live By

Jamarion Senior, "That's Gracie and her mother, and family."

"Why is Gracie with our governor's family?" Mike asked.

Solace, "The first lady is her mother."

Jamarion II, "Isn't she white?"

Solace, "Be quiet, here she comes."

Gracie, "Hi family," they all hug her,

Challis, "Come on Sassy, I'll take you to your class after you meet my other family, is that alright?"

Challis, "Of course."

Jamarion Senior, "Who is following who?"

Solace, "Tell me about it, Gracie is always going to do what's right, look Challis, he loves her and Sassy, look at both of them running to him, yes love at its best."

Jamarion III, "When did all this happen? Isn't that Maxie?"

Jamarion Senior, "Yeah."

Mike, "Well, young bros she's off the market."

40 minutes pass, and Bishop Neil's Connors IV enters,

"Well tonight, we're going to on **Exodus 13:17**"When Pharaoh let the people go, God did not lead them on the road through the Philistine country, though that was shorter. For God said, "If they face war, they might change their minds and return to Egypt. And Mark$^{2:1}$When he entered again into Capernaum after some days, it was heard that he was in the house. ²:²Immediately many were gathered, so that there was no more room, not even around the door; and he spoke the word to them. ²:³Four people came, carrying a paralytic to him. ²:⁴When they could not come near to him for the crowd, they removed the roof where he was. When they had broken it up, they let down the mat that the paralytic was lying on. ²:⁵Jesus, seeing their faith, said to the paralytic, "Son, your sins are forgiven you. "Now let's pray Lord speak to us that we might hear from you and not I let them go home tonight take over in Jesus mighty name amen.

"Look at somebody and say You can do this!"

The congregation, "You can do this!" to each other.

"This is talking about times as now, it's very important for you all to downsize and upgrade, see sometimes your family, maybe it's been you all along, it's also time to drop some people off, it's time now, more importantly, to have people in your life that will put you through the roof,"

Bishop Neil's Connors IV, "See at one stage of your life, certain people were fine, but then you started feeling a certain way about them, either you had to leave, or you had to bring them."

Constance, "Hallelujah!"

Bishop Neil's Connors IV, "Sometimes, religious people are the worst you can have on your team, because they have so much spiritual man-made baggage that they don't want to do now."

"Give me a crack head that over-came, give me a single mother or father that raised all her or his kids by themselves and worked 3 jobs and volunteered, yell, let's get deeper, see, your head is saying no because you always had a husband, or a boo, or you ain't never been on drugs. But see, all of us got something in our back yard that we have that has not been revealed, see you can keep on going, being comfortable with what is wrong, see I'm doing better than you all. Amen."

See, you can make these alternative parameters over a thousand up that we won't confront. Keep sitting I'll be down your aisle right in a minute, how many made up beds do you have in your life? Just keep on laying there, there is no way you can go out from here and go right down the street all slain in the spirit, but I'll tell you one thing right now, no color is in this. See people, you all make beds every day, I'll do this, I'll do that, and then do nothing. You must get out of your comfort zones, don't just sit right there smiling and taking pictures to celebrate an anniversary, but you are not connected. Some of you all sleep too much, when a person in needs comes to your home, you are going to miss their blessing, because you are too busy,"

Bishop Neil's Connors IV goes to Maxie and Gracie, "excuse me what is your name?"

He asked the two of them.

"Maximillian and Gracie."

Bishop Neil's Connors IV asked them, "Both of you are engaged?"

Maximillian, "She just said yes."

"What do you mean?"

Maximillian, "I asked her three days ago, and she said not now."

Gracie, "But I did say yes now."

Bishop Neil's Connors IV, "Do you have a ring?"

Gracie, ''Yes."

Maximilian, "No."

Maximillian, "Not now."

People laughed

Bishop Neil's Connors IV, "Hold on after bible study."

Challis, "The ring is right here." standing up.

Bishop, "How come?"

Challis, "I picked it."

Maximillian, "I got upset, and I threw it away."

Bishop, "Do you come for counseling here?"

Gracie, "I do."

Maxie, "I guess we do."

Bishop, "How old are the both of you?"

Gracie, "I'm 19."

Maximillian, "I'm 21."

"Okay. The reason why I centered them out was because you all saw her run with Challis's little girl to him,' Bishop points at Maxie, "and it looked just like in the movies.

He picks her up like the leading man."

First Lady Collate, "That's right!"

Bishop, "Some of you men and women should better do the same, pick up the right people."

Bishop, "It's time to man up because, you see, this is no time to sit on the couch, and let life that you've prayed for just slip past you by being with all these people who are up to no good, we have good people that have been in all our lives, and we may have made a mistake, you people have to go back and do whatever God has told you to do, because take a look at him, he was made, but he came right up in here, right here to find her, he wasn't settling on, 'not now,' as an answer. A whole now life is here and either you want to flourish, or you just want to sit on the sideline, there is everything that God can do but he needs you all to take a step or two. Before I forget, Maximillian and Gracie, after Bible study, go to the office to fill out counseling and member documentation,"

They both say yes.

Then Bishop continues, "There are people here, like men, some of you have old girlfriends 3, 4, 5, 15 years ago, come on, and you still got some of them in your contacts."

The women laughed.

Bishop continues, "then you ladies, I 'm coming right down your own lane too, you all have shoe boxes filled with old letters from some of your old boyfriends."

The congregation laughs.

Bishop, "You all don't know why nothing is going right, it's because you are not 100% in it, so don't try and come see me when you haven't done the work for yourself. I don't have that time, look at Maximillian,

He asked her once, she said, "not now," he got rid of the ring, but he came here looking for her. See? That's what I'm talking about. What did you say?" He asked someone in the congregation.

Raymond, "I said she would have been fresh out of luck."

People laughed.

Celeste, "Bishop, don't let him deter tell you, I said no 4 times, and we're here now, 5 kids and 20 years later."

Bishop, "And I have married you two twice."

Raymond, "Yes, but I told her this is it."

Bishop, "Sit down Raymond."

He does and people burst out laughing.

Bishop, "See, right now in life, think about the team you have, and if they aren't doing nothing, then you need to move on, get rid of them, because I can bake my own cake, and buy my own candles, and blow them out too."

A lady, "That's right."

Bishop continues, "See I don't need nobody that is not in with me, see when I wrote a book, my wife, she sold cakes, and got a sponsor, and wrote a recipe book. She got published,"

Some people yell, "Have I told you this before? When I wrote another book, she wrote 4 songs, and one of them got a Grammy, then our kids published their own magazine. This life is no time for trophies, we are all grown in here, sex is only going to get you so far, and you can go bowling and win one of them and then put it on the mantel or a trophy case. You all can sit here and think you got money and that you don't care, blow your mine to the wind, a team works together, Mark 2:2-5,

When they could not come near to him for the crowd, they removed the roof where he was. When they had broken it up, they let down the mat that the paralytic was lying on."

People shouted, "Hallelujah, bless God."

"See that man was a paralytic and could not get up, but he had enough sense to do something every day, I'm sure people walked by him every day. He was working in his own transgression, see he wasn't playing; he got his blessing, if I could walk just like him, and can I walk with you? One may say no, but the right one will say yes. Don't play with me now, there are a lot of members that are not doing anything, and yes we know you are going to say, 'it isn't so', you can keep your money, we're in the business to save souls, and you all coming to church ,It's like beating a horse."

Collate yells!

Bishop bends down and looks under the pews, "see we help clean Gods house, but we do the work of our kids also. What time is it baby? Come and pray. We're going to carry this on next week."

First Lady Collate stands up and prays. Then Gracie brings out Sassy.

Maximillian hugs and kisses Sugar, "I'm sorry." and then he hugs Jamarion Senior and apologizes also to him.

Grace, "After we go register, we would like to see if you all would like to come to dinner tonight, me and my mother cooked, and mama Sugar, she's very clean." she hugs her again.

Sugar, "Ok, I will wait in the foyer till you finish."

Gracie, "Okay ma'am."

Maximillian grabs her hand and says, "Let's go do it."

They leave.

Time goes by, they are back, and Gracie says to Challis, "May we go? And can Sassy ride with us?"

Challis, "yes."

2 hours goes by and the food is impeccable.

Gracie, "That's my Grandma."

Sugar, "She was gorgeous, you look like her a lot, but really now I see your mother, you are almost twins,"

Jamarion II, "Look at Queen B, she is really being sweet."

Challis, "She looks really happy mama."

Sugar, "And this food is all delish, I guess white black girls can cook."

Jamarion II, "She still looks white to me."

Mike, "I'm happy for Gracie. and look at her dancing with Sassy mama."

Sugar, "She knows Gracie loves her and us."

Challis, "They really look like they love her."

Jamarion Senior, "Who would not, she's breath taking."

Sugar, "Yes, she is."

Gracie, "Mama Sugar, can you please come and pour the bourbon cream and brown sugar? For the rice pudding, I got an apron for you. I told my mother that is your favorite."

Sugar, "Okay, yes."

They both enter the room.

Governor Clark, "Cigar and a chilled glass of Brandy anyone? I have a cigar wine house up in here."

Jamarion Senior, "Yes, thank you."

Challis, "I won't mind if I do."

Mike, "Yes."

Jamarion II, "Me as well."

Challis, "Maximillian we're going to the Cigar House, tell Gracie."

Maxie, "We got Sassy," as they left the room.

A month goes by.

Bishop Neil's Connors IV contacts Challis, "Hello! I have sent you your Bible study, marital study as to what it takes to be a husband father in God."

Challis, "The Book and Workbook came yesterday."

Bishop, "Okay, Monday we will begin, read chapters 1-4 and answer questions."

Challis, "Yes sir," and they hang up.

His mom, Solace comes in.

"Mrs. Mustier is here to see you."

Challis, "Yes ma'am,"

"What are you going to do?"

Challis, "She's going if she can keep up with Gracie and her nanny."
Solace, "Isn't that the truth? Oh, the nannies."
. Challis, "They are on paid call as needed for all our children."
"Hello sir," Mrs. Mustier said, coming into the room.
Challis, "Yes she can do all."
Mrs. Mustier, "Today may I take her to be tested."
Challis, "How long will the test be?"
Mrs. Mustier, "They assured me that the test would take no longer than 30 to 45 minutes."
Challis goes to intercom, "Nurse Kelly-Anne, please send Sassy down and pleases dress her to leave."
Nurse Kelly-Anne, "Yes, she'll be down in 10 minutes."
Challis, "Okay," and clicks off the intercom "Okay, Mrs. Mustier have a seat, she will be down in 10 minutes."
"Okay, thank you."
In 10 minutes on the dot, Sassy comes down with around collar bell bottom jumper, with yellow suede patent leather sandals, hair in three ponytails with yellow rhinestones ribbons, and she has on a white summer rhinestone sweater and her toes nails painted yellow, and a yellow suede patent rhinestone eye bear back pack.
Solace, "I'm coming also, if that's alright."
Mrs. Mustier, "The more the better."
20 minutes goes by, and Solace comes back down, she has on a mint green maxi dress, with mint sides, back out flat rhinestone sandals, purse to match, and a white linen blazer on also, and a page boy black blonde wig.
Challis, "Gracie made this."
Challis, "That looks good."
"Thanks."
With mint green makeup and her eyebrows arched in natural black, Mrs. Mustier has on a powder blue linen dress, with a powder blue summer sweater on her shoulders, and pearls around her neck, and a flat baby blue mint jeweled sandal. And they all leave.

Jamarion Senior, "Where are you off to son?"

Challis, "Over to the University, I have to pick up my books for my law degree classes."

Jamarion Senior, "Way to go, do it all. Who is it?" He asked as the intercom beeped.

The security, "Gracie."

She comes in crying.

Challis, "What's wrong?"

Gracie, "May I stay here for the weekend? I have some things to work on."

Challis, "Yes of course, but dad is the only one here."

Gracie, "Okay, thanks."

She goes into the house.

Mike, "What is it, little brother?"

Challis, "College."

Mike, "What? You are going back?"

Challis, "Yes. A couple of days a week, and one online night class for law degree."

Mike, "How long?"

Challis, "A lot of my credits transferred over, so 18 months."

Mike, "That's alright, bless you," they hug and Challis leaves.

Jamarion III, "You are going out?"

Challis, "Yeah, dad and Mike are inside."

Jamarion III, "Okay. Everything good?"

Challis, "Yes."

Mike, "What is going on?"

No one said anything. "What's wrong with you?"

Jamarion Senior, "They found out who attacked her."

Mike, "Who?"

Gracie, "Excuse me," and goes to the sewing room.

CHAPTER 20

Attackers

Mike turns to his father. "What's wrong with her?"

Jamarion III, "Hey dad."

Jamarion Senior, "Get us a couple of cold ones out the fridge, game will be on in 20 minutes, I'm going to watch on the closed in patio deck."

In 10 minutes, they got beers and waiting for game to start.

Mike, "So what's up?"

Jamarion III, "Damn, I'm hungry."

"Go to the fridge, and bring out 3 subs, and then chips from the pantry," Jamarion Senior said to him.

"Wait till I get back, I want to hear also," Jamarion III said to them as he stood up to go.

10 minutes go by,

Jamarion Senior, "Shut the patio screen doors."

Jamarion III does that.

Jamarion Senior, "She found out that Maximillian's ex-girlfriend had her brothers jump her."

Mike, "Why?"

Their dad, "Because that's what Maximillian told her."

Jamarion III, "So?"

their dad, "He stopped sleeping with her, that is the ex-girlfriend, the day they became engaged."

Mike, "Well, have they?'

Jamarion Senior, "No, that child is a virgin."

Jamarion III, "Oh okay."

Mike, "So what? They're not getting married?"

Their dad, "She said that she doesn't want him,"

Mike, "Where is her mother?" Mike asked.

Their dad, "Overseas. She said that she has to work on her orders, and all her stuff is here, we gave her the big room in the back, this is her home too."

Mike, "I know."

Jamarion III, "Yes, that's cool, but she still needs to marry Maxie, these women kill me, they keep themselves, and then they expect us to have not indulged in the difference, that's just what I had to clue Karen, either you love me or oh well."

Mike, "How old is she again?"

Jamarion Senior, "19."

Mike, "Where is Maxie?"

Jamarion Senior, "On TV right now."

Jamarion III, "Oh, this is his college team, they'll work this all out."

Sometime goes by, and Gracie comes out,

Pappi, "He says yes,"

Gracie, "The quants are getting so big, and I have some special things to make for them and Sassy's fur piano cover case."

Pappi, "Challis told her he would do that."

Gracie, "No sir, he won't be able to find the fur. I'm going to make a slipcover for the bench and then the piano cover, I told him all about it, and I will also make it to transcend with her dress ensemble."

Pappi, "Oh, okay."

Gracie, "I'm meeting Lynn at the airport tonight, and I'll return in a couple days."

Pappi, "Where are you going?"

Gracie, "To join my mother in Paris, so I can gather my products for show."

Pappi, "Okay, but let security take you and let Bartholomew and Casey accompany you, you got your phone?"

Gracie, "Yes sir, and a new number, I'll call you with it right now." she pulls it out and calls him.

Pappi's phone rings,

Pappi, "I got it, okay, I'll call Challis."

Gracie, "Thanks, and I'll pay them," and leaves.

Mike, "Maxie is winning."

Jamarion, "He should better go to Paris."

Jamarion Senior, "Let me call Challis because he got her Bartholomew and Casey," as he dials his son's number.

Challis, "Hey dad."

Jamarion Senior, "Call Bartholomew and Casey so they can accompany Gigi to Paris for a couple days."

Challis, "Cool, I will this time."

Jamarion Senior, "And she got a new number, I'll send it to you."

Challis, "Okay, they'll be there in the next hour."

They both hang up.

Mike, "And you know it is strong, but that man got nothing to do, look game over he won."

On the T.V Maxie was saying, "This win goes out to the only love of my life ever, my future wife, Gracie Le Marie Cherish, I'm sorry baby."

Mike, "See women. Game over!" Looking at the T.V screen.

Chef Mavis, "Excuse me. What will it be? You all got me. Tonight, I'm at your service."

Jamarion III, "It's going down right here, you all are doing it over here."

Their dad, "Where are your families?"

Mike, "My wife is at the hairdresser, but she should be done."

Let me call her, picking up his phone, he calls his wife, "hey baby you done?"

Cindy, "Yes, I'm on my way home."

Mike, "Have her drop you at my parents, we are going to have dinner here."

Cindy, "Okay."

Jamarion II picks up his own phone and calls his wife too,

Mike, "Baby, I 'm coming to swoop you."

Karen, "I'm at the book club. Rhonda picked me up."

"What about our sons?"

"They are at Donavan's spending the night."

Jamarion III, "Okay, have her drop you here at my parents' around the corner from her."

Karen, "Okay, I 'm hungry."

Jamarion III, "Come on."

They hang up.

Their dad, "What are we going to eat?"

Mike, "Ribeye's, citrus, Salmon, sweet baked potato, loaded casserole, greens, beans, tomato, cucumber, and onion salad rolls, cheesecake."

Their dad, "All he said,"

Chef Mavis, "Okay, it will be done in 2 hours, I have horde's, drinks, lemonade out already, and also cocktails.".

In thirty minutes, all is back.

Challis, "Smells good."

Jamarion Senior, "Were you enrolled?"

Challis, "Yes sir."

Solace, "We also, she is starting next Monday."

Gracie, "Excuse me, may I take Sassy to Paris with me for a few days?"

Sassy, 'Yes, yes, please daddy."

Challis, "Her school begins soon."

Solace, "What are you going to Paris for?"

Gracie, "To get stuffs that I need for Sassy and my Lady B and clients."

Challis, "No because I want her to know how to swim by the time school starts and ride a bike."

"Daddy," Sassy called.

Gracie, "I'll bring some stuffs back girl."

She bends down and picks her up and kiss her.

Solace, "Have a safe trip. Who will be with you?"

Gracie, "Lynn. And we're meeting my mother, she's already there with security."

Solace, "Okay. Have a safe trip, we're here."

She hugs her.

Mike, "Come on Sassy, let's bath for dinner, it smells so good," Solace said to Sassy. Mommy you are popping."

Solace, "Thanks to my Gracie."

Jamarion II, "Dad you better watch out."

Jamarion Senior, "I'm a paying customer, Gracie, hook your Pappi up."

Gracie, "On me, and wait let me measure you."

She runs inside and gets a measuring tape.

Challis, "Let me check on my loves," and he runs up.

Time goes by; everyone is now eating, and Gracie is in the wind Security winning.

Maximillian, "Hello family, is my future wife here?"

Mike, "She's in the wind Security."

Maximillian, "Where?" confused.

"She'll be back in town on Friday."

Jamarion Senior, "She's overseas with her mother,"

Maxie, "Well, thanks. Can I eat?"

Challis, "Of course."

Solace, "This is all so delicious," with her slippers off displaying her natural bare feet,

Jamarion Senior, "That school is out of this world, it's really exceptional Janice."

Challis, "Who is that?"

Solace, "All your daughter's liaison, she already has put all your children on the list to enroll in 2022."

Challis, "How did Sassy do?"

Solace, "She can read now on a 3rd grade level."

Mike, "I knew she was advanced."

Karen, "Our boys are going there in the fall also."

Jamarion II, "Yeah, 7th through 12th they are going to be heavy weights, that school has everything right."

Mike, "Yeah. How much a month?"

Jamarion II, "$20,000."

. Mike, "Damn, that ain't college."

Jamarion II, "They have gotten so many donors for success, once proven we are going to have a free ride."

Solace, "Even Sassy is $10,000 a month, your counsel paid her up for the next 7 years."

Challis, "Good, because we are about to hit it."

"Thanks, she did not remove her necklace, but it says… wait she is here," Maxie said.

Solace, No, her necklace is here."

"She laid it on the table over there," she points to a table at the far corner of the room.

Mike, "How are you tracking her? You both are not married yet."

Maxie, "She's mine, and that's nothing but a technicality. I'm going back, so I can go to bed."

Challis, "Okay man, we'll see you."

He hugs Solace and leaves.

Mike, "Gracie is young. She really does not need to be marrying right now, she's got all the time in the world."

Solace, "I would feel that way if…"

Solace gets interrupted by Sassy.

Sassy, "Excuse me, may I be excused?"

Challis, "Okay."

Sassy kisses her dad, and entire family, and leaves the room.

Cindy, "She is so sweet, and a cutie pie."

Karen affirmed, "Yes."

Solace, "Anyway, she has been on her own since 16, she needs to marry."

Mike, "He's good for her, they can wait on children, and just enjoy each other."

Challis, "Bishop Connors is going to counsel them."

Jamarion Senior, "That's good, because they on the outs right now."

Challis, "I thought it's odd he did not know where she was, what happened?"

Solace, "Yes. What?"

Jamarion Senior, "I don't know who, but they found out that Maxie's other woman had her brothers to jump Gracie."

Challis, "That's not his fault," Challis said.

Jamarion Senior, "It is because he did not break it off with whoever she is until Gigi said yes."

Karen, "Who is Gigi?"

Solace, "Gracie."

Karen, "Oh, that's cute."

Solace, "Good. Let him sweat a while."

The security intercom beeps.

Security, "Maxie is here."

Maxie, "Fam, do any of you have my bride to be's number?" As he entered the room.

Solace, "She must have changed it, but no."

Maxie, "Okay, thanks."

Mike, "Dad."

Jamarion Senior, "I am not getting in that, she gave me her number for us, she must not want to talk to him."

Karen, "Wow,"

Solace, "She's tough, because she is going to be with him,"

Challis, "Just like my baby."

Cindy, "Young love."

Jamarion II, "Watch him fly to Paris tonight."

Jamarion Senior, "I hope not."

Mike, "Daddy, you just want all your stuff."

Jamarion Senior, "I'll get all my stuff, she's dependable. He can't take her off from what she must do. You see she's in Paris shopping, and did not give him her number."

Challis, "She's been trained well by the best, yes, our counsel has been her counsel since she was 16."

They all laughed

Solace, "I know I saw Ethel at the hospital, and she did not look like she thought too highly of Maxie."

Challis, "She still doesn't like me. Is she married?"

Solace, "Duh, Attorney Salomon is her husband."

Challis, "Figures. He lets her act any kind of way," and they all laughed.

Solace, "They have six attorney sons."

Challis, "Thanks, they all work for us too."

Jamarion Senior, "That counsel is deep."

Challis, "Yes, it is. I'll take Attorney Solomon Senior out to dinner next Thursday."

Mike, "Why?"

Challis, "I want to know the ins and outs of all our businesses, and other things, such as for our kid's upbringing."

Cindy, "I saw Janice today with Sassy, she's married to their youngest son, Larry."

Solace, "I did not see you, we were together, oh, when they went next door to size Sassy, I stayed to speak with Chancellor Dr. Walda Huckleby over the primary."

Jamarion II, "They brought her in from The Ohio State, the middle school and high school Chancellor is Langston Divenchy V, he was Morehouse's President."

Solace, "Who is the Chancellor President?"

Challis, "Caine Harmon III from the United States Congress."

Karen, "This, I believe is the best money we will spend, and I like their uniforms."

Solace, "There are kids from all over the world trying to get in that school, Sassy is really smart, she finished their entry test in 20 minutes with time to spare, all her teachers will be speaking in English, and Spanish, and Chinese."

Challis, "She has been doing both of those tutorials."

Karen, "Where did you buy them?"

Challis, "At Grains Bookstore for Education, but she had several already with her."

Solace, "They have ice skating, piano, violin and ballet per semester for gym credit and art credit, we put her in all."

Challis, "I like that she's going to be strong in mind, body and soul."

Karen, "You say it, Giselle can hear you, and your kids have told her about Sassy."

Challis, "They already know each other, and no because I don't know what to say yet. I have never told her about my past life."

Solace, "Well, what are you waiting for?"

Challis, "I am, but every night Sassy is in her bed sleeping, I wake up and she is in our bed right under my Butter, she calls her my lady B, it's a mess."

Jamarion Senior, "Truth is the best vessel."

Challis, "As much as Sassy talks to them all every day, morning and night, Gigi does also."

Mike, "What will your family do?"

Challis, "Just really smile."

Cindy, "Well, they are receptive of them."

Challis, "Yeah. Well, fam, I got to hit it."

Solace, "It's only… oh midnight, okay let me go."

Jamarion Senior, "What you got to do?"

Solace, "I'm getting up at 5am to jog with Ethel, Janice and Walda at the school track, and they have an early riser's summer, water aerobics, and cycling M-Thursday at 6am till 8am, 3 miles."

Karen, "How did you get into that?"

Solace," They asked me, but its open, do you want to go? Cost is $100 per month."

Karen, "Yes, every day."

Cindy, "Me too."

Solace, "I'll have our driver grab you all at 4:30."

Karen, "Oh thank you."

Cindy, "Oh yes, we better clean up and go."

Mike, "Challis, you going to that?"

Challis, "No, I got to get up, and teach my daughter how to swim, and ride her bike before school, because by the time we move home, all our kids will swim at 6am and ride their bikes to school with us."

Solace, "They got mega bikes, and racks there, as well as toddles, oh they have lockers for each kid, and don't forget your swim suites towel ladies."

Night falls and morning comes, everyone has left, and Jamarion Senior has joined Challis and Sassy, so they can teach her.

Challis to his daughter, "Okay, put your face in the water.".

Sassy, "Dad look!"

Challis, "What dad?"

Jamarion Senior, "She can swim already."

Challis goes to swim with her, they reach the wall, and his dad does the same.

Challis, "Who taught you?"

Sassy, "My baby sis, and Lady G taught me when I was a baby."

Challis, "Okay, we are going to swim 6 laps, wall to wall, what about deeper?"

Sassy, "6ft, I can't dive yet."

Challis, "Okay later, let's go long ways and swim, you still keep on your stuff."

They swim with his dad for an entire hour,

Challis, "How do you feel dad?"

"Great, I'm going to jog a couple of miles."

Challis, "We can go, come on Sassy."

They all change and jog for 40 minutes and 4 miles, and Sassy kept up.

Challis, "Bike."

Sassy, "Training wheels."

Challis, "Okay later, after breakfast we will go buy some bikes for our family."

"I'll go buy one for me and my baby, and couple extra for the house."

They all shower except Sassy who is bathed by her nurse Kelly-Anne. After they dressed, by then time had passed, they have a light breakfast and leave for the bike store. Solace and her daughter in-laws shower at school and all go get manicures and pedicures, and facials.

Constance, "This fabric is gorgeous."

Gracie, "And it holds shape well."

Lynn, "They have this in all these colors."

Gracie, "Let me see."

Lynn, "Sense all that happen to you all the orders are still coming in, but people are leery about the accrual store traffic."

Gracie, "I have been thinking an actual store in New York, California, Chicago, high end sales any more I don't want except by appointment only rest online with sizing charts and those in Cincinnati, Columbus, Ohio, Cleveland down scale managerial staff area general manager you if you want."

Lynn, "Yes."

Gracie, "And sales people, customer service, call center, California and Chicago that handle all calls and upgrade, a straight 100 seamstress that I will work with, and our fashion shoes, fashion week," as she goes to her mother.

Constance, "I think that will suffice, mommy owned a diamond mine all these years in Louisiana, Oil and Gas Wells, mineral rights."

Gracie, "She talked about it often, but she did nothing. But now in her will, we have to do it." Constance, "I still, can't believe she wanted this for me," she cries,

Gracie hugs her, "She willed everything to us both."

Constance, "I know I still don't feel right to do anything."

Gracie, "Mommy, she understood you."

Constance, "Yes she did."

Gracie, "I know that you and I met many days, you sent her money and she just willed it all to me."

Constance, "Well I want us to fight for what was my mother's.".

Gracie, "We will, I'll tell my counsel about it, they can do the work, but out of our inheritance use a million."

Constance, "I have some money saved."

Gracie said, "Mommy, it's our inheritance."

Constance, "Let me do something good for my mommy, God bless her soul, let me," she runs away in tears.

Lynn, "Is she like this all the time?"

Gracie, "My mom thinks I don't know, I hear her in the night weeping about me, I have to comfort her."

Lynn, "Yeah, she loves you so much, I can tell."

Sales Rep comes in.

Gracie, "All these rolls, those over there, and there, and the stuff at the cash register and the written order ship to address on documentation."

Mac, "Hey son, what blows you in?"

Maxie, "Dang, they are getting big. Hey little bro's we are going to be hanging out."

Mac, "That's on you, and you gone have to clean it up."

Maxie, "Latrice and her bros are in jail, their father called me, they are trying to say I put them up to it."

Mac, "Like hell they did the act, tomorrow we are going, no let me call Jackson."

Maxie, "Dad, will you represent me?"

Mac, "No we need an outside counsel."

'Hello,' Attorney Kenneth Jackson said.

Mac, "I need some council for my son."

Attorney Kenneth Jackson, "About what?"

Mac, "He's fiancée is Gracie Cherish and his ex- had her brothers jump her and leave her in back of her truck ports but Maxie my son found out his fiancé."

Attorney Kenneth Jackson, "Who found out it was them?"

Mac puts the phone on speaker.

Mac, "Who found out it was them?"

Maxie, "Her mother's security team found out by a camera that was hidden over the adjacent store by a tree limb."

Attorney Kenneth Jackson, "Were you in the picks?"

Maxie, "When I, Lynn and Rudolph found her and called the police."

Attorney Kenneth Jackson, "Who is Lynn and Rudolph?"

Maxie, "Oh he works for Gracie and Lynn, she does also when I went to the store, he opens the dock to show me where the alley port was that she sometimes parked and we both saw her."

"Was that your first time to go to the alley in question?"

Maxie, "Yes, when you go in the store, you can't tell which part from which, it's dead ends and the buildings to the side port closes it."

Attorney Kenneth Jackson, "Will you take a poly-graph?"

Mac, "Why?"

Attorney Kenneth Jackson, "I have a connection at the FBI that can do it, I believe him, this will clear it all up."

Maxie, "Yes, I love her I would not do this to her."

Attorney Kenneth Jackson, "I just texted him, he said 4pm today."

Maxie, "Okay."

Attorney Kenneth Jackson, "You still stay near the hospital?"

Mac, "Yes."

Attorney Kenneth Jackson, "Well, it's the yellow door, office building next door. I'll meet you there."

Maxie, "Thanks."

Two hours passed; It's now 15 till 4pm, Maxie and his dad walks down the street to the next door.

Maxie, "Dad," as they walked down the street,

"I almost forgot. When I broke up with her, I made sure to do it outside our locker room, and she said something off, like, how's your little wifey? I said, what did you say? But by then she was on her way out, and Coleman said as he was walking up, that she said something off, like, how's your wifey to be, Gigi?"

Mac, "The stadium will have that, when we get in here, write that down just like that, and give it to Attorney Kenneth."

Maxie and his dad fist bump each other. Attorney Kenneth walks up to them, "Come on, they're waiting for us, and anything else you remember write it down, and give it to me." The FBI office was very professional, as soon as they came in through the door,

'Attorney Kenneth Jacksons," FBI Foreman Guy Freeman said.

He greeted them, "Is he ready?"

Attorney, "These are the questions to ask plus anything else."

An hour goes by, and Maxie came out, FBI Foreman followed him out, and then turned to go grab the test result, when he came back, he handed an envelope to Attorney Kenneth Jackson who says thanks. Then they all do the same.

Attorney Kenneth Jackson opens the envelope and read it, "He said you passed, you're telling the truth."

Maxie, "Here is the rest of the evidence I have," and hands a paper to the attorney.

Attorney Kenneth Jackson takes the paper from him, and reads it, and then he says ok and gets out a paper. They all go sit down, Maxie signs and gives 1million dollar retainer.

Attorney Kenneth Jacksons, "These results will be sent to Columbus Ohio Police Department and let me do my job."

They all shake hands and agree to Attorney Kenneth Jackson's terms.

Attorney Kenneth Jacksons, "Now stay with your parents and this wifey."

Maxie, "I'll reach out to her and have her stay with us."

The attorney, "You people should stay together on good terms."

They all leave the building.

CHAPTER 21

No respect

Maxie, "She's in Paris," as they were walking back home.

Mac, "You are mad."

Maxie, "I'm not, she has changed her number, and is in Paris with her mother."

Mac, "I'm sure Challis can reach her, and get her back here," he reaches into his pocket, brings out his phone and calls Challis.

Challis, "What's cracking?" on picking up.

"Can you reach out to Gracie and let her know that she has to get back here, because we just had to retain Jack," Mac said.

"What?" Challis asked.

Mac, "Latrice Hamas is trying to say Maxie had her do it. Gracie has to come here, and stay with us, we just cleared his polygraph with the FBI."

Challis, "We in there then, I'll reach out, and have her call Maxie," and they hang up.

An hour passes, Gracie did not want to call Maxie, but she does.

Maxie, "Babe, I need you to come back tonight."

Gracie, "I will be home tomorrow at the Calms-Ways, I have stuff to do."

Mac, "You're not hearing me, I need you here at my parents' house with me."

Gracie, "Okay, what's going on?"

Maxie, "I'll have all your stuff delivered to my parents' house."

Mac, "Let's all just go to Challis's house, I'll call his parents, they have room for all of us," and they all agreed.

A day goes by. China comes in crying.

Maxie, "Baby, we will be fine. I hired us 2 nurses. We'll be fine, we just need one front, and Gracie has orders to work on."

China, "You know that's cool because we have orders to."

Time goes by. Gracie is back, and she is not happy.

Maxie "You did not miss me?" Asked her.

China, "Son, leave her alone."

Gracie, "Can you move mommy? Thank you."

Constance, "Love you my baby."

Gracie goes to hug and kiss her.

Her mother, "Maxie is right here."

Grace, "I cannot stay here with him."

"No sir and no ma'am, I am not marrying him."

Maxie, "What? Your mother just started loving you, she cares nothing for you."

Gracie, "What goes on between me and my mother is none of your business, have I ever disrespected your parents ever?"

Maxie, "They're way better."

Gracie, "Sassy come let me show you all the stuff I got you."

Maxie, "I'm sorry,"

Gracie, "See what I got us."

She sits on the floor and Sassy sits right by her.

Sassy, "Ok, these books."

Sassy, "They're empty," as she turns the pages.

Gracie, "They're supposed to be, I thought that me and you, if it's alright with your dad, should write a coloring children's book about what you told me."

Sassy, "My sleeping babies and Lady B the Queen, and I'm keeping the secret witch away, and I have to find the Christmas secret from far away to awake them."

Gracie, "Yes, and we're going to publish it. I already ran it by our counsel."

Sassy, "7 books?"

Gracie, "Yes, and we will have first edition done by Thanksgiving."

Sassy, "That's not Jesus Birthday."

Gracie, "You're right, but remember I told you about what kind of shoppers."

Sassy, "Black Friday, ooh ooh, I want fat crayons, and skinny to go with each book, and a candy stocking filled with goodies like our book, ooh, can we put our recipe? You said for our gingerbread cookie, candy apples, what my mommy made us that one year you got tummy sick."

Gracie, "You know I will love to have some, and sure."

Sassy, "Daddy, can we?"

Challis, "Yes, I like it."

Gracie, "Okay, our price will be whose favorite number?"

Sassy, "Ooh, mommy's 24, her graduation day."

Gracie, "Yes, and who else's?"

Sassy, "Lady B is 77."

Gracie, "So $24.77 will be your price and these books I will help you with them, but they're whose?" Sassy, "Mine."

'What?" Gracie asked. Sassy's Sapphire's Christmas tree spins, and they both screams.

Maxie, "Okay good, we have to talk."

Gracie, "You've said all I want to hear,"

China, "Maxie does not mean half of the stuff that comes out of his mouth."

Gracie, "Excuse me? Can Sassy go with me so I can measure her stuff to sew?"

Challis, "Yes. Dinner is in an hour, and a half."

Gracie, "I can bath her for dinner."

Challis, "Thanks," and they leave the room.

Maxie, "I'll go stay with Gigi," and goes after them.

Time goes by. Everybody is playing with the babies. Gigi and Sassy goes and sit between Pappi and Sugar, they all say grace.

China, "Gracie, Maxie loves you."

Gracie, "That does not make it right."

Maxie, "I don't know what is wrong with you,"

Gracie, "You never had to like my mother, I never asked you to,"

Maxie, "This is about Constance?"

Gracie, "Excuse me?"

Sugar said, "Just go on, say it, and be done."

Gracie asked Sassy, "Okay, are you finished?"

"Yes, can I go write about my book?"

Challis, "Yes, but bring it back, so I turn on cartoons for you."

Sassy, "No sir, please a movie."

Sugar, "I got her the Disney movie channel now, and 6 new DVD's."

Challis, "Okay. Cinderella."

Gracie, "No please, I bought that one. I want to watch with her."

Challis, "Okay, sleeping beauty, no, okay."

Time zooms by, and Sassy skips back in, her nurse has bathed her and changed her into a Paris big t-shirt and foot jammies.

Sassy, "My baby sis, is this how it goes?"

Gracie, "Come here!"

She comes, and she puts her on her lap, and pulls up and says, "The robe."

Sassy runs and gets it, she puts it on her.

Sassy, "I like that."

China, "That is very cute."

Sassy lays down on a big carpet blanket and opens her writing color case with colored pencils.

China, "I want my daughters all that."

Gracie, "I got you all some stuff, Pappi, I put all your stuff in your closet."

Pappi, "Okay. Thanks."

Gracie, "I will not marry a person that disrespects my mother."

"She spoke to him, and he said nothing Just stared at her. No."

Maxie, "Just because you kiss her…"

His mom cuts him off, and hits him again, "but I love you, and I'm never going to forget what she has done to you,"

"It is none of your business, she's my mother, and I know just who my mother was, but because she chooses to be that way does not mean that I should forsake her."

Gracie, "Honor thy father and thy mother" that is one of the Ten Commandments in the Bible, and in Deuteronomy, I believe God, and were not equally yoked."

Maxie, "What does that have to do with anything?"

Sugar, "A lot,"

Gracie, "We don't possess like mines, you're you and I'm just me, and right now in my life, I have just been the happiest in a long time. You will not disrespect my mother and wed me."

Maxie, "I respect you."

Gracie, "No, you don't, and to be truthful, I'm quite sick of you. Let's take a break, you can date and do you, and I'll do the same for 21 days, after then we will meet back up. You might find someone else, and I'll be over you, truce. I got stuff to do."

Maxie, "That's what? Else I'm sitting here, I was almost about to go to jail, and you…"

Gracie, "I'm here. I came, didn't I?"

Maxie, "But you did not want to,"

You know, Maxie, that's one thing. My mother does not say one thing about you to me, I said I have to leave to get back to Maxie, and my mom asked if everything was okay, I told her that I didn't know, and she said, 'well, let's leave early,' so here I am.

Then you come to my family's home, you said if she is going to be here that I have to be with her, they let you in, and you still did not say one thing to my mother. I will not tolerate you, no, she's my mother.

Mac, "Maxie that's true, that's her standard," Mac said to his son.

Gracie, "Let me," getting up.

Maxie, "I will take your mother out to dinner, how about that shopping?"

Gracie, "You don't have to do that, no genuineness fake."

Time goes by, and Gracie and Sassy are knocked out on the long sofa chaise with matching ottoman.

Maxie, "Where am I supposed to sleep while everyone else plays card?"

Pappi, "You can have that blue room you always have."

Maxie says thanks, then he goes. Gigi yawns, wakes, and gets up to get some water.

Maxie, "You are all just sleeping," and everybody burst out laughing.

Gracie, "Now, I'm not supposed to sleep? Move."

Maxie, "I'm upset."

Gigi grabs cold water, yawns, "I'm sleepy, so what are you?"

Maxie, "I'm going to sleep."

Challis goes to get Sassy.

Gracie, "No, I promised her we would have a slumber party when I got back."

Challis, "Tomorrow, before Maxie cries," amused.

Gracie, "Yeah, I'm going to my room, and he's going to his. Goodnight."

Maxie follows her as she leaves the room.

She gets on the couch, "I really have to take this call, wait, say nothing, it's my mommy."

Maxie takes the phone.

Maxie, "Hello!"

Gracie tries to get it from him, "I'm really sorry, and I would like to take you to dinner, and shopping on Friday."

Her mom, "With Gracie?"

Maxie, "No ma'am, just me and you."

"As long as Gracie is okay with that," her mom said.

"She is okay with it. Have a good night, here she goes," he gives the phone to Gracie, she takes it, "Mommy, yes ma'am."

Constance, "I was just checking in on you.".

Gracie, "I love you mommy, and thanks, wait, Pappi and mama Sugar, can my family come to dinner tomorrow? I can cook and Maxie can help me."

Maxie, "I will if they say yes."

"Mommy, I want you all to come to dinner around 7pm, bring your bowling shoes, they have a bowling alley here." She hangs up.

"Can they?" Gracie asked.

Mama Sugar, "Yes, and we all can play."

China gets one of her daughters, summer.

Gracie, "Ooh, let me see, they have gotten so big, she looks so pretty, who is back up?"

But Sassy is mad and is folding her arms, "daddy slumber."

Challis, "Okay, in there," and she gets right under her cover.

Gracie, "Get your own cover, we're in this slumber bag."

China, "Where did you get that?"

Gracie, "I made these, two years ago for her, it's really warm inside."

She yawns, "Excuse me!"

China, "And Gracie, marry our son because you don't know this, but he does respect you."

Mac, "Yes."

Gracie, "I will one day."

China, "No soon, he's not your child, he's mine."

Gracie, "I know,"

Maxie comes back,

Maxie, "No cover."

Gracie, "you said you made just two, I want my own."

"See child," she gets up and pulls, and there is one for him, and he gets in it. She shakes her head, "God help us!"

Mama Sugar, "He will, Maxie is going to be a great husband."

In minutes, they are all sleeping. China is with her other son,

China, "Your poor brother is so in love, but you know Gracie, I like her, she brings the best out of him."

Pappi, "We see he sure did correct himself with her mother."

Mac, "She's right, he should respect her mother."

China, "Gigi is a grown woman now, he has realized how he hurt her, I love my daughter in law to be, thank you Jesus, one down one to go."

Mac, "You are late Lynn."

China, "When?"

Mac, "Been MacArthur my son."

China, "Beautiful, I got it made, no crazies."

Challis, "You?"

China, "You better be glad I got mommy's Mandell, who's going right back to sleep?"

She goes to put him back to bed.

Sugar, "You spoiled them."

Mac, "No, my wife has."

Challis, "Well, it happens."

Night falls.

Solace, "Morning son, how did you sleep?"

Challis, "Alright, I told my wife to be last night about all about me, and everything, and she has been frowning ever since."

Solace, "Let me see, well, I don't know what to tell you." As she goes into the room,

Challis, "Now our babies are upset."

Solace, "Looks well, the truth shall set you free."

CHAPTER 22

Time to explain

Up the steps come Sassy, "daddy,"
    Challis, "Yes?"

"How are you? My dad and Lady B's to be husband were you and my mommy married?"

Solace, "Let me go."

Challis, "No, we weren't,"

Sassy, "Well, how am I me?"

Challis, "Sit."

She does, and he does too.

Challis, "Me and your mother had an encounter, and made you."

Sassy, "What's an encounter?"

Challis, "When grown people have sex without being married."

"So, you had that with Lady B because you are not married yet?"

Challis, "Something like that, at times people that love each other make love to seal their commitment."

Sassy, "So, you did not have no commitment with my mommy, but I'm here."

Challis, "As you get older, you will understand better one day."

"Renee at my old daycare said when her mom was pregnant, that her dad said"

Sassy, "that kid is not mine,' Renee said because her mom was having a baby not by her dad,"

Challis, "You are mine, and sometimes people make mistakes,"
Sassy, "Me and my mom was a mistake?"
"No, I love you."
"Do you love my mommy?"
Challis, "I cared very much about her wellbeing."
"Why didn't you marry my mommy?"
Challis, "I was married to someone else."
"Who?"
"To a bad lady."
"To Jay Bird?"
Challis, "How do you know that?"
"I heard Jay Bird's mommy say that you were Jay Bird's husband."
Challis, "Yes."
Sassy runs and gets under the bed screaming,
"You are going to hurt me!" She screamed.
Gigi runs up the steps, Challis squats down, "we're alright."
Sassy gets out and jumps into Gigi's arms screaming and crying.
Challis, "Please sit down."
His mom, "What is wrong?"
Challis, "She told me who my wife was, and I said yes."
Sassy, "He's Jay Bird's husband."
"Take me and hide me, baby sis."
Challis sits on the ground, "have I hurt you since you
Sassy, "No sir."
Challis, "Do you think I would harm you? Because JayBird is dead, what she did to you I'm sorry, but if I had known, I would have stopped her."
Gracie, "Your dad loves you,"
Sassy, "I just want you; I was supposed to live with you, you promised my mommy."
Gracie, "I know, but do you think I would be here if your dad was going to harm you?"

Sassy plays with her hair, "I don't know what is true."
Gracie, "What is true is that your dad helps you every day."
Sassy, "Yes."
Gracie, "Indeed, your dad has never hurt you."
Sassy, "Yes."
Gracie, "So if I'm here, your dad, Pappi, your mama Sugar, your family are here. What do we all have for you?"
Sassy, "Safe. I'm safe."
Gracie, "And you are loved,"
Sassy gets down and runs to her dad, his mom smiles. Challis picks her up and hugs her real tight, "I love you, and I will never let anyone, God so help me, hurt you."
Sassy, "Daddy, I love you."
He smiles, Gigi and his mom claps. Challis kisses her on the cheek.
Sassy, "Put me down please, I'm sleepy, I want to go back to sleep with my Lady B and our babies."
Challis, "Okay, we'll be right downstairs. Do you want to put on the T.V?"
"Yes sir, Moses please,"
He puts her in the bed with Giselle, Giselle, and their babies all smile. Sassy gets right under lady B. Gracie, "I'm a little sleepy also, I'll lay up here in the chaise lounge, if that is alright with you."
Sassy, "Yes."
Challis, "Okay."
Sassy, "Bye dad."
They all go.
Mama Sugar, "Thank you Jesus."
Couple of days goes by, and it is Labor Day.
Solace, "Is the Chef here?"
Challis, "Yes, but Chef Michael and Chef Gray are going to cook outside at that place we put up, I was thinking have him grill up a bunch

of different meats, clean back the grill, he been smoking a lot of meats though, and cook several sides."

Solace, "That will be nice."

"We can freeze our meats that we don't eat, ok let's have…"

She writes potato salad, Cole slaw, deviled eggs, bake beans, green beans, potato, onion, greens, cabbage, peppers, onions, and 4 sweet potato, and 2 cobblers peach, 1 apple, lemon, curd, coconut cake, cookies, fresh lemonade, and tea, and pop, and here. Challis takes the list and goes gives it to his chef.

"Bishop will be here; I got a bible lesson."

His mom, "Okay, where is everybody?"

Gigi "Rava, Bear and Cliché said they can do our hair and nails, and we would be out in 2 hours or so."

Mama Sugar, "Well tell them yes, and let you, me and Sassy go."

China, "Go where?"

Gigi, "To get our hair and nails done."

China, "Husband?"

Mac, "Yes baby."

China, "Wait, can I come?"

Gigi, "Yes."

Mac, "Oh go ahead."

Within 20 minutes, they leave, and the men set everything up while all the nurses take care of Giselle and all the babies.

Challis, "We can put our staff food over there, in the cafeteria."

Mac, "Okay."

Maxie, "My attorney just called me, he said I'm in the clear, he said Gigi doesn't have to testify either, because they have the entire recording, and they all pleaded guilty. It's a done deal, what are you doing?"

Mac, "Cook out we set on drinks."

Challis, "Let me see," and he goes to the beverage, beer, wine, liquor closet fridge."

"Chefs just have to make the ice lemon tea, and we're good."

The Security intercom beeps, "Bishop Conner's and Lady Collate."

Challis, "Put them in my parents downstairs conference room, let me go!"

"Where is Solace?"

Lady Collate asked him immediately he got into the room.

Challis, "They all went out, wait…"

Lady C, "Hello Solace, I just asked about you."

Solace, "Have security drop you, or do you need hair and nails to be done?"

Lady C, "Yes, I have not had time at all'"

Solace, "Let me speak to Challis."

She does.

Challis, "Ma'am."

Solace, "Let one of your security drop her."

Challis, "On it," and gives her back her phone.

Challis, "Tank, please drop Lady C where you dropped my fam." To the driver this time.

Security Tank, "Okay."

Lady C, "Honey."

Bishop, "Go on, okay."

They leave.

Challis and Bishop goes in and sits at the end of the meeting table. There are windows all around that no one can see in.

Bishop, "Let's pray!"

They bowed. "Heavenly father, we're here Lord, and we need a true word from you, allow me to step back so that Challis can have a clarity call of the word that brushes right up against the purity of your Salvation. Lord there is so much going on, but you still stand clear of the stone. Lord we come to you this day that you have made, and we thank you Lord in Jesus mighty name, Amen, Amen,"

Bishop prayed.

Challis, "Amen!"

Bishop, "Proverbs 3:6, Living Bible (TLB) In everything you do, put God first, and he will direct you and crown your efforts with success. Being protected and corrected by God Jesus is real, Challis, and even though you have your homework, I'll look at it, but I'm just moved to share that have dreams but have goals its nothing wrong every day."

"I have to have a goal daily to not let people take me there, through hard work in discipline means that you're getting a lot done, because I went by your property the other day, and I asked your guys if I could walk your land, and pray, and they said fine, and you know materialistic things comes and goes, and I prayed that you always get on your knees and thank God for whatever his blessed you real good with, or your true desire is the proof that it's yours, always in him, that's God's indication that is good you can have if you take hold of it each one inspire to make a soldier for Christ an effort in you put God into in your life, and I want to say you're doing sensational thus far, remarkable not by mere works. Now let's open our bibles to, amen, James 2:14-26, New King James Version (NKJV)"

They both do.

Bishop, "Faith Without Works Is Dead."

[14] What *does it* profit, my brethren, if someone says he has faith, but does not have works? Can faith save him? [15] If a brother or sister is naked and destitute of daily food, [16] and one of you says to them, "Depart in peace, be warmed and filled," but you do not give them the things which are needed for the body, what *does it* profit? [17] Thus also faith by itself, if it does not have works, is dead. But by your faith to keep going I see you clear and I know it's hard son, you're doing it, don't confuse what you do with doing but what you accomplish along the way, let the success stand in you, as to what you always do for your family, how you love, how you get down on your knee's every night, that you live every morning, that's the man you can stand on to help your children. See the Lord's man, that's

what you show the good life is in God, not man, see being a real man of God is no joke, see, understand that not some but everything you have is a gift from God up above, hallelujah."

Challis, "Amen!"

Bishop Connors continued, "You, your intermediate family is going to move the world, and people know it, do you?"

Challis, "I believe that."

Bishop, "I saw that your daughter played the piano at the re-pass."

"I thought she is just what you all needed."

Challis, "Yes, my wife to be, and our babies smile for her, and Sassy has her own room, but through the night she always comes gets under Giselle, and I leave her there to sleep, she often is talking to her, then she talks to all our babies."

He talks for some hours, "I'm still so sorry for whom I was, but I'm happy now she's here. I love our baby girl."

Bishop, "I'm glad to hear that."

Malcolm intercoms, "sir Challis, your attorney, Salmon and Ms. Mustier are here."

Bishop, "We're done."

Challis, "Send them down," and they click off.

Bishop, "Let's pray!"

Challis, "Yes!"

Bishop began to pray, "Lord, thank you for this time for which we had in you, Jesus Lord we realize that this life we live at times are monstrous individuals, our heart is here, our ear is here, Lord stay with Challis and his family.

Lord you said in your word, Isaiah 54:17[17,] No weapon forged against you will prevail, and you will refute every tongue that accuses you. This is the heritage of the servants of the LORD, and this is their vindication from me, declares the LORD in Jesus mighty name, Matthew 18:20[20,] For where two or three gather in my name, there am I with them, amen.

Challis, "Amen."

Bishop Connors stands to go.

Challis, "If you don't mind please stay."

Bishop, "Okay," as he sat back down.

Attorney Salmon and Mrs. Mustier comes in,

Challis, "Have a seat."

They both do.

Mrs. Mustier, "It has been brought to my attention that Dr. Karon Ortega will be Sassy's go to Psychologist for the school."

"They have 6 now, I switched her, she gets out info to Dr. Deborah Olshan, now Dr. Karon Ortega complained, because she looks albic end names, now I do not think that I should speak to her although she tried to challenge me."

She takes out a card, "this is her card now, the Superintendent can reroute her over to the high school."

Challis, "Our daughter is a child, and I would like it to be handled it quietly."

Mrs. Mustier, "Okay, I will be at Sassy's school off and on weekly to peep in on her."

Challis, "If that is all, have you eaten?"

Attorney Salmon, "We're eating with my family."

Challis, "Okay, and thank you both."

Mrs. Mustier, "May I see your intermediate family?".

Challis, "Yes, just come, they are all out, Nurse Lucy, please show them my family."

Sassy runs down, "Hi Mrs. Mustier."

Mrs. Mustier, "Hi."

Sassy, "Can you pick me up?"

Mrs. Mustier, "Of course, I have missed you."

She picks her up and says, "You are getting so big and beautiful."

She twirls around.

"Now, let's go see your family."

Sassy, "Ooh yes, come, and Mr. Salmon you too."

Sassy, "Hi Attorney Salmon."

He greeted back, "Hey Sassy,"

Some time passes, and the men are watching the game, and the ladies are all playing cards, bid whisk, and listening to some slow jazz music. Bishop and First Lady are still there. All the men are watching Monday night football, and Sassy is dressing her dolls all over the floor, and coloring, she is sort of watching the football game too.

Challis, "I thought to myself, the woods, all my damn woods, Jesus keep them from our children. Please I give them all back to you, just please keep them Lord, amen."

Next day.

His mother asked, "What was Mrs. Mustier and attorney Salmon doing here?"

Challis, "Mom, it's all good."

Solace, "Right, another bone from the past."

Challis, "Yes, short lived."

Solace, "Okay, you better put every last woman made fire out."

Challis, "Sunsets, all my intermediate family and you."

his father, "I hope so!"

The intercom beeps,

Security Vernon, "Mrs. Tina Albright, and Taylor, and her baby sis Shonda."

Solace, "Show them in."

Challis, "Who are they?"

Solace, "I think they are our neighbors."

Mrs. Tina walks in with her little kids, "hi neighbors, our little Taylor, and baby Shonda, would like Sapphire to come over, and play, we just saw that her, and Taylor our classmates."

Challis, "Sassy, do you want to go play?"

Sassy, "No sir, but can they come over here?"

Mrs. Tina, "I don't have a problem with that, if you all don't,"

Solace, "Fine, play date for 2hours."

Mrs. Turner, "Okay girls,"

They both jump up and down. Sometime spins by, and the girls are all coloring, and dressing dolls, and eating snacks.

Taylor, "Are you being in our church's pageant?" Taylor asked.

Sassy, "No, I have another pageant coming up."

Taylor, "So you can do two, we looked you up, you play piano, and your mommy is dead."

Sapphire, "Yes, but I have a new mommy."

Taylor, "You can't do that, she will be your step mommy, just like our neighbor, Nicole's new mommy."

Sapphire, "No, she is my mommy now."

Taylor, "How my mother said she is going to sleep till Christmas, same as your stepbrother and sisters."

Sassy gets up and goes to her father.

She called. "Daddy?"

Challis, "Yes."

Sassy, "Can we have popsicles?"

Mama sugar, "I'll get three,"

She gets up and hands each one to the girls. All sit at the table and eat their popsicles.

Taylor, "Your real mommy should have you and a little sister."

Sassy thought to herself, "I'm getting sick of her. How much time is left? One more hour?"

"I have two baby sisters."

All done with their popsicles,

"Sticks."

They all give them to her, and no one see's Sassy, as she goes open the door, and start throwing Taylor's and her sisters' stuff out the door.

Challis, "What the…?"

And was cut off by Sassy.

Sassy, "It's time to go, I hate her."

Gig, "Who?"

China, "Her play dates."

Taylor, "We are not going anywhere till our mother comes back to get us."

Sassy, "Oh yes, you are a big mouth," she tries to pull her, and sister out the door.

Challis, "Wait, let go of them."

Sassy screams, "Stop it. I don't like them, Taylor, she is bad."

Challis, "Wait, all three of you, sit at the table."

He grabs Sassy.

Security brings back in all their stuff.

Mama Sugar, "She has been picking with her the whole time."

Challis, "Mom please."

Mama Sugar, "I'm just saying."

China, "They so cute."

Solace, "Don't let…"

Challis cuts her off.

He said. "Mom,"

She says ok.

Challis, "Now, what's wrong?"

Sassy, "Is Lady B my mommy now?"

Challis, "Yes."

Taylor, "How? She is not."

China, "That is none of…"

And gets cut off by Mac.

Mac, "Baby."

China, "Let me go check my kids, and sister," and left the room.

Sassy, "I do not ever want her to come over her baby, her sister is alright."

Taylor, "My mommy said we are going to be best friends."
Sassy, "No, no! I don't like her," shaking her head, she pats her dad,
Taylor, "My mom saved you a spot on the church pageant, didn't you?"
Her mom, Shonda, nods her head.
Shonda, "Yes."
Sassy, "You are in it right?"

CHAPTER 23

Pageant

Taylor, "Of course, and I'm going to win, I won last year."

Sassy, "Baby sis, can you make me some quick pageant stuff?"

Gracie, "Yes, what's the date?"

Taylor, "It's next week, on Friday, and you're too big to be her baby sis, how old are you?"

Shonda puts up two fingers.

Gracie, "Alright, then we are going."

Challis, "She likes it?"

Sassy, "Yes sir, let me go."

Sassy starts cleaning up their mess.

Challis, "Taylor you can help her."

They both do. Time goes by quickly.

Solace, "I don't beat other people's kids, but I wanted to beat her, 'no she's your stepmom,' who asked her? Lord help me!"

Gracie, "Yes, she is a mess."

China, "Sassy was serious, threw all their stuff out," she laughs, they all do.

Mac, "I just looked like, 'what the hell."

Challis, "We are going to have the best life."

His dad, "The best life ever, that was too funny, you know why she's in that pageant,"

"Sassy, why are you in the pageant?"
Sassy, "I want to beat Taylor."
Challis, "Okay, bedtime."
Gracie, "I got her."
China, "Sassy is tough."
Solace, "She will have to be with overbearing Taylor in kindergarten," she gets up, "talks too much. I can't blame my grand-daughter because I was about to throw her little behind out myself."

(psalm 23 - King James Version)

First Lady Collate, "The Lord *is* my shepherd; I shall not want, He maketh me to lie down in green pastures: I'll have a talk with Taylor."
Two days goes by.
Sassy, "I want to look like a sapphire butterfly."
Gracie, "Sapphire butterfly you will be."
"come on, we got a lot of work to do. I just got in some lovely material, but the wings, yes, here we go, Sassy."
The intercom beeps,
Security, "Taylor is here."
Taylor, "My dad is watching me from across the lawn, he's waiting for me, I just want to know what color Sassy is using for the pageant."
Sassy, "No. No."
Gracie, "Yes."
Challis, "You will have to wait till the day of the pageant, okay?"
Taylor, "I can wait, but can Sassy come play?"
Sassy, "No."
Challis, "She has a lot of work to do."
Taylor, "Can she spend the night?"
Sassy, "Never."
Challis, "It's up to her."
Taylor, "You're her dad."

Challis, "Okay, Bryant Security, please watch her back."

Taylor, "I'm supposed to call my dad when I'm ready to come back."

Challis, "Okay, call him."

Taylor gets out her phone, and dial's her daddy's number.

Taylor, "Daddy, Sassy has a lot of work to do."

Her dad, Thomas, "Coming."

They hang up. Within minutes, he's at the door. Challis goes and opens the door.

Thomas, "Well, hello, are you Sassy's dad?"

Challis, "Yes. Nice to meet you."

They shake hands, and Taylor leaves.

Solace, "See."

Challis, "No come on."

Jamarion Senior, "She is too grown for me."

Mac, "She has to lose, I got $100 on her. Here is my $100, on my God daughter, she's going down."

Solace goes to her purse and gets out a $100.

"I am not supposed to bet, but what the hell is $100 to my grand baby, and the cash goes to her."

Everyone agrees

. Solace, "I like her, she goes all the way out."

Two days goes by, and his parents have gone.

Gracie, "Okay, let me."

She puts sassy up on stool in front of a mirror.

Solace, "That's gorgeous."

Gigi , "Thanks, this is her final dress, we also collaborated over this butterfly bodice long gold shimmer Rhine-stone print skirt, with deep pockets, rhinestone belt, and with a eyelet white lace bottom, and this bow tie, white light rhinestone gold shimmer lace ruffle cuff, rhinestone cuff links, with these matching white gold rhinestone spur heel, white suede gold rhinestone boots."

Solace, "I just love this," she touches it, "you have been really working up a storm day and night."

Gigi, "Oh her suede diamond gloves, and rhinestone white suede and gold cowboy hat, we still got to do her entry dress."

Solace, "Please let me design it."

Gigi, "Wonderful, yes but I have to have it by tonight."

Solace, "And I'll do all the accessories also."

Gigi, "Okay, now we have over here lots of one of a kind shoes I bought up."

Solace, "I love these rhinestone golds feathered."

"ok let me take these shoes and go."

She does, she goes straight to the table with her laptop and goes to town, she draws Ball Gown Ankle-length sequined pearl rhinestone top with Tulle/Sequined Sleeveless Scoop Neck With Sequins/Bow(s) white feathers full bodice with a rhinestone pearls gold two tone feathered button by one big rhinestone cape simple but uniquely beautiful to be worn with hair up in rhinestones and sequined pearls with pearl rhinestone gold tiny earrings and nails rhinestone pearl gold Ombre.

Challis, "Mom, what you are doing?"

His mom has a table full of swatches also.

Solace, "Just finished designing your daughter's entry gown."

Challis, "Let me see."

His mom, "No, not till the pageant,"

Challis, "Okay, let me go peep in on my fam."

Solace, "Their hair is growing to the floor, and their tone is gorgeous."

Challis, 'Yes, I hope our sons would wake again, so I could cut it low again, but, oh well," he runs up the steps, doing 3 at a time.

Nurse Jamia, "Hello."

Challis, "Hey, how are they?"

Nurse Jamia, "Fine. Other than a slight rash that all of them have."

Challis, "Yes, I noticed that. What are you doing for it?"

Nurse Jamia, "We're keeping it clean, and applying a light sab mixture,"

Challis, "I'll contact Dr. Brimer for a good dermatologist."

Nurse Jamia, "That should do it."

Challis, "Okay."

He checks each one of his loves, and then he kisses Giselle, and gets out his phone.

"Hello Dr. Brimer, here."

Challis, "Hello, my wife and our kids are having an allergic reaction to something, and I would like a referral for a dermatologist to come over."

Dr. Brimer, "My colleague, Dr. Tasha R. Vernell. I will speak with her; she is a dermatologist."

"Okay, thank you," Challis said, and they hang up.

Time goes by, and it is dinner time. All are seated at the table.

Gigi, "This is delicious."

Solace, "Yes, it is so tender and juicy."

Challis, "This texture is so delicate."

Solace, "Have you started on her design by me?"

Gigi, "Yes ma'am, I'll have it finished by tomorrow, the particular pearls feathers should arrive morning, which will be good, because I need to work on more of Sassy's musical routine."

Sassy, "One pianist and one solo with puppets."

Gigi, "Yes the song will be a song, she has routines with Mr. Dover's WILL CONTROL THE PUPPETS, he'll arrive tomorrow to work with her she use to sing and dance with his puppets, together with her mother."

Solace, "Good, she should know that by heart, oh so how many dresses?"

Gigi, "3."

Challis, "How many more to go?"

Gigi, "Just the presentation, one your mother designed, and the lace pants set she'll wear to there, the one for the tuxedo pants, formal and top hat I had my seamstress do, it arrived today. It's gorgeous, entirety is Sequins."

Challis, "Sounds all good, I have to go now, it's almost 7pm, my only night class."

Gigi, "What time are you getting out?".

Challis, "9pm, that's the only one they had open, so I can graduate in 18 months."

Jamarion Senior, "Go on, we got Sassy."

Gracie, "I'll bath her, and put her to bed, and also stay up in the room, till you come back."

Challis, "Thank you, but I alerted the night nurse, she will pitch in also, here they come," and he leaves.

Three days pass, and it is the pageant day.

Mama Sugar, "You all ready?"

Sassy, "Yes ma'am."

Gigi, "Yes, we are, time to dress."

They have hired her for a makeup and hair artist. Finally, Sassy has on her lace white feather design.

Challis, "My baby girl, you look beautiful."

His dad, "Yes, you do."

And they are all packed and left for the pageant.

An hour goes by, they arrive at the church, and it is packed on the side where Bishop allows gospel concerts. Lady Collette comes up, her dressing room is in the back, the one with the red door right off from the stage.

Mama Sugar, "Thank you, and don't you look lovely?"

Lady C, "I have had this going on for 14 years, it's from The Madame Collection."

Mama Sugar, "Turn around, that cut is original."

Lady C, "I just love how you ladies, and Sassy are dressed."

All says thank you.

Gigi, "Let's hit it."

She and mama Sugar go, and within an hour its pageant time. All Sassy's family is in the first row, off from the judges, which are, Josephine Bridge Water, Ashanti Shutters, Katherine Devore, Randee Waters and Cedric Collins.

The magistrate is Mrs. Justine Logo, she stands, "Thanks for coming, it's so nice, we can all get together at this time in fun, and yes I'm sure we have raised our goal for our sick, and shut in church team?" As they all clapped.

Lady Collette stands, and nods yes.

Mrs. Janet, "Okay, we have a yes from our good looking, quite lovely tonight, first Lady C, let's give her an appreciative round of applause."

All the invites cheered. Some of whom Lady C knew, and many she did not.

Mrs. Janet, "Now where's our Bishop?"

He waves in the back and starts coming down. People cheered.

Mrs. Janet, "Now, let's get right down to it, our judges' tonight are, Randee Waters, renowned model."

She stands.

Crowd cheers!

Mrs. Janet, "Katherine Devore, outstanding fashion magazine DEVOE, which will do and entire spread on the pageant."

She stands,

Crowd cheers!

"Cedric Collins, not too far from his home, the number one comedian,"

He stands,

People claps!

"Singer and songwriter, 2-time Grammy winner, Ashanti Shutters,"

People stand and clap!

"And Josephine Bridge Water, author and poet the beards award twice,"

She stands and people really clap!

Mrs. Janet, "Now next, we will introduce our contestants, please hold all applause to the end, introducing contestant 1, 6-year-old Sandra Bare, okay, what do you wish to use your winnings for?"

Sandra Bare, "To help my mommy fly me and my class to South Africa."

Mrs. Janet, "Okay, stand right here."

The little girl does, "Okay, now next is Violet Vans, she is 5 years old, okay now, what is it you wish to use your winnings for if you win?"

Violet, "I want to open my own only cats' shelter."

Mrs. Janet, "Why just cats?"

Violet, "Because when my cat TEE TEE ran away, nobody cared to take her into their home, and when we got her back her right paw was gone."

The crowd says awh!

Mrs. Janet, "I'm sorry to hear that, stand right there.

Okay, next is 5 year old Taylor Tanner.

Okay now, what would you like to use your winnings on if you win?"

Taylor, "I will use my winnings to hire a lawyer to fight for no height limit rides."

Mrs. Janet, "Explain."

Taylor, "When me and my family went to Disney world, they kept measuring me, and I could not ride with my parents, me or my little sister."

"Okay, right up there, okay, Bethany Caddell, okay, what will you do with your winnings if you win?"

Bethany, "I want to use my winnings to get my dad a surgery, so he won't snore."

The audience cracks up laughing. Mrs. Janet laughs too.

"Okay, please quiet, right over there, okay, Tajine Jamie, okay, now if you win what will you use your winnings for?"

Tajine, "Parachute jumping forever."

"Okay, right here, now Sapphire Calm-sway, what would you like to use your winnings for if you win?"

Sapphire, "I would like to start a religious card line for the poor."

Mrs. Janet, "Elaborate."

Sapphire, "Each poor kid can receive money for everyday life to help be have nurtured."

Mrs. Janet, "Well, alright, okay, this will be our last contestant, take a bow ladies."

They all do.

Mrs. Janet, "Okay, we will be out with our first talent showing in 10 minutes."

Curtain closes.

First up is Taylor Tanner, "Good evening."

She is playing drums with a yellow puffy party dress, with her hair in two big matching bows, and she sounds good.

She is playing the star-spangled banner, and she is really jamming, and the audience is into it. She jams for 15 minutes.

Mrs. Janet, "Remarkable, come on, let's give it up for drummer Taylor Tanner. Okay, next up is Violet Vans, and she is going to do a mine dancing."

Her music is slow, but nice and welcoming. She mines around, dances softly in white face she has the audience enchanted.

Mrs. Janet, "Nice, real nice, let's give it up, mine oh mine, yes she did. Come on for Violet Vans.

"Next up is Bethany Caddell.' She is doing a baton routine, dancing around, giggling, kicking up her leg, throws baton in air, and catches it.

She runs, does a buck down to one knee, catches baton, twirls it between her legs. The audience is amazed, then she twirls it behind her back, and catches it, the music is just what she needed, thriller, finally she jumps, smiles, twirls and throws up, catches, and does a split.

Mrs. Janet, "Very nice, let's give it up to Bethany Caddell, nice."

The crowd claps, then she says, "right there. Now next up is Tajine Jamie, doing harmonica, let's do it."

Music starts and Tajine plays right along not missing a beat or note, she is skilled, and it shows on her, she is now doing solo, she is on high, then balance, then Simba.

Mrs. Janet, "Great."

The crowd claps for Tajine Jamie.

Mrs. Janet said, "Wonderful, right over there, okay, a soloist music for Sapphire Calms-ways."

On roller skates, she takes off, as the Soloist sings, she jumps up, and twirls, the crowd is almost out of their seats, she does an air buck skates around fast, does a one leg twirl around. Then she goes around real fast, then jumps real fast in midair, she is good. She then dances across in sync with soloist, and you have would have thought she was on ice skates the way she made the stage at her command, and all a sudden she goes skating around real fast, nothing can contain her, then she twirls, and twirls around non-stop, over and over, then she takes off. Nobody saw trampoline, she skates full force, and jumps off stage, hits the trampoline and twirls in air.

Gigi throws her a rose, she catches it in her mouth, and lands twirling, cape up, and one side down a rose in mouth. Everyone is out of their seats, and cheering, and clapping. Challis is stoked about his baby girl; the entire family is out.

Mrs. Janet said, "Done, spectacular. Can someone help her?"

Gigi does Challis hugs Gigi, "Thanks."

Mama Sugar, "She tore them up."

Jamarion Senior, "Yes, our grand baby did it."

Mike, "She was amazing."

Cindy, "Yes, she was like a little grown woman."

Karen, "That entire get up was the bomb, yes, my niece was bomb."

Some time goes by, and its now time for next round talent. Out first, and out the gate is Sapphire Calms-way with an all-white judge robe with a Kenya turquoise ribbon, and she has a judge hammer, and a two tone loafers one side, and her other side is dressed in a plushy flaunting chiffon gold sparkly dress with magazines all over, and with tape around her neck, a pin bobbin for ring designer hose, and patent gold metallic flats.

Mrs. Janet, "So what are you going to grow up to be?"

Sapphire Calms-way, "A 4th circuit federal judge first, then Supreme court justice, and fashion designer, and business owner."

Mama Sugar, "You go Gigi."

Gracie, "All her ideal, I just made it."

Challis, "You know you are our daughter also; we love you."

Gracie, "Yes, and I love you all."

Mrs. Janet, "Alright now, right over there."

Now, Taylor Tanner, an Oscar winning actress/drummer, okay, right over there now."

Bethany Caddell is dressed as a dog, rabbit, cat, snake, and doctor. She is going to be a veterinarian.

Mrs. Janet, "Okay, right over there now."

Tajine Jamie, she is dressed as an Olympian, with a leotard, with a balance beam arm, and 4 fake gold medals.

Mrs. Janet said, "Now, right over there, now Violet Vans."

She is dressed as a world-renowned painter with all painter equipment attached to her, and a picture.

Mrs. Janet said, "Yes, right there. Now its next up for last talent." 10 minutes go by. Bethany Caddell is up dancing this time, and she is rocking, giving it to them, flipping and parting down, smiling, and happy. She's dressed in a top hat, and shorts with a vest under long coat, all red and white, with white design stockings, and white tap shoes. People clapped.

Mrs. Janet, "Nice, okay, next up is Violet Vans."

She is singing to birds, she calls, and its screechy to all ears, but cute, she has on a blue full cinder Ella dress, with a Blue bird on her shoulder, and blue suede flat shoes. People clap.

Mrs. Janet, "Okay, very good, yes."

Taylor Tanner is singing all out to the ball game, and she sounds good, with a baseball cap, and ball dress on. She is in tune, and not missing a note, right on beat. People clap.

Mrs. Janet, "Okay, yes you, next."

Tajine Jamie is doing bow and arrow shots to target, dressed in a mint colored flowing formal chiffon dress, with sparkly shoes. People clap. She hits every target.

Mrs. Janet, "Okay, yes, ok now."

Sapphire's grand piano comes up, and with a long flowing white dress, with a white stow on, she bails out one note before music that hits her target audience in a special way, and then she sings alto. Then she plays the music, it's addicting and mesmerizing, and just lovely mildly arranged with a soft shadow Ombre, with one light on her. The entire audience stands up. She has hit their hearts in a spectacular way.

Gracie, "Oh mommy, I did not know you were here?"

Constance, "We're in the back, this child, she is blowing us away."

Mrs. Janet said, "somebody did not come to play, ok next."

Formally, all the girls go back, then in 10 minutes, they all come back. Violet Vans is on Silver all formal dress bow sleeves. Taylor Tanner is on a red sparkly full dress, and Sapphire Calms-Way has on a soft one shoulder rose closure blue turquoise teal, psychedelic formal rose pedals, and an entire bodice huge train.

Constance, "That's popping."

Gracie, "Mommy."

Mama Sugar, "It is a wow."

Mac, "Astounding."

Jamarion Senior, "Beautiful."

Then Tajine Jamie comes out in an all milky white formal halter puffy dress. Bethany Caddell has on a purple ball gown taffeta dress.

Mrs. Janet, "Okay, all look so lovely."

The Judges gives her an envelope, she says, thank you, okay now, 3rd runner up is Bethany Caddell," she said, and they give her a bouquet of roses, and a sash.

Mrs. Janet, "2nd runner up, and don't be upset, because all of you were sensational, and contestants will get a prize, Taylor Tanner."

She gets a bouquet, sash, and she is mad.

Mrs. Janet, "No reason to be mad, you did a great job,"

She takes another envelope and says.

"Our Princess is Sapphire Calms-Way."

Taylor Tanner stomps away, Sassy gets a rhinestone crown, they pin it on her head, and a sash that says, 'Princess' and she walks forward, does the Mrs. America wave. She is smiling.

And she comes back, whispers to Mrs. Janet.

Mrs. Janet, "You won, it is yours. She wants to give her crown to Taylor, parents?"

Challis, "If she wants to."

Mama Sugar, "No."

Challis, "Mom."

Mama Sugar, "That is hers' and Gigi's crown."

Gracie, "And yours,"

Constance, "Daughter, you keep on amazing me."

Gigi hugs her mom. Two hours later, all are out to eat.

Mama Sugar, "You know I got a bone to pick with you."

Sassy hugs her.

Mama Sugar, "All this work, girl, you did it."

The Tanners are out at the same restaurant. Taylor's mom comes over with the crown,

"Hi, I'm Brooklyn, Taylor's mom."

They all speak, and she says, "her behavior was terrible, so she cannot have this."

Mama Sugar takes it.

Brooklyn, "Okay, thanks, nice meeting you."

All says thanks, and nice meeting you.

Mama Sugar, "This is nice."

Constance, "Very pretty."

Karen, "Let me see, this thing is heavy."

Cindy, "You worked for this girl."

Sassy, "We all worked hard, pageants are fun, but so much hard work, daddy, may I sleep in?"

Challis, "Yes."

Mama Sugar, "Well, you beat her."

Sassy, "Yes ma'am, but winning hurts people's feelings, and I don't like that."

Cindy, "You can in the future, put on your own show."

Sassy, "Fund raisers to help feed kids,"

Bethany comes over.

Bethany, "Hi."

Sassy, "Can she sit with us? We're all sitting together in the middle."

Challis, "Do you want to?"

Sassy, "Yes sir, but my food."

Challis, "I 'll have them deliver it over there, do not get up without telling me."

Sassy, "Yes sir, come on baby sis."

Gracie, "No, you'll be fine."

Bethany, "Come, everyone wants to talk to you." and she grabs Sassy's hand, and they leave.

All the parents have waiters and waitresses deliver their food and desserts, they eat laugh and talk. Waiters gave them all coloring pages, and crayons, they color, eat and chat.

Mama Sugar, "I'm crying, her first set of friends, despite Taylor."

Challis, "Yeah, well, they all will be competitive."

Mike, "But Sassy is the star."

SEASONS OF LIFE AND THE ALTAR CALL OF CHRIST

Mama Sugar, "No picture?"
Challis, "Yes, I hired Donavan, we'll have all by tomorrow."
Jamarion Senior, "This was really a nice experience for her."
Jamarion II, "Baby girl put in the work."
Karen, "She was so poised, and disciplined."
Constance, "Just like my Gigi."
Gracie, "No, her mom demanded her work ethic, it's in her, and what I appreciate about Sassy is that no push she gives 100%, in mind, in technique, she thinks what she wants to do, and as she gets older it'll be, yes look at her."
Challis, "See Donavan still works, yes smile. Okay he got us."
Constance, "Come, I want one with just my daughter, I'll pay."
Challis, "No, go."
They go over to Donavan.
Jamarion Senior, "Hey Cobb and Leslie."
Solace, "Yes hello," all her families and daughter in-laws speak too.
Cobb, "That was your granddaughter that won?"
Jamarion Senior, "Yes, our youngest son, Challis's baby girl."
Cobb, "Well, you saw ours, Taylor."
Leslie, "I'm here to tap her behind my son in law."
She walks away.
Solace, "It happens."
Cobb, "Nice seeing you all."
Leslie, his wife, "yes it was."
Jamarion Senior, "Small world, they will get Miss Taylor together."
Solace, "I did not know that was their Brooklyn, Taylor looks just like her."
Jamarion II, "Sassy just a yapping."
Solace, "They all like chattering Kathy's,"
Karen, "They look too cute, good your photographer got them."
Solace, "All of them were on the list."
Jamarion Senior, "What list?"
Solace, "Oh incoming students."

Challis, "I like that, I still contact them, you know Haz and Simon?"

Mike, "Yeah, me too. I still talk to Pollard and Craig," Mike said.

Bishop, "Hey all."

his wife Collette, "Hi."

"I wasn't supposed to have a favorite, but you all know my heart went straight to the grace of Sassy,".

Solace, "Thanks you all, just got here?"

Bishop, "No, we have a meeting with Cobb and Leslie, we will see you."

All says, "Okay, good."

Pageant night came and morning gallivanted in. Challis and Sassy were both sleeping in.

Solace, "I tried, I just got up."

Jamarion Senior, "Me and some Joe had to get it on."

Solace, "What are you talking about?"

Jamarion Senior, "Chef, put on a nice pot, and breakfast spread, I'll dig in a few, where is Challis?"

Solace, "They are all still sleeping."

Mike, "Hello, my favorite parents."

Solace, "Your only parents."

Mike goes and hugs and kisses his mother, then he hugs his father.

Jamarion Senior, "What brings you here?"

"I just was in the neighborhood."

Solace, "Doing what?"

"Oh, I came to look at you and daddy's and Challis penthouses."

Jamarion Senior, "What? You are downsizing?"

Mike, "Yes, the upkeep is relentless, and we're both ready to be downtown, it's going to be really something when all you get finished."

Jamarion Senior, "Challis's penthouse is going to be more of a fit for you, because we're getting older, seniors fifty, single or married year old, and no kids."

Challis, "I'm doing adult living as well."

Mike, "Our kids."

Challis, "Older children, no one under high school age,"

Mike, "Cool, I like that, maybe, but teenagers is a story as well."

Challis, "Most likely, they will be from the high school, and their schedule will be gruesome, so cool."

Mike, "Summer."

Challis, "Adults will be my main profile, but kids can come visit during periods."

Mike, "But aren't we going to own them?"

Challis, "Yes, each person on their own, I'm spinning building owner ship, and we will do all up keep for a monthly fee, as well as other things like, pick up, cleaning, laundry, grocery shopping, oh I'm having attendees."

Mike, "I like all that."

Solace, "I am so ready, I think I'll cook dinner today,"

Challis, "Mom, you want some help?"

Solace, "Yes because there are some things I want to learn."

Challis, "The Chef, Marion will be here, he can assist you."

Solace, "What happen to the other chef?"

Challis, "Oh, it's my man Gabe's agency."

Mike, "Sellars?"

Challis, "Yes, so he has upcoming Chefs because we need steady, but not now, you know?"

Solace, "Yes, who is that?"

Challis, "I don't know, probably wrong number, let me go check my family." They just hung up.

He jumps 3 stairs at a time.

Solace, "I got to start ordering our stuff for Thanksgiving."

Jamarion Senior, "I'm sure Challis will have that covered."

Solace, "I want prime rib this year wait… hello."

CHAPTER 24

Dinner Guest

Monroe, "Hello baby,"
 Solace, "What? Who is this?"
Monroe, "You know who it is."
Solace, "30 years."
Monroe, "So my wife has passed, and I'm coming after my next option."
"Really?" Solace asked.
"Yes, I know you're still married, but baby aren't you tired of the same ole…" Monroe said. "Baby, I'm going with Mike, golfing," he bends down and kisses his wife on the lips.

She kisses him back. They leave.

Solace goes to the backroom,

Solace, "I'm telling you just like this, lose my damn number, I didn't want you when I had you, remember I left you."

Monroe, "Don't fool yourself, I got what you want, and I got my self-fixed up, so you better get on why you can."

Solace, "Next time I'll have my husband deal with you."

Monroe, "I saw you, who goes to my grandson's school? Your sweetness."

Solace hangs up, then her house phone rings. She answers.

Monroe, "You know you love me," Monroe said.

Solace, "How the hell did you get my phone number?"

Monroe, "You know me, I got little thing on the side. Let's do the swing thing."

Solace, "Okay, I'm not going to play, I have your number too and I'll have my husband nip this in the bud," said and she slams down the phone.

Challis, "Mom, who is that?"

Solace, "Some ole nigga from my past."

Challis drinking lemonade, and almost chokes,

"What?"

Solace, "Won't take no for an answer, I'll tell your daddy."

Challis, "See, that wig I told you was popping has gotten you in trouble,".

Solace hits him, "boy stop playing, I'm serious."

She cries bitterly.

Challis consoles her, "Mom I'm sorry."

Solace, "I don't like nobody messing with our family."

Challis, "Mom don't tell dad, let me handle it."

Solace, "No, I and your daddy don't have secrets, and this is what you need to learn, tell it all while it's still fresh."

Some time goes by, Solace cooked. She sent the Chef home. She was not in the mood. They are having lemon roasted chicken, all different pieces on a big platter, with cream spinach, plus potato au gratins, with bacon chicken noodle soup, and big salad rolls, and she made fruit cocktail, home-made ice cream, sandwiches and cupcakes, and potato chip, pretzel cheese, and popcorn mix.

Jamarion Senior, "Smells good, let me go and shower."

Sassy, "Daddy, I'm hungry."

'You go on and eat, I need to shower myself and her. Jamarion Senior leaves.

Challis knew his parents well he knew his mother had waited to bathe to tell his dad. Jamarion II and Karen his wife, and both their sons, Jamarion III, Jam for short, and Joshua, Jos for short, came just in time.

Challis, "What's cracking nephews?"

Jam, "Hey uncle."

"Hi Jos," he fist bumps and hugs their uncle.
Jam, "Hey, pretty Sassy."
"Hi, Jos, she is cute."
Challis, "These are your big cousins."
They both hug her.
Jam, "Can we go see?"
Challis, "Yes, right up the steps, hey, Sassy introduce them to our family."
Sassy goes, and they follow her."
The intercom beeps,
Security Dobbs, "What's your name?"
"Monroe."
Challis, "All hell no."
Mike, "Come on in."
Challis, "What the fuck, damn, I'm hungry."
Jamarion II, "What's going on?"
Solace comes down in a green black moo moo, with her hair all up into a ponytail.
Jamarion Senior, "Now, I know this mother fucker has not come over our house."
Challis, "Dad, I got him, come on man."
Jamarion Senior, "No, we are going to handle this right now."
They all knew their dad was mad as hell.
"Let him in, he came all the way over here."
Monroe, "I'm just here,"
He starts singing a song, 'for what's truly', he hits high note, "mine."
Mike, "What?"
Jamarion II, "Who…" and 1, 2, their dad leaped over their stairs and knocks Monroe the fuck out.
Challis and Mike grabs their dad.
Their dad, "No, let me go," they did, while Sassy said her grace, and was at the table just eating with her cousins, and auntie Cindy, and auntie Karen.

Then their dad, "get this piece of shit off my damn foyer," and the Security guys, Nick and Vargas picked Monroe up.

Challis, "Let me wash my hands."

Mike, "Dad, are you alright?"

"Yes."

Jamarion II, "I'm have to come over here more often."

"This was all the way to live."

Solace, "I'm sorry."

Jamarion Senior, "You have nothing to be sorry for, let's eat."

They all ate in silence because they knew their dad was pissed. A couple of days goes by.

Mike, "Challis, was that nigga stalking mommy?"

Challis, "Trying to, but all is quiet over here."

Mike, "I guess so, daddy is lethal."

Challis, "You come over people's houses, and that's what you get."

Mike, "Let a mother fucker think he is going to step into mine, I'm going, just come over, I think we will have to move into mommy and daddy's building,"

They laughed.

Challis, "Yeah, if you want Showtime because even a pin is not going to drop in mine."

Solace, "Come on, we are going to be late."

Challis, "Church, later."

An hour goes by.

CHAPTER 25

Worship

Bishop, "Greetings members and newcomers, my sermon this Sunday is "Winning" 'Psalms 108: 13 – With God on our side we win; he will defeat our enemies. 1 John 5: 4, for everyone born of God; overcomes the World.

This is the Victory that overcomes the World, even our faith. Now I hear everything, and I know that. 1 Corinthians 10: 13No temptation has overtaken you except what is common to mankind. And God is faithful; he will not let you be tempted beyond what you can bear. But when you are tempted, he will also provide a way out so that you can endure it. John 16:33. "I have told you these things, so that in me you may have peace. In this world you will have trouble. But take heart! I have overcome the world."

"Winning" this is my Sermon, now I do not like when people mess with my parishioners, but I want you to know that God battles for you, and I will too. I heard some disturbing news, but today I want to share with all of you, that you're all winning, we're on the right path, but know this. Jesus had his own sorrows, but he kept the faith, and that's what we must do. Keep going just like Jesus did for us, see no matter what your age is, trouble is planted right here on your forehead just because of who you choose this day to serve."

Congregation says, 'amen Hallelujah.'

Challis, "Hell no, this fool," as he watched as Monroe took his seat 4 rows down from them with a brace on his neck.

Solace looks then at Monroe, she prayed, "God please let him stop," then out the corner of her eyes at her husband, she could tell he was steaming. She just kept pleading the blood in silence.

Bishop Connors says, "Hebrews 4:13. Neither is there any creature that is not manifest in his sight: but all things *are* naked and opened unto the eyes of him with whom we have to do. I want you all to take heed to this if there is something or someone you think getting the best of you, rebuke them by the blood of God. **Isaiah 54:17**[17]**Noweapon** that is **formed** against thee shall prosper; and every tongue that shall rise **against** thee in judgment thou shalt condemn. This is the heritage of the servants of the LORD, and their righteousness is of **me**, saith the LORD. That's stands in us from the word of God now if you the one causing harm. Romans 8:1[1]Therefore, there is now no condemnation for those who are in Christ Jesus, now if you causing strife then this does not apply to you this is for Gods people that are standing with a pure heart from God just trying on all accord to live right. Matthew 25:46. 46 "Then they will go away to eternal punishment, but the righteous to eternal life. Psalms 121:7 -

The LORD shall preserve thee from all evil: he shall preserve thy soul. See God shelters his own Congregation." Parishioners shout, 'amen and Glory to God,' Bishop Conner continues, "I'll tell you all, we are not out here walking the blind, leading the blind," parishioners shout, "but God, you are right about that. Yes but God, we are, Deuteronomy 7:6

"For you, us, we are a holy people to the LORD your God, me, you; the LORD your God has chosen you to be a people for His own possession out of all the peoples who are on the face of the earth."

People are up really shouting to God, even the Calms-Way family.

"I' m telling you all this, mark my word, Jesus is real and just as quick as nonsense came, nonsense will be gone," and on that mark, the police comes in with some men, with a straight jacket. Monroe sees them, and darts out the pew, running.

Bishop, "Lord have mercy."

Bishop, "Monroe, just stop, go on, and get the help you need. I'll be out in the morning."

"Thank you, Doc.,"

Bishop, "He is gone."

The church goes quiet as they throw him down.

Bishop, "you don't have to do all that."

They get Monroe up, as the cops and men leave with Monroe.

Bishop Connors, "sometime life is over whelming, and if I was in a car, and my wife or daughter chooses to drive, and it blew up with my wife and daughter in it, I would be a little off as well, and so would you if it happen to you."

CHAPTER 26

School

Time goes by, and Solace and her hubby are relieved, not in the sense of what has happened. Solace prayed for Monroe, she does not know his entire story, but she knows everyone needs a prayer to the highest one, Jesus.

Sometime goes by, and Sister Rea comes, "Hey family, me and Frank."

He speaks and all say hello.

Rea, "I went on with your Chefs, and made dinner, and you all can pick up snack, which is on the table, soup, oyster, crackers, and relish tray, its fresh lemonade also."

Solace, "Ooh, that's gorgeous."

Rea turns around and said, "Gigi sent me this, I just love it, and she made me these slides."

Solace, "All those colors are beautiful,"

Rea, "It's so comfortable."

She twirls around.

Solace, 'Let me go get comfy, I'll be back down."

Challis hugs his auntie and shakes Frank's hand.

Jamarion Senior, "Drink anyone?"

Frank, "I'll get it, go on and change," Frank said.

Jamarion Senior, "Just wine for me."

Frank, "Okay."

Rea, "Me also."

Solace, "Nothing for me."

Challis, "Zero, and come on."

Daughter Sassy runs up the steps and her nurse Jamie greets her and Challis. They all speak, and she goes to change with her nurse Jamie.

Challis, "Jammies, please school is tomorrow, her bike lesson, we'll just practice this week after school."

Sassy, "Yes sir."

Time goes by.

All are at the dinner table.

As they all said grace and ate.

Rea, "So you got school tomorrow?"

Sassy, "Yes ma'am."

Rea, "You scared?"

Sassy, "No ma'am, I love school."

Frank, "That's good because you have a long way to go."

Challis, "And our babies have longer."

Rea, "Mark my word, they are going to be skipped a lot."

Challis, "I don't want that, I want our kids to remain in their proper grades, and really enjoy."

Solace, "With Sassy's birthday," Solace said, "she really should be in pre-kindergarten."

Rea, "Isn't she five?"

Challis, "Yes, but she's a January baby,"

Rea, "What? Did they test her?"

Solace, "Yes."

Rea, "This child can hold her own, the way she hangs with Gigi."

Challis, "That's the truth, but its fine she makes friends."

Solace, "Yes, she does, because most of the pageant girls are blowing up our house phone for Sassy."

Challis, "They can stop, that, it's all on lock. School is in, no chatting, maybe one or two can call, heck, conference call one day on the weekend for an hour, that's it."

Dinner ends, and night falls. Everyone is tired and goes in to sleep. Wee morning comes, Sassy and her dad jog, and then they swim next. Sassy goes bath with one of their nurses, Jasmine, and she ponytails her hair up, while her daddy showers, and puts on business casual. He packs a bag of his construction clothing, and combat boots, and they both come down. Sassy is wearing her burgundy pad suede elbow sleeves, peter pan white collard dress shirt plain, Criss Cross burgundy tie with pearls, and a plaid jumper burgundy thick tights saddle suede, and leather toss led front black and grey ankle boots with big burgundy plaid bows on each side of her three ponytails, with zig zag part. She is wearing her necklace from her mom, and a burgundy gps watch and, dog tags. Her dad puts small strands of pearls around her neck.

Rea, "Don't you look too cute?"

Solace, "Here is your book bag, Gigi made hers with fashion tags plus stickers, and pen with message of love, peace and happiness all over, and pics of her family.

Rea, "Look at that."

Solace, "Gigi made this, I just love the thick suede and leather."

Rea, "The straps got that."

Time goes by, and Challis walks his daughter to the office. Secretary Mrs. Tasha Reiner greets them.

Challis, "This is my daughter, Sapphire, Garnier- Calms-Way."

"Okay."

The secretary said, she gets up.

"I'll show you room 10. And her teacher is Mrs. Hatchway, and this," she grabs a brown envelope, "she says this is her take home package for your dad to fill out, and her room is right around here."

Challis loved the décor of the entire school.

Mrs. Hatchway, "Well, hello."

Secretary Reiner, "This is Miss Sapphire Garnier-Calms-Way."

Mrs. Hatchway, "Okay, dad I'll take her from here."

This is our room, now go sit on your name.

Sassy, "Bye dad."

He says, "See you later."

Sassy, "Yes sir, see you later," and she goes sit on a turquoise square with her name Sapphire.

Hatchway, "At the end of school, Mr. Calms-Way, you can gather her out front on the red star end."

Challis, "Okay, thank you," and he leaves.

On his way to his own classes, he thought, "looking good," as he glanced at the men working on their home and their hotel and some other properties of theirs.

Hours pass and Challis was getting in the swing of purchasing his books and notebooks, he already had brought his nice laptop, and he entered his class, pre-law, and went and sat down. The room was around 50 large.

Time went by, and his parents both swam, Rea and her hubby did too.

Solace, "Let's go pamper."

Rea, "Yes, down in 20 minutes."

And they left. The men went golfing.

Solace, "I'm going earth tones with 613, and brown brows, and facial, nails, and pedicure."

Rea, "I'll do auburn, and dark brown brows, tinted also, nails and pedicure, and facials too."

They get to the salon.

Rea, "Good, no one is in here."

Solace, "Because it's early, but all are really good."

Rea, "Who are you going to?"

Solace, "Felix and Ronald."

Felix, 'Hello Mrs. Calms-Way, what will we be having today?"

Ronald, "Hello, and you."

Solace, "Hey Ronald."

Rea, "Everything."

They each go with their beautician, before they know it, it is noon. Solace, 'You look gorgeous."

Rea, "And you too, that brings out your eyes."

Solace, "We can eat over there, I'm famished." Rea, "you and me both. "The hostess seats them down. Solace, "I made another appointment for next week, I'm upping my game." Rea, "I'll do the same back home." Solace, "I have been thinking, let me and you order over 50 lines of clothing." Rea, "yes, but sexy." Solace, "and I'll enroll in a fashion course." Rea, "I'll take a marketing course; my business degree will come in handy now." Solace, "plus all the early years we worked in the mall back home." Rea, "right." Solace, "but I'm thinking more on online, where we don't have to be so bulged down. This way we can hire, and we can design the line this year, hire our seamstress, and by next two years we will have all we need." Rea, "I am all in, I and Frank talked, we're going to sell our house, and move in with you, and Jamison's building." Solace, "yes, I'll make sure we have an office meeting room, plus work area, and display." Rea, "yes." Challis was thinking to himself, "I really like this course, it's very interesting, and let me put my syllabus in here now." Jessica, "hello, you don't remember me?" Challis, "oh yes, hello." Jessica, "what about coffee for your old friend's sake?" Challis "no, it's good seeing you," and he bounced. Challis, "let me keep my focus, and cut them at the knees," he thinks to himself as he leaves. Mrs. Hatchway, "now, every day when you arrive, we go to where…" She gets interrupted by Kevin Dander, who raised his hand. Mrs. Hatchway, "okay, Kevin. "He answered to the carpet. Mrs. Hatchway, "where our name is? " Correct, now where each desk you are sitting is at, now, where each of your name is, you sit. " Sapphire raised her hand. Mrs. Hatchway, "yes? "Sapphire "I want to do well this year, so may I please move from Taylor? She keeps talking to me." All the kids nod their heads. Mrs. Hatchway, "Taylor is that true?" Taylor ", I just wanted to change places so I could sit by Sassy." Mrs. Hatchway, "who is that?"

Taylor, "Her." Pointing at Sapphire. Mrs. Hatchway, "Sapphire." Sassy, "yes ma'am, my nick name." Mrs. Hatchway, "do you prefer that?" Sassy, "no ma'am, not in school." Mrs. Hatchway, "okay. Now Taylor you need to ask Summer if she would like to switch." Summer, "no ma'am." Mrs. Hatchway, "well there it is, also Taylor you may not talk when I'm talking, understood?" Taylor, "yes ma'am." Mrs. Hatchway, time went by, and it was lunch time. "Now on that note, packers in this line, behind the red line, and payers behind this blue line." Mrs. Hatchway, all the kids except Sapphire did accordingly. "Sapphire." "Ma'am, I do know." "you come with me. The rest go with Mrs. Tovey, the room helper." Mrs. Hatchway and Sapphire goes to the office. Mrs. Hatchway, "hello Mrs. Reiner, we got one without a lunch. Mrs. Reiner, "sit her there, I'll call her. Mrs. Mustier comes in, and says, "Hello." She sees Sassy, and says, "Your lunch. Mrs. Reiner, "Thank you I was just going to call you. Mrs. Hatchway, "come Sapphire. "Sassy takes her lunch, hugs Mrs. Mustier, and then she leaves. Mrs. Reiner, "Now will you be bringing her lunch every day? Mrs. Mustier, "No, but here is a check for her lunch through the year. Mrs. Tasha Reiner takes the check, and says, "If she is a packer, you won't need to."

Mrs. Mustier, "I will decide on that later, but for now, please retain."

Mrs. Tasha Reiner copy's the check, signs it, and gives it to Mrs. Mustier.

Then Mrs. Mustier leaves. Time goes by. Sapphire is having the best time, and she loved her chicken wrap for lunch, and fruit and chocolate milk, and juice on the playground. She is jumping rope, when Kevin and Justine pull her hair. Sassy runs after them along the playground, her second-grade playground monitor.

Mrs. Alayna Sparks stops her, and asks, "what is your name? There will be no running here, you could have hurt yourself, and others." Sassy sees Kevin and Justine laughing, and she said, "they pulled my hair."

Mrs. Alayna, "next time, tell me. What is your name?"

Sassy, "Sapphire."

Mrs. Alayna, "now, come here you two."

The boys walk over to her.

Mrs. Alyana, "I'm Mrs. Alayna Sparks, what is your name?"

Kevin, "Kevin Scott."

Mrs. Alyana, "and yours?"

Justine, "Justine O'Connor."

Mrs. Alayna, "why did you two pull her hair?"

Kevin, "I don't know."

Justine, "I don't either, but she was in our way."

Mrs. Alayna, "for you running, and you all pulling her hair, you go for now, I will tell you when to get off."

They leave. Sapphire is crying. Time goes by, and her dad is waiting in the red star area.

Mrs. Mustier walks up to him.

Challis, "hi, I got her."

Mrs. Mustier, "just checking,"

Challis, "thanks."

Mrs. Mustier, "I brought her lunch today, and paid up for the year."

Challis, "wow, I totally forgot. Thanks, I'll see if she wants to pack or not."

Mrs. Mustier, "okay."

She leaves.

Sassy comes out of her class.

Mrs. Hatchway, "Sapphire has a note with her about today."

Challis, "okay."

Sassy starts crying.

Challis, "hey, Sassy I'm sorry."

Challis picks her up. He takes her bag from her, and she continues crying on her dad's shoulders. He straps her into the car.

Taylor and her parents are passing by and Taylor says, "Sassy was bad today, she had to get on the wall."

Taylor's mom; Brooklyn, "okay, tend to your business."

Taylor's dad; Greg, "yes, we're sorry."

Challis, "it's cool."

They shake hands and leaves.

Challis and Sassy had to stop at the college bookstore for one more book. And after that, on their way driving home.

Challis, "so what happened?"

Sassy cries again, "Kevin and Justine, while I was jumping rope on the play-ground, pulled my hair hard, and I chased them to hit them, and Mrs. Sparks put us all on the wall. Here is my note."

Challis, "keep it till we get home, but stop crying, you are not in trouble."

Sassy, "but I missed recess."

Challis, "you're okay, daddy will handle this, is there anything else?"

Sassy, "I love school, I just don't want nobody pulling my hair, and dad I don't want to sit by Taylor."

Challis, "why not?"

Sassy, "daddy, she talks the whole time. I need to hear my teacher."

Challis, "okay, I'll see what I can do, but I'm glad you like school."

Sassy, "do you like your school?"

Challis, "thanks for asking, and yes I do. But the best part of my day was taking you to school this morning and picking you up."

Sassy, "I like that also, but dad I need to pack my lunch tomorrow."

Challis, "I will handle your lunch, we're cool."

They get home.

Sassy, "dad you're dirty."

Challis, "dad has been working on our house."

Sassy, "you went to school like that?"

Challis, "no."

Sassy, "When can I see our house?"

Challis, "When it's finished, but tomorrow I'll show you our progress."

Sassy, "Will we have a girl's room?"

Challis, "Yes, daddy has to think on that."

Solace, "Dinner is ready in one hour."

Rea, "hey girl, how was your first day?"

Sassy, "I liked it, but I got in trouble."

Rea, "Somebody bothered you?"

Sassy, "Yes ma'am, they pulled my hair."

Rea, "that's one thing about school, bad ass kids."

Challis, "go up, tell your nurse to put you on a jogging suit. We have to practice bike riding."

Sassy, "no training wheels."

Challis, "no training wheels, and let me change also."

And he runs up, Sassy follows him. They check on their family, they both kiss all of them, and then they both leave the room. Twenty minutes pass, and they are outside.

Challis, "okay, I got you, just peddle, and those brakes, use those when you're ready to stop, just peddle."

Sassy, "Dad with my feet like that?"

Challis, "right, okay, peddle, peddle."

Sassy, "daddy don't let go."

Challis, "I'm here, just peddle."

They go around, and around the circle drive for ten minutes as the family looked on out of the window, and the security guys securing the area, and watching.

Sassy, "this is fun."

Challis, "you peddle on your own."

Then he lets go and Sassy is riding on her own. Challis runs closely behind her; she peddles by herself and more by herself.

Challis, "stop."

She does perfectly. Rea and Solace come out.

Rea, "girl you got that bike riding."

Challis, "you went all around by yourself."

Sassy, "I did."

Challis, "one more round."

He helps her climb her bike, then he lets go. Sassy rides and rides till her dad yells.

Challis, "stop."

And she does.

Challis, "okay, I got your bike, go in and tell your nurse to bath you."

In thirty minutes, she comes back with rolled bangs, and twenty big twist up braids in ponytail and baby hair out with light shimmer.

Rea, "that's too cute."

Sassy, "thanks, Nurse Jamia said she is going to be stocking cap, and then tie it up, so that in the morning I don't have to get my hair done for the next two days."

Solace, "I like that, it'll last very pretty."

They all say their grace, and they all eat.

Sassy, "Dad I'm finished, may I listen to my beats, and watch cartoons, and get in bed with my mommy Lady G?"

Challis, "yes."

He gets up, gets her beats. He puts her Spanish beats on her, and says, "Wait, any homework?"

Sassy, "no sir, she said not till next week, but dad you have homework, the papers Mrs. Reiner gave you."

Challis, "right, I got them. I'll do it tonight."

Sassy, "okay," and she leaves. Her dad goes back to eating, his dad and Uncle Frank comes in, they both speak, and then goes to shower and come back to dinner.

Challis reads the note, "Sapphire is on the wall for the next two days, no recess."

"I will be damned."

Solace, "what's wrong?"

Challis, "the world. They have the nerve to put my daughter on the wall for the next two recesses. No."

Solace, "just calm down."

Rea, "that's what they do, punish them all, and they pulled her hair, bad ass brats."

Jamarion Senior, "when you take her to school tomorrow, ask to see the principal."

Rea, "It's not going to make a bit a difference, mark my word, they are going to still punish her, that's those little boys, pulling our hair."

Solace, "yes, remember Heber? You kicked him."

Rea, "I was doing just what our daddy told me, he kept on and on, and then pushed you, that was the last straw, I let him have it."

Solace, "yes, you did."

Rea, "I had to stay in for recess for two weeks."

Solace, "but daddy let his father have it."

Challis, "this is the first day, and she wants to be moved from Taylor."

Solace, "why?"

Challis, "she said she talks the entire time."

Jamarion Senior, "well, you got 18 years times, 5 to go."

Frank, "that's what was so cool about raising sons, they just do their schoolwork, fight, and go on."

Rea, "but we had some stuff to do with Miss. WY Tina, talking about that, Frankie called her a bitch, I knew she was lying, now if she had said David Anthony, then I might have believed her."

Frank, "I ended that, just sent them to military school, game over."

Challis, "I think I prefer our girls to go to an all girl's schools, or home school, because I'm not going to put up with this."

Solace, "this is a remarkable school, it'll get better, just stay involved."

Challis, "I forgot her lunch, but Mrs. Mustier brought it, and paid up her lunch tab."

Solace, "she has to eat every day."

Challis, "mom I know, I'll make her a sub wrap for tomorrow, and veggie chips, fruit chocolate milk, water, and two straws."

Solace, "It's on top of the fridge."

Rea, "Gigi made her a cold hot compartment tag lunch bag." "Nephew! You've being a great dad."

Challis, "thank you, I'm trying."

Solace, "you are."

Challis, "she even has a container for hot and cold stuff? I like this, plus it can hook onto her book bag, good she sewed her name in it. What will we do without Gigi?"

Solace, "Friday is her fashion show." Rea, "where?"

Solace, "somewhere in Manhattan, she decided to have it there, it's been all over the radio and TV."

Rea, "social networks with her advertisements keep flashing up on my phone."

Challis, "let me see, okay, now shots in."

Rea, "she needs her shots."

Solace, "she already has them on file from Chicago medical."

Challis, "okay, good, now I have to find her a doctor here,"

Solace, "call your committee person, Mrs. Mustier, I'm sure they have picked one."

Challis, "let me call her." He dials her number. "Hello Mrs. Mustier, I 'm calling to see if you already have a pediatrician picked out for Sassy."

Mrs. Mustier, "I was going to run it pass you for Sassy and the other children, my sister, PHD. Dr. Jakeiah Price for the girls, and her husband, PHD. Dr. Hamilton Price III for the boys."

Challis, "are they local?"

Mrs. Mustier, "yes, they've been in practice little over 10 years, plus both are International Medical doctors."

Challis, "okay, please forward to my email to them, so I can add Sassy's information, that will be all, and thanks for today. I will pack the rest of the days, if not I'll call you."

Mrs. Mustier, "you're welcome, oh and the dentist is Dr. Ayesha Walls and Barron, her husband."

Challis, "sure." and they hang up

Solace, "who? I might know them."

Challis, "Doctors Hamilton and Jakeiah Price, Mrs. Muster's sister and brother in-law, both are International Medical doctors."

Jamarion Senior, "that's good, they cover all bases,"

Challis pulls up out of his email the information, "Good, their practice is just 4 blocks from the school, and the dentist is in the same building, Dentist Ayesha and Barron Walls, husband and wife. She said the women will do all our girls, and the men will do all our sons."

Rea, "that's good, all the information in one place, plus they are all married, leaves the nonsense out."

Frank, "just as long as they do their jobs."

Challis," I need a pen." Then he goes out.

Solace, "It's in the drawer right there," as he shouted after him.

Midnight falls and morning comes. Challis and Sassy runs, and then they go swimming, when they finished, they go to shower. Sassy baths and dresses up.

Challis prepares her lunch bag, "perfect."

He goes to eat his breakfast. Sassy comes in, washes her hands, and eats.

Solace, "come here." she puts an apron over her, "don't you look cute."

Sassy has on a white pilgrim collar grey corduroy jumper, plaid burgundy, white blazer, burgundy tights and grey suede burgundy belt strap boots to calf.

Rea, "they aren't going to have nothing on Sassy, with a two-tone suede grey burgundy satchel purse."

Frank, "look at you!"

Nurse Jasmine comes down. "HI,"

Challis, "how many uniforms does Sassy have?" \

Nurse Jasmine, "fifty, mixed kinds, they all look like they should be dry cleaned, though they say you can wash them."

Rea, "you better dry clean."

Challis, "yes, there is a shoot I installed for laundry crew for dry cleaning."

Nurse Jasmine, "I saw that, okay, I'll send them down, but I came down because Miss. Calms-way, and all the babies, are running an elevated temperature of 101 degrees steadily." Sassy joins the rest.

Challis, "eat let me go and see."

Nurse Jasmine, "the doctor is 20 minutes out,"

Challis goes into their room; he touches each one. They are all warm.

Challis, "I have to go to class, text me the details!"

Nurse Jasmine, "I will,"

Challis goes back down, "mom are you going to be home today?" He asked his mother.

Solace, "yes, we got to work on some things, I and Rea."

Jamarion Senior, "I'll be here also."

Challis, "okay, come baby, I have to drop her at school, and speak to the principal, and then go to class. I have a test." Solace, "they probably have a little bug."

Sassy runs and grabs her fun fur grey burgundy scarf cape, with her leather gloves.

Challis, "okay, let's do this."

Rea, "that is beautiful, wait, her name needs to be in that."

Solace, "let me see, I thought Gigi sewed it in. Sassy keep up with your stuff!"

Sassy, "yes ma'am."

Rea, "yes, because kids steal, she even put a silk lining in it? That girl is bad!"

Challis and Sassy leaves.

Rea, "I want that cape, it's too cute,"

Solace, "that must be the doctor, Rea, wait."

One of the doctors, "hello, we're Dr. Jakeiah Price and Dr. Hamilton Price, we are here for our patients, the children."

Solace, "you know they are in a sleeping coma."

Dr. Hamilton, "we have been filled in."

Dr. Reynolds, the main doctor comes is.

Solace, "these are now the children's doctors."

Dr. Reynolds, "come, I 've been brought up to speed."

The doctors both go. Gigi comes in she goes and kisses Solace and Rea.

Mama Sugar, "yes, where have you been?"

Gigi, "getting my fashion line together for the show."

Rea, "you know we're starting a fifty-up line."

Solace, "yes,"

Gigi, "that's nice, can I ask for a favor?"

Rea, "what?"

Gigi, "my mommy is dying to start the same thing, could you bring her in?"

"Sure, if she wants to, but I'm taking a fashion course or two," Solace said, "and we are launching in two years."

Rea, "and I'm doing a couple of marketing courses."

Gigi, "great, because my mom just enrolled in a textiles fabric course."

Solace, "at where?"

Gigi, "at the college, it starts next month."

Rea, "we need that,"

Gigi, "you are moving here?"

Rea, "yes."

Gigi, "you all can apply online, just forward or scan your other credentials that has everything to do with education."

Rea and Solace high five each other, "we are doing this girl," as they hugged each other smiling.

Gigi., "what are you doing now? You could go with me."

Rea, "we…,"

Solace interrupts her, "no, the men are here."

The doctors comes in.

Dr. Jakeiah Price, "the girls just have a taste of a cold, they have antibiotic and Ibuprofen, alternating Tylenol, and some has been administered in them, now the nurses will repeat this in 6 hours, no milk but Pedialyte They should be fine."

Dr. Reynolds, "same for their mom."

Dr. Reynolds, "and for boys."

Solace, "okay, thanks."

Jamarion Senior, "hello," they all speak.

Gigi runs, and hugs Big Daddy. She also hugs Frank.

Sugar, "Honey we're leaving with Gigi,"

Jamarion Senior, "I'll be here."

"Let me go see my peeps," Gigi said, and she runs up the steps.

She kisses each one of them, then she comes back down, and they leave.

Gigi, "we're flying to New York."

Rea, "see? That's what I'm talking about."

Solace, "whose plane?"

Solace asked., "Challis. I texted him. He has been letting me use it,"

They wait for her mother, Constance, to meet them there. Before they know it, they are all in Manhattan Museum of arts.

Rea, "this is gorgeous."

Constance affirms, "yes, it is."

Challis is waiting in the office for the Principal, the assistant principal, Coby Parcel comes in," I can see you now!"

They go into her office, "have a seat!"

Challis, "my daughter is Sapphire Garnier- Calms-way, and I do not feel that my daughter should have her recess taken away twice."

Principal Coby, "because Kevin and Justine choose to pull her hair. I have been brought up to speed, and this time, I will over ride Sapphire's punishment solely because the boys pulled another little girls hair, so I realize that they are the coo berate, but please let Sapphire be aware that there are teacher's attendees that are out to assist her. No running. I will pull Sapphire before recess aside to explain no running to her."

Challis, "okay thank you."

They shake hands and he leaves. Time went by, and assistant principal Cody pulled Sapphire aside,

She is like, "hello Sapphire."

Sassy, "hi."

Principal Coby, "your recesses, you have it back, but no running, if someone does something to you, tell one of the teachers on the playground."

Sassy, "yes ma'am."

Principal Cody, "come on, so I can tell the teachers on the playground that you get to play."

They go. Teachers are notified, and Sapphire chooses to play tether ball with summer. She is good at it. Kevin and Justine are on the wall, the reason why they team up so much is because their fathers are brothers, and they are first cousins.

Gigi, "now all my staff is already here."

Solace, "are the chairs set and runway set for you?"

Gigi, "yes ma'am."

Solace, "how did you get it so fast?"

Gigi, "my mommy."

Constance explained, "the person that runs the museum is my husband's cousin,"

Rea, "well, that's nice."

Solace, "all your invites are out?"

Gigi, "yes ma'am,"

Gigi, "I did all online through a Local ticket organization, and it's much better, only my VIP's receive paper invitations, such as you all. I will give you all, but there will be a list that people must be on prior to entering, because it's full. I also had to hire several cops to secure the area."

Rea, "you need that!"

Gigi, "each set of models will come out by lighted coloring; I also had all these made to surround the outer back corridor."

Solace asked, "who drew those?"

Gigi, "students from my Fashion College, their names are listed on each."

Constance, "the floors have all been done I see they gloss."

Gigi, "yes, they did them last night."

Challis, "oh, here she comes again."

Jessica, "well, hello."

Challis, "hello," and he sprints off. "Give it a rest," he thought to himself as he left.

Jessica, "one day he'll come around," then she thought, "maybe he is gone, yell, probably we'll."

Jessica greets Ace, "hello!"

Ace, "hello baby, how you are doing?"

Jessica, "fine now, you are going to class?"

Ace, "yes, let's go together."

He takes her hand.

Rea, "wow, you got so much, and it's all so gorgeous."

Solace, "this is a store, all this stuff, and color coded."

"I have so much, because the same day feature each will receive a fashion magazine, which will really be in an order form, they can log on to it, and purchase for the next 3 weeks, till all customer service, and shipping will operate from here."

Rea, "you got all this down."

Gigi, "mommy helped, thanks."

They all hugged Lynn, "oh Lynn, you made it!"

Rea, "hello to all, customer service is already set up, just the body's show night, working the phones in 3 shifts for the three weeks, and weekends, as well as I have all the employees list I sent you for the Virginia base field office, and call center."

Gigi, "I received it, managers."

Lynn, "two per shift, and one head and Tonya's general called me."

They all walk around.

Constance said, "you're going to be fine."

Gigi smiles and hugs her mom. Couple hours pass, the ladies are out for lunch. Challis remembers that he forgot to switch Sassy's seat. He sits, and between classes, he calls the school and asks for Mrs. Hatchway.

Mrs. Reiner, "I can give her a message, oh hold on, Mrs. Hatchway, telephone parent, on line one."

Mrs. Hatchway, "hello!"

Challis, "Hello, Taylor Tanner is talking so much, and it is bothering Sapphire."

Mrs. Hatchway, "I will give it the rest of the week, if that is alright, and then I will."

Challis, "okay."

Mrs. Hatchway, "because we are getting into our work next week, and she will not have time to breathe, let alone talk, I know she is chattering a lot, most of them, except your Sapphire, she is so attentive, I've heard."

Challis, "okay, thanks."

They hang up.

Jamarion Senior, "how are they doing?"

Nurse Jamia, "their fevers are down."

Jamarion Senior, "very good."

Nurse Jamia goes back up the stairs.

Chef Craig, "would you gentlemen like some lunch?"

Jamarion Senior, "yes, steak burgers, cool."

Frank, "yes."

Chef Craig, "well done."

Both men, "yes."

Chef Craig, "French Fries, salad."

Both say fine, and ranch dressing. They go to the back of the house to bowl. Some hours go by, and Challis is now picking his daughter up from school. He is in the red star spot waiting for her. Sapphire comes out of her class in a few minutes.

Challis, "how did your day go?" As they were walking to his car.

Sassy, "fun."

Challis, "good, what did you do today in school?"

Sapphire, "we colored a lot, and our teacher read us a story. We also did a real fun math game, and spelling game, which look," she shows both her gold stickers to Challis.

He sees one for math champion and spelling champion.

Then he turns to the corner, "wonderful."

He parks straight down.

Sassy, "where are we?"

Challis, "our house."

He gets Sapphire out, and they both walk down the rock path.

Sassy, "I love all these huge trees, it feels like Jesus to me."

Challis, "yes," amused.

Sassy begged, "wow, horses, water, pick me up dad, please, so I can see the horses better." Challis lifts her up.

Sassy, "Is that an open range?"

Challis, "yes, and we own them as you can see."

Sassy, "how is an open range? My mommy told me that it means horses are wild and free." Challis, "They are, but the dirt under their hoofs belong to us."

Sassy, "oh wow! Our house is going to be that big?"

Challis, "yes, but comfy."

She yawns and falls to sleep.

Challis, "party pooper."

He takes her back to the car and he zooms off. They get home; Challis gets her book bag and picks her up. He goes into the house. The women are back.

Challis, "she only needs to sleep an hour, she has to go to bed early, you up?"

Sassy, "daddy, I'm thirsty."

Solace, "hi."

Sassy, "hi mama Sugar."

Solace, "come here, so you can get some water."

Challis gives her to his mom and goes upstairs to see how his family is doing.

Nurse Kimmie, "their fevers are down."

Challis, "good, no problem all day?"

Nurse Kimmie, "no, I just came in; the reports are on their usual."

Challis gets the report and reads it. It sounds well to him, he reads the doctor's messages again, and he is pleased.

He kisses his family, "thank you Lord," and goes to shower.

Sassy comes up to change.

Nurse Kimmie, "come on Miss. Sassy."

Sassy does, before they know it, they are both back downstairs and changed. Solace has also changed too. Rea and Gigi comes out. Sassy runs and almost knocks Gigi down.

Sassy, "I missed you."

Gigi, "I missed you more, and I'm sorry I was swamped."

Sassy, "I love my school."

Gigi, "Good," and puts her down.

"Dinner is done," Chef Craig said.

The doorbell rings,

Security, "Taylor Tanner."

Sassy runs, "dad we just got home."

Challis, "hold on Taylor, through the week, she cannot have company."

"But what about her helping me with our spelling list for tomorrow's game?"

Sapphire, "I don't want to,"

Taylor, "my parents then."

"Brooklyn Tanner," the security announced.

Brooklyn, "Taylor come, I'm sorry."

Taylor, "mommy please,"

"No," Brooklyn said, she picks her up and says,

"I'll help you, let Sassy be." And she says sorry again, Challis and his family says, "no problem."

An hour pass and they were all eating Prime Rib mash potato, cream peas, and rolls. Sassy ate very well because she liked her food. Gigi was munching also.

Rea, "so do you like Taylor at all?"

Sassy, "no ma'am."

Solace, "I can't blame her."

Gigi, "she is too pushy."

Sassy, "yes."

Solace, "I hope she changes as she gets older, but truly I don't think that's possible, and really I'm fine with how my baby girl feels."

Sassy, "excuse me, I'm finished," standing up.

Challis, "okay, your tutorial cartoons."

Gigi, "can she sew a little? I brought her sewing machine."

Challis, "okay, so after your tutorial, go with Gigi."

Sassy, "yes sir."

She leaves.

Gigi, "let me go as well and set up for her."

Challis, "I have been around a lot of women and most start out just like Taylor and they turn into aggressive women that hurt people along the way."

Rea, "tell me about it, remember Peppermint?"

Solace, "do I ever forget? She was the worst."

Jamarion Senior, "bowling my brother."

Frank, "yes,"

Challis, "what did Peppermint Pattie do?"

Rea, "screwed almost every guy that liked me in high school, I beat her tail, not because of the guys in high school, but because she was my best friend all through kindergarten up."

Solace, "I never liked the goose's neck heifer."

Rea, "I knew that summer before kindergarten, that she was no good, and that she going to lie on me. Mama tore me up."

Solace, "I told you."

Challis, "what happened?"

Solace, "Her ball came in our window, I went out to give it back to her."

Challis, "why didn't you throw it back?"

Rea, "Because of our mama, and her freshly starched and pressed curtains, no, plus I went out to tell her to stop playing by our windows, and she said, 'play with me,' I said no, so she bounce the ball to me, I told her to stop, she did it again, after it hit the mud, I moved and it went into our mama's window, dirtied up our curtains, our carpet and she ran. I tried to tell but mama saw my hands and the rest is history. I say this to every new parent, let your children plead their cases."

Challis, "will do."

Solace, "I never knew why."

Rea, "I felt sorry for her, she was the baby girl with all those older siblings, the sway back whore."

Challis, "That is maybe not the sleeping part but everything else that is Taylor."

Solace, "you see her mother had to come over here to get her."

Rea, "she is too much."

Solace, "just like the pageant, she lost and then made a scene."

Challis, "Sassy felt sorry for her, I was so glad her mother said she could not keep her deserved crown, and I told her teacher she is talking up a storm."

Rea, "In class?"

Challis, "yes, Sassy wants to be moved from her."

Solace, "what did the teacher say?"

Challis, "she said she would decide in a week, I said okay. She thinks she'll stop once their workload next week picks up."

Rea, "If she is talking now, she is still going to be talking, Sassy will have to cut her off right now, ooh you know what, sister."

Solace, "what?" As she eats pie.

Rea, "let us while we are doing all our other stuff write some kids books about this stuff."

Solace, "It would sell because my granddaughter is not going to get tangled up with her, I'm so glad you're moving downtown."

Rea, "watch when you move, watch them move downtown, where all the action is."

Solace, "well we are going to be like sealed lips."

Rea, "she is a just sneak into the office and find out, Lord Jesus help talking about this child, Lord."

Challis, "no, God help my daughter, let me go do my own homework, mom, what kind of pie is that?"

Solace, "It's 4 different ones in the kitchen, this is mixed berry."

Challis, "I want that," He goes to the kitchen.

Rea, "bring me a piece, and one scoop of vanilla ice cream."

Challis does and grabs his satchel bag and goes upstairs.

The security announced, "the black caucus is here,"

Solace, "put them in the living room."

Rea, "what do they want?"

Solace, "let's go see in our Moo Moo's."

"well, hello, hello," they both greeted.

second family Maxine Waters, "hello sisters."

They all hug.

Rea, "Sit," Rea said to them.

Maxine Waters, "Well we are all here, because you have downtown on lock, and next year we want to have one of our main offices in your store front buildings,"

Solace, "yes, yes."

Elijah, "and what about us having a huge party for our Virginia Candace launch in your ball room?"

Solace, "of course, I'll run all by my husband."

Jamarion Senior, "you will run what?" as he walked in, "hey." All the Black Caucus gets up, all the men shake hands, and the ladies hugged Jamarion Senior and Frank.

Elijah, "we want to use your store front establishment, and ball room next year, we wish to lease."

Jamarion Senior, "sure,"

Solace, "okay."

CHAPTER 27

Fashion show

A month pass by, and it is the day of Gigi's fashion show and all her second family is in attendance, and her family, with her mother, her brothers, and stepdad, the Governor is all in attendance. Out comes Ombre, Ombre is a transgender man whom is known all over the World, because of his personality.

Ombre, "well loves, thank you, thank you loves, sit, sit, we have a fascinating evening tonight."

Someone yells from the crowd, "WE LOVE YOU OMBRE!"

Ombre, "I love you all, thank you baby, but tonight, are you ready?"

The crowd, "yes!"

The music really gets banging, out comes the first tall attractive beautiful bald head dark model, wearing a lemon yellow long chiffon wrap around with lots of jewelry, with long collar dress with splits a floral embroidered wool blazer, with paunchy 4 inch suede orange stilettos working the walk with much pazzass.

Rea, "that is bad."

Next a gorgeous Indian woman with a half-tattooed face, and sea blue suede pants, and silky halter top, with a 10 colored suede silk jacket, with red toe out 4-inch boots. She is strutting as she makes the runway.

Solace, "oh yeah, that's talking."

Then out a white woman, with hot pants, bust v to the navel, out cross 5-inch suede heels, with ribbons, as she cascades in true form down the runway.

Constance, "you go my toasty baby."

The fashion show went on and on, one bad outfit after the other and then, finally brides of palms model, white lace wedding gown with purple stilettos, bold silk knickers, with Sassy sporting Minnie me, bring all working the runway is their slave and out comes breath of air, Gigi wearing a full body con red turtle neck suede back out to the but long dress high front with high water suede stilettos jeweled out with, Maxie with 2 bull mastiffs jet black dogs, with huge diamond collars, a red to bone high water tux no socks suede red shoes.

There is a standing ovation.

Challis, "she got down."

Jamarion Senior, "yes she did."

Mike, "five stars."

Cindy, "she's going all the way."

Jamarion II and Karen, "yes,"

Frank, "just sensational."

Constance, "let me go see."

She cries and hugs her husband and hugs Solace too.

Solace, "she did it."

Oval, "excuse me, Gigi has requested for both of her families, please come."

They all follow her.

Karen, "so lovely."

Constance is already back there hugging her daughter.

Sassy runs to them,

Sassy, "daddy, daddy, did you see me?"

Challis picks her up, "yes," and kisses her on the cheek, he hugs her tight.

Mike, "come here," and takes her from her dad.

Sassy, "hi Uncle Mike."

He tickles her and she laughs.

Jamarion Senior, "look at you, Sassy,"

Sassy, "hi, my Pappi."

Frank, "Our new movie star."

Sassy, "hi Uncle Frank."

Jamarion II, "She is getting too big for me."

"Pure doll baby," Cindy said.

Sassy, "hi Auntie Cindy."

Cindy, "hi, you were so awesome."

Sassy, "thank you."

All screams, "Yeah!"

For Gigi, Gigi cries a little bit. Maxie hugs her tight.

Constance, "my baby is just so on the top."

Gigi, "thank you mommy," and they hugged.

Constance, "I am to the moon over you."

Solace, "Come here, just gorgeous simply."

Days go by, but night has set.

Challis, "come Sassy,"

Sassy, "yes sir."

They go up and get on their knees and say their prayers. Matthew 6:9–13 (ESV) "**Pray** then like this: 'Our Father in heaven, hallowed be your name. Your kingdom come, your will be done, on earth as it is in heaven. Give us this day our daily bread, and forgive us our debts, as we also have forgiven our debtors. And lead us not into temptation but deliver us from evil." bless our family in Jesus' mighty name, amen." Then Challis goes sits in his big chair. Sassy gets in bed with her Lady G and Challis begins to read his bible out loud, Sassy's ears are keen, but he knows in a few she will be asleep. "**1 Corinthians 13:1-8**[1]If I speak in the tongues of men or of angels, but do not have love, I am only a resounding gong or a clanging cymbal. [2]If I have the gift of prophecy and can fathom all mysteries and all knowledge, and if I have a faith that can move mountains, but do not have love, I am nothing. [3]If I give all I possess to the poor and give over my body to hardship that I may boast, but do not have love, I gain nothing." Solace as she makes her way upstairs, she hears Challis reading, and is very pleased, she stops and sits in a rocker in the hallway, and listens."⁴Love is patient, love is kind. It does not envy, it does not boast, it is not proud. ⁵It does not dishonor others, it is not self-seeking, it is not easily angered, it keeps no record of wrongs. ⁶Love does not delight in evil but rejoices with the truth. ⁷It always protects, always trusts, always hopes, always perseveres. ⁸Love never fails. But where there are prophecies, they will cease; where there are tongues, they will be stilled; where there is knowledge, it will pass away.1 Corinthians 9:29²³And this I do for the gospel's sake, that I might be partaker thereof with *you*. ²⁴Know ye not that they which run in a race run all, but one receiveth the prize? So run, that ye may obtain. ²⁵And every man that striveth for the mastery is temperate in all things. Now they *do it* to obtain a corruptible crown; but we an incorruptible. ²⁶**I therefore so run, not as uncertainly; so fight I, not as one that beateth the air:**²⁷But I keep under my body, and bring *it* into subjection: lest that by any means, when I have preached to others, I myself should be a castaway. Am I not an apostle? Am I not free? Have I not seen Jesus Christ our Lord? Are not ye my work in the Lord?

1Corinthians Chapter 9: 2 If I be not an apostle unto others, yet doubtless I am to you: for the seal of mine apostleship are ye in the Lord.

3 Mine answer to them that do examine me is this,

4 Have we not power to eat and to drink?

5 Have we not power to lead about a sister, a wife, as well as other apostles, and *as* the brethren of the Lord, and Cephas?

6 Or I only and Barnabas, have not we power to forbear working?

7 Who goeth a warfare any time at his own charges? Who planteth a vineyard, and eateth not of the fruit thereof? Or who feedeth a flock, and eateth not of the milk of the flock?

8 Say I these things as a man? Or saith not the law the same also?

9 For it is written in the Law of Moses, Thou shalt not muzzle the mouth of the ox that treadeth out the corn. Doth God take care for oxen?

10 Or saith he *it* altogether for our sakes? For our sakes, no doubt, *this* is written: that he that ploweth should plow in hope; and that he that thresheth in hope should be partaker of his hope.

11 If we have sown unto you spiritual things, *is it* a great thing if we shall reap your carnal things?

12 If others be partakers of *this* power over you, *are* not we rather? Nevertheless we have not used this power; but suffer all things, lest we should hinder the gospel of Christ.

13 Do ye not know that they which minister about holy things live *of the things* of the temple? And they which wait at the altar are partakers with the altar?

14 Even so hath the Lord ordained that they which preach the gospel should live of the gospel.

15 But I have used none of these things: neither have I written these things; that it should be so done unto me: for *it were* better for me to die, than that any man should make my glorying void.

16 For though I preach the gospel, I have nothing to glory of: for necessity is laid upon me; yea, woe is unto me, if I preach not the gospel!

17 For if I do this thing willingly, I have a reward: but if against my will, a dispensation *of the gospel* is committed unto me.

18 What is my reward then? *Verily* that, when I preach the gospel, I may make the gospel of Christ without charge, that I abuse not my power in the gospel.

19 For though I be free from all *men*, yet have I made myself servant unto all, that I might gain the more.

20 And unto the Jews I became as a Jew, that I might gain the Jews; to them that are under the law, as under the law, that I might gain them that are under the law;

21 To them that are without law, as without law, (being not without law to God, but under the law to Christ,) that I might gain them that are without law.

22 To the weak became I as weak, that I might gain the weak: I am made all things to all *men*, that I might by all means save some.

23 And this I do for the gospel's sake, that I might be partaker thereof with *you*.

24 Know ye not that they which run in a race run all, but one receiveth the prize? So run, that ye may obtain.

25 And every man that striveth for the mastery is temperate in all things. Now they *do it* to obtain a corruptible crown; but we are incorruptible.

26 I therefore so run, not as uncertainly; so fight I, not as one that beateth the air:

27 But I keep under my body, and bring *it* into subjection: lest that by any means, when I have preached to others, I myself should be a castaway."

Challis, "Amen, thank you God; sleep let me put you baby girl in your bed."

As Challis was getting into his room, his mother tip toed to her and her husband's room, she did not even see her husband come to bed, and yes, he was knocked out. She went and showered quickly, then dried, oiled, applied deodorant perfume, and wears her silky nightwear, she says her prayers, and she goes to bed.

CHAPTER 28

Challis Seeks God

Time pass and morning slowly came in. Challis wakes and says 1 Corinthians 9: 24 Know ye not that they which run in a race run all, but one receiveth the prize? So run, that ye may obtain.

25 And every man that striveth for the mastery is temperate in all things. Now they *do it* to obtain a corruptible crown; but we an incorruptible.

26 I therefore so run, not as uncertainly; so fight I, not as one that beateth the air:

27 But I keep under my body, and bring *it* into subjection: lest that by any means, when I have preached to others, I myself should be a castaway

In compliment, "thank you Jesus for watching over us through the night and keep us safe today forever more thank you."

Then he kisses his sleeping wife and all his children, he then takes his shower. There is a full walk in closet in the bathroom, of all his stuff with mirrors galore. He dresses fully and comes out. Sassy is now fully bathed and dressed, her dad smiles.

Sassy, "good morning daddy."

Challis, "morning."

And they go join their family for breakfast.

Sassy, "today is show and tell."

Challis, "why are you just telling me?"

Sassy, "Mrs. Mustier had my puppeteer ensemble, and when she came to my school, and peeped in my class, she asked to speak to me. Just on how school is going. And she said that she was picking up my puppeteer from being fixed, she said it broke in the move, but I told her no ma'am it had been broken, so I asked her if she could bring it to me today, and she said yes, and she would take it back and drop it off."

Challis, "okay good, because I have a test today, you finished?"

"Almost," Sassy said.

"Let me drop her, you go on," Sugar said.

"Okay," Challis said, "but I will pick you up."

"Yes sir," Sassy replied.

"This French toast is good, Chef Juan," Challis said.

The chef says thank you, and Challis leaves.

"While you finish that, let me go," Sugar said, she goes in, after some minutes she is back fully dressed as her sister is.

"My stomach, I 'll just have a pop," Rea said.

She goes and gets it.

" Where you are going?" she asked Sugar.

"To drop Sassy at school, and then to our spa appointment," Sugar replied.

"Oh okay, I'm still going," Rea said.

"Here is an acid blocker," Sugar said to Rea. Rea takes it.

"Where is Frank?" Jamarion Senior asked.

"Right here," Frank replied.

"You ready?" Jamarion Senior asked him.

"Yes," Frank replied.

"Oh, I forgot fishing," Sugar said.

"Yeah," Rea said.

They all get ready to leave, and Gigi comes in, she hugs all of them.

"I have work to do," Gigi said.

"You here all day?" Sugar asked.

"Yes, till tonight. I got to fly out to the Hamptons," Gigi replied.

"Who is going with you?" Sugar asked.

"My mom and Lynn," Gigi replied.

"That's good," Rea remarked.

They all leave. Gigi runs upstairs, and hugs, and kisses her sleeping loves.

"Okay, let me park here," Challis said. He gets out and he see's Bishop Connors.

"Well, hello," he greeted.

"Hey, hello, off to class?" Bishop Connors asked.

Challis goes to him and shakes his hand, "Yes sir," he replied.

"Right over here," Professor Daniels said.

"One second," Bishop Connors said, "Challis will you be able on tomorrow evening 6pm to teach a session on riches is not what all it looks like?"

"Definitely, how long?" Challis asked.

"No more than thirty minutes per person," Bishop Connors said.

"Okay, I will be there," Challis said.

"Also, have you been seeing a red caravan around the school when you pick up Sassy?" Bishop Connors asked him.

"No sir, why?" Challis asked.

"Because the police thinks he snatched a lady Professor from here, name is Charlotte Hathaway, that has a daughter that is also missing from your daughter's school," Bishop Connors said.

Challis looks at his time. He startled and says, "Wow, I'll be praying for their return, but I'm sorry, I have to go to my first test."

"Don't let me keep you," Bishop Connors said.

Challis runs off. "God protect my family and daughter," he prayed as he ran.

"Okay, hello," Sugar said.

Lady Teacher Mrs. Rhonda Ephrata turns to look at them, and says, "Hello. "She opens the door.

"Hello Mrs. Ephrata," Sassy said.

"Hello, and don't you look amazing today," Mrs. Ephrata said.

Sassy goes to her line. Sugar and Rea pull off a little way but stop and watch as Sassy's class goes to enter the building, when Sassy is in Sugar and Rea look both ways and pull off. Rea turns on the radio.

The commentator was saying, "Professor Charlotte Hathaway, and her 6-year-old daughter, Chelsey, that attends the Montessori extension primary school, witnesses saw the kidnappers jump out of a red caravan License plate number S132TZ. If you know or remember anything, contact your local police special number at 1800-463-4775."

"People are going straight to hell," Rea said.

"We need guns, I have made a wrong turn," Sugar said, "I didn't know this service road went in this circle."

"I never been down here, and yes we do," Rea said, "I got me look some of this mace on my key chain."

"Damn, they almost ran us over," Sugar said.

"People are so much in a rush," Rea said.

"Wait, look, isn't that the license plate?" Solace said.

"My glasses, I got it written down," Rea said, "let me see, okay, ZT071."

"That's them, the only red caravan I ever seen," Solace said, "Call 911."

"No wait just follows it around, and see where they go," Rea said.

"I don't know this way," Solace said.

"Just keep on, stop, look," Rea said.

They pulled into a business garage, and then two Iranian men come out in dress suites.

"They're looking this way, go," Rea said.

Solace pulls forward and goes straight, and turns, and just drives. The road takes them back to town.

"I'm glad these windows are tinted," Solace said.

"They couldn't see us; you think we should still call the police?" Rea asked.

"Yes, that building was 1010 East Shrine Road," Solace said.

They call the police and leave a tip. Then they go on to the spa.

"Those two bitches in Persian," Sama said.

"I got theirپلاکماشینقنلهی *license plate number,"* Osama said.

The men get into a Mercedes with tinted windows and goes out looking for them.

"I think we need to go home with security," Rea said.

"Just to make you feel better, I will call someone," Solace said.

Sometime goes by, security has arrived. Soma and Osama have spotted Solace's car, they go to the valet guy,

"Excuse me, please I see my wife's car, I keep calling her. Did she go in here?" Sama asked the valet.

"Sir, what car?" the valet asked.

"Oh sorry, the Bentley with Solace license plates," Sama said.

"Oh, they went in the spa right there," the valet said.

"Thank you," Sama said.

They left. Finally, all done. "Pretty are you about to finish?" Rea asked.

"My manipedi is dry now, let me slip on my shoes," Solace said, "Who is paging me?"

"Wait," Security Bose said to her.

"Ma'am is that them? Security Crush asked.

"Yes," Solace replied.

"Okay, cool, call the police," Security Dobbins said, "stay with Bose, and let us do our job."

Crush goes outward, and around, and then Dobbins flacks left of center.

"Lord Jesus, this is too much," Rea said.

"Just stay here," Crush said.

"Move and I'll put 2 in both your skulls," Crush said.

"And I'll light two in your ass, move," Dobbins said.

Crush checks them and takes each one's gun and says, "sit the fuck down."

The police has arrived.

"Put the guns down," the officer said.

"Those two were following us, and they have a red caravan parked at 1010 East Shrine," Solace said, "I believe it's the kidnappers van."

"Take them," Officer Delamare ordered.

The other 4 cops arrest Soma and Osama, "What's the charge?"

"You have the *right* to remain silent. Anything you say can and will be used against you in a court of law," Officer Fritto said, as they led them out, "You have the *right* to an attorney. If you cannot afford an attorney, one will be provided for you." "Can you and…," Officer Delamare said, and gets interrupted by Rea, "I'm here."

"My sister," Solace said.

"She was with me," Rea confirmed.

"Okay, can you both come down to the station?" Officer Delamare said to them.

Some time goes by.

"You two busted this kidnapping case wide open," Detective Malbury said.

"I knew it," Solace said.

"Me too," Rea said, "they looked guilty."

Some more time goes by and in comes their family, as well as the Professor and her daughter, whom have been rescued. They were gagged in the back of the caravan.

"I don't know what you were thinking," Frank said to them on their way home.

"We weren't thinking," Rea said.

" Look at the good side, the Lord was in this, yes he was," Solace said.

"It's about to be Halloween," Challis said, "I don't even know if my daughter will be participating."

"You have an entire month," Solace said to him.

A day passes, and its Challis night to speak with the young men and men of all ages, plus his brothers, father and uncle are in attendance.

"Just sit back, and listen to the billionaire businessman, producer, novelist, son, father, widower and married," Bishop Connors said, everyone claps.

Challis comes up, "Good evening Men of Valor,"

Challis said, "everyone, in your bibles, smart phones, tablets turn to it, and read with me in Luke 18:27," he waits for them to find it, "when you all have it say amen." Majority says amen and he reads, "That Jesus, referring to salvation, told those who questioned him that what is impossible for man is possible with God. … But what is impossible for man is made possible with God. <u>Ephesians 6:11 Put on the full armor of God, so that you …</u>

Put on the whole armor of God, that ye may stand against the wiles of the devil. Webster's Bible Translation: Put on the whole armor of God, that ye may be able to stand against the wiles of the devil. Weymouth New Testament Put on the complete armor of God, to be able to stand firm against all the stratagems of the Devil Challis I have not always lived a life of God

Order my steps in thy word: and let not any iniquity have dominion over me. Deliver me from the oppression of man: so will I keep thy precepts. Make.

Challis, I want to talk about "The iniquity of dominion that transcends within each one of us when we're not living a life of God" Dominion 1. sovereignty; control. "man's attempt to establish **dominion over** nature"

synonyms: supremacy, ascendancy, dominance, domination, superiority, predominance, preeminence, hegemony, authority, mastery, control, command, power, sway, rule, government, jurisdiction, sovereignty,

Death the action or fact of dying or being killed; the end of the life of a person or organism.

"I don't believe in life after death"

synonyms: demise, dying, end, passing, loss of life;

Death and Dominion go right hand in hand with Sin, the wrong kind of living. I'm not going to try to downplay my past life, it was truly the worst life ever, regardless if I was, and I'm still a Billionaire if I had to work every-day for a life. But in God every day and have my children all healthy, to marry a woman of God's very own hem, that I love with all my heart is way more valuable to me than mere money. Yes, it cost to live a life of God, but it's worth every living notion now I'm not going to say that life does not get me, but I realize that every transgression that my previous wife did, no matter how foul my hand was the cause, and in it all. At first, I blamed my wife for all the discourse I allowed her to do, and I gave her the stamp of silent approve. Let's read, turn to Genesis 3." They all do. "Genesis 3 King James Version (KJV),

3 Now the serpent was more subtle than any beast of the field which the LORD God had made. And he said unto the woman, Yea, hath God said, Ye shall not eat of every tree of the garden?

² And the woman said unto the serpent, We may eat of the fruit of the trees of the garden:

³ But of the fruit of the tree, which is in the midst of the garden, God hath said, Ye shall not eat of it, neither shall ye touch it, lest ye die.

⁴ And the serpent said unto the woman, Ye shall not surely die:

⁵ For God doth know that in the day ye eat thereof, then your eyes shall be opened, and ye shall be as gods, knowing good and evil.

⁶ And when the woman saw that the tree was good for food, and that it was pleasant to the eyes, and a tree to be desired to make one wise, she took of the fruit thereof, and did eat, and gave also unto her husband with her; and he did eat.

⁷ And the eyes of them both were opened, and they knew that they were naked; and they sewed fig leaves together, and made themselves aprons.

⁸ And they heard the voice of the Lord God walking in the garden in the cool of the day: and Adam and his wife hid themselves from the presence of the Lord God amongst the trees of the garden.

⁹ And the Lord God called unto Adam, and said unto him, Where art thou?

¹⁰ And he said, I heard thy voice in the garden, and I was afraid, because I was naked; and I hid myself.

¹¹ And he said, Who told thee that thou wast naked? Hast thou eaten of the tree, whereof I commanded thee that thou shouldest not eat?

¹² And the man said, The woman whom thou gavest to be with me, she gave me of the tree, and I did eat.

¹³ And the Lord God said unto the woman, What is this that thou hast done? And the woman said, The serpent beguiled me, and I did eat.

¹⁴ And the Lord God said unto the serpent, Because thou hast done this, thou art cursed above all cattle, and above every beast of the field; upon thy belly shalt thou go, and dust shalt thou eat all the days of thy life:

¹⁵ And I will put enmity between thee and the woman, and between thy seed and her seed; it shall bruise thy head, and thou shalt bruise his heel.

¹⁶ Unto the woman he said, I will greatly multiply thy sorrow and thy conception; in sorrow thou shalt bring forth children; and thy desire shall be to thy husband, and he shall rule over thee.

¹⁷ And unto Adam he said, because thou hast hearkened unto the voice of thy wife, and hast eaten of the tree, of which I commanded thee, saying, Thou shalt not eat of it: cursed is the ground for thy sake; in sorrow shalt thou eat of it all the days of thy life;

¹⁸ Thorns also and thistles shall it bring forth to thee; and thou shalt eat the herb of the field;

¹⁹ In the sweat of thy face shalt thou eat bread, till thou return unto the ground; for out of it was thou taken: for dust thou art, and unto dust shalt thou return.

²⁰ And Adam called his wife's name Eve; because she was the mother of all living.

²¹ Unto Adam also and to his wife did the Lord God make coats of skins, and clothed them.

²² And the Lord God said, Behold, the man is become as one of us, to know good and evil: and now, lest he put forth his hand, and take also of the tree of life, and eat, and live forever:

²³ Therefore the Lord God sent him forth from the garden of Eden, to till the ground from whence he was taken.

²⁴ So he drove out the man; and he placed at the east of the garden of Eden Cherubims, and a flaming sword which turned every way, to keep the way of the tree of life.

See just like Adam aloud Eve, I too, became the tail, and at the end of day it was all my fault that on my birthday, my wife brought me a gift to bed. Yes, she brought 3 more, 4 more, faked her death to me, because I never desired to take control. I always thought that I was in control, but I wasn't, because I was not in God. See [Psalm 1:1-6ESV](),

Blessed is the man who walks not in the counsel of the wicked, nor stands in the way of sinners, nor sits in the seat of scoffers; but his delight is in the law of the Lord, and on his law he meditates day and night. He is like a tree planted by streams of water that yields its fruit in its season, and its leaf does not wither. In all that he does, he prospers. The wicked are not so, but are like chaff that the wind drives away. Therefore, the wicked will not stand in the judgment, nor sinners in the congregation of the righteous;

See I was walking in the counsel of the wicked, a wicked man with no regard to the Lord, just not even nothing. I was just feeling as if I was on top of the world, but I tell you all this day that I wasn't. I have 3 daughters, and the worst thing I have to do is tell my daughters about the man I was before, you all tell them the worst, I already had a trail run with my oldest daughter. She confronted me about her mother, not my sleeping fiancé, but the kicker, my sleeping fiancé will wake on Christmas. Glory to her God, daughter, my daughter, she'll awake to know that I was the cause that got my daughter's mother killed. My daughter's mother, she would not give it up as to where our daughter was, and at the time, my wife that died from her hand to her lover played a vicious part of killing my daughter's mother. See this is all so devastating to you all, but take living it day to day, it's all so messed up, I would not even have our daughter if she had not been killed. She never told me about her. Couple of days ago, my 4-year-old daughter cornered me, and she just told me, 'you're her husband,' she was so scared of me, but I told her the truth. Talked her down to where she could finally know I was not going to hurt her, finally she was able to come to me. She lives with me, being raised by me, I say all this to say that fame, money, ain't nothing compared to living a life for Jesus. It's the Salvation of Christ, the reason I stand here now, it's no way easy, but it's getting so much better to stay in there. Let's read, 1 Corinthians 9:24-27 [24]Do you not know that in a race all the runners run, but only one gets the prize? Run in such a way as to get the prize. [25]Everyone who competes in the games goes into strict training. They do it to get a crown that will not last, but we do it to get a crown that will last forever. [26]Therefore I do not run like someone running aimlessly; I do not fight like a boxer beating the air. [27]No, I strike a blow to my body and make it my slave so that after I have preached to others, I myself will not be disqualified for the prize.

In life, mistakes are made but in God we can start over fresh. In the Society, there are no passes, but in God there is freedom. Hallelujah." Others share in salutes of Hallelujah to Jesus. "There is a God that rises up in us day to day, our vessel of Christ soars within whatever trouble the Lord says.

SEASONS OF LIFE AND THE ALTAR CALL OF CHRIST

Brothers, men of Valor, this is life, the race, I'm in it now, and it fells so Hella good. I've lived since we in church pretty lousy, I want to say but anyway this is life, this is truly living, to rise every morning, and thank Jesus, to put my daughter to sleep, while reading to her, and our sleeping family the word of God. I don't even look at the time anymore, I just wait til I'm tired enough or just fall to sleep, the best, it's nothing else before this, everybody I thought cool with me always something now. I got 1 true friend that has been the same all the way through, and I don't need no more, it's the quiet, I like it, to get up every day, and take my daughter to school, to have my mother not have to worry about me. I've seen so much of God, that I'm deathly afraid of my Lord and Savior, he's nothing to play with, I just keep my ear on. "The men all stand, and cheer. The rest of the night went on, speaker after speaker. At the end, they meet and greet, and Challis had a line almost wrap around to the sanctuary.

CHAPTER 29

Halloween

A month passes and it's Halloween.
Challis, "are you ready?".
Sassy, "yes sir," as she comes down dressed as a Genie, she looks so cute.
He loves her costume Gigi made her.
Solace, "I like that."
Challis, "let's do it."
They go trickery treat door to door.
Taylor answers her door.
Sassy, "trickery treat."
Taylor, "stay here with us, we're not allowed to trickery treat."
Brooklyn, "excuse her here you go Genie, too cute."
Sassy, "thank you," and they left.
Their neighbor dressed as Dracula scares Sassy, and so many kids out. Time flies, Challis takes his daughter to the Children's hospital, to have her candy x-rayed for free, and a lot of other kids did the same. Sassy could not stay awake, so she fell to sleep on the ride home. Her dad carried her and her full to the brim bucket basket in.
Solace, "aww, she could not hang on."
Rea, "wow, all that candy!"
Challis, "and I took her to get it all x-rayed at the hospital."

Jamarion Senior, "That's the best way."

Gigi, "I'll take her and bath her, and also put her to bed."

Challis, "thank you, I'm starving."

Solace, "chili dogs on warm in the kitchen."

Challis, "I'll go shower and eat."

Night comes, all sleep. Morning flosses in on high.

Gigi, "I am starving."

Challis, "me and you both."

They go sit and says the grace. Sassy and Solace comes in, and sit, say their grace and eat.

Gigi, "morning everyone."

They all speak.

Challis, "come on baby, this is weekend, we're doing nothing."

Sassy, "daddy, I have ballet piano, and ice skating."

Challis, "I know."

They finished by 1pm with Mrs. Mustier. Then there was nothing else, and they all go home.

Challis and everyone sleep in."

Before he knows it is time to get up and take the children to school. He gets the car ready and in minutes reach red star, and Sassy is whisked away by her teacher, Mrs. Reiner. Challis does not have class, but he must go over for the day, and check out how their home is coming along, and downtown properties. He thought he would have a catch up a day out of it, first thing Challis noticed, was the progress, and he is happy. Their home now is all glass, and in two months or so, it will be all finished.

Rea, "thanksgiving is right around the corner."

Solace, "yes, I know, I've been putting together a list for us to prepare."

Rea, "I thought you would have your Chefs cook."

Solace, "I'll have them help us sister."

Rea laughs, "okay, yes put me down for candied yams and mama's pecan pies, I'll make three."

Solace, "and I'll do mama's cream peas, dressing, two peach cobblers."

Rae, "I can't wait, cream peas delish and mama's dressing."

Gigi, "what are you ladies chatting about?"

Solace, "thanksgiving dinner."

Gigi, "oh I can make her Me Mauls rolls."

Rea, "I thought you would be with your mother?"

Gigi, "definitely, but I'll be with my two families."

Solace, "girl, you know your mother is looking forward to seeing you all day."

Gigi, "my mother knows, we're having an early thanksgiving at 1pm."

Solace, "right, and ours is going to be at 4pm."

Gigi, "see it all works out, but know this, my family may follow me here."

Rea, "girl we love you."

Solace, "why don't you see if your mother wants her family to eat with us."

Gigi, "let me call my mommy."

She dials her mom's number.

Gigi, "hello."

Constance, "yes love."

Gigi, "mommy, I would like both my families together for thanksgiving."

Constance, "Clark, my baby wants us together for Thanksgiving with her two families." Clark, "there or here?"

Gigi, "over here."

Constance, "over there."

Clark, "okay, fine with me, it's her time now."

Constance, "you heard?"

Gigi, "yes ma'am, love you, and may I speak to Clark?"

Constance gives the phone to Clark; he takes the phone.

Gigi, "hello, thank you."

Clark, "no problem daughter."

They hang up.

Gigi, "so we are in here, wait my mommy again, hello mommy."

Constance, "let me speak to Solace," Constance said.

Gigi, "my mommy wants you," handed the phone over to Solace.

Solace takes the phone.

Constance, "hello, I would like to make the Turkeys and the mash potatoes plus my mamas mix berry pie."

Solace, "you can prepare two and our Chefs will do three, and the rest is fine."

Constance, "okay, thank you."

They hang up.

Gigi does a buck and screams yes.

Rea, "girl, calm down."

Gigi still excited, goes and hugs and kisses them both and dances around.

The phone rings.

Solace, "are you cooking?"

Gigi, "hello, hold on, yes ma'am, I'm making deviled eggs, baked beans, potato salad, all that my Grandma taught me, okay, we're having Thanksgiving right here. That is perfect; my parents are finally moving here. Alright. Okay, kisses let's talk later."

They hang up.

Challis, "come on, we have to check on our home," addressing Sassy.

Gigi, "oh leave her here, I'll watch her."

Solace, "and we will also."

Challis, "okay, thanks."

He grabs a jacket and darts out. Before he knows it, he is at his house site, but before he goes in, he goes and peaks at his parents' sensational creation, the Grand Ballroom through the window, and he is aroused and happy as to the luxury defined décor.

Challis, "okay, let's get down to business," and he jets back across the street, and almost gets hit by a car due to a horse that ran across from his open range. But the horse got confused and ran back. The lady was startled but apologized and went on her way. Challis was a little uneasy, but he went on. One thing he knew was that, he was going to build a fence to stop them from coming into town. Challis also thought about what else might be out there lurking around. He hoped it wasn't lions, tigers or bears. Here are his properties, and he was in amazed at all the work his men had done. He could walk on the stone path that led to their home. The structure was huge, but solid; he loved the detailed crafts of the glass.

Daniel the Foreman came up to him, "hello sir, it's coming right along on schedule."

"Yes, it is ahead of schedule," Challis said, "I'm a happy man."

"We'll have the garage doors up and on later tonight, because…" Daniel said, Challis shifts, "we're around the clock."

"I like that," Challis said, "when do the appliances get here?"

"All the built-in ones will be here Friday," Daniel said.

"Will you be finished?" Challis asked. "Yes, we're starting wiring tonight," Daniel replied.

"Okay, now also, we have to do a bob wire fence around the open range from coming in traffic," Challis said.

"Someone cut a huge hole in the fence that was already up," Daniel said.

"Have you seen any other animals?" Challis asked.

"A couple raccoons, possums, deer, rabbits, but that's about it," Daniel replied.

"Okay," Challis said.

Time goes by, he looks around some more and heads home. On his drive he notices, the same car that almost ran him over stopped on the side of the road, lights out, and he thought, 'nope, no trouble, dash cam is on, and he zoomed right on' soon he was home. Night comes in full force and morning gently peeks through, after a couple hours or so.

Security Damon intercoms in, "Mr. Challis."

"Who is it this early?" His mom asked.

"Mom I got it," Challis said to her.

"The cops are here about you involved in causing someone off the road," Security Damon said.

"I'll be right down," Challis said.

"What is going on?" His mother asked.

"Cool mom," Challis replied.

"Like hell, come on baby," Jamarion Senior said.

They both follow Challis down. The officers are inside.

"Hello, I'm officer Jimmy Fallon," one of them said.

"And I'm officer Ted Lemons," the other said, "a Sheila Edwards said you caused her to go off the road and damage her car."

"I have a dash cam, and car cam that records the entire road I travel, and I saw the car earlier last night, and she almost ran me over downtown where I'm building and have other business," Challis said.

"Your building on the old Shining property?" Officer Ted Lemons asked.

"Yes, come I can show you from my car cam," Challis said to them.

They follow him, within minutes Challis is cleared. He comes back in; his parents and his daughter are eating.

"What was all that?" His mom asked.

"It's cool people, and Sheila Edwards, remember Sunny Edwards sister?" Challis asked.

"She always liked you, how did you know it was her?" Solace asked.

"The cops showed me her picture, I told them I only know her from her older brother," Challis replied.

"They all moved to California your junior year, that's going on 20 years or so," Jamarion Senior said.

"Right, and I don't care what she's on, but from now on, I'm rolling with detail, starting today, everywhere I go, it's too close to time," Challis said.

"You got that right," Solace said.

Hours pass and Mrs. Mustier had arrived for Sassy,

"Are you ready?" Mrs. Mustier asked.

"Yes ma'am," Sassy replied, "what will I practice in?"

"I have all your things, and first, may I change her into her ballet stuff?" Mrs. Mustier asked.

"Yes," Challis replied.

Within minutes, they are back fully ballet dressed. Sassy looked so cute and they leave. "We better start prepping today," Rea said,

"Thanksgiving is this Thursday. "Sassy comes out." Probably Wednesday early," Solace replied.

Sassy is dancing like a pro instead of a beginner, her mother had been training her just as much ballet as piano, and ice skating, and regular skating.

"Mom, can you and auntie meet today at the house in a second? Cake tasting, I forgot several bakers are coming by," Challis said.

"Go on, I 'm game for that," Rea said.

"How many bakers?" Solace asked.

"I've settled on four," Challis replied.

"Okay," Solace said.

Time goes by. Challis is in the wind and the first baker, Tova Cakes has arrived with a custard filling lemon base tart cake, with buttercream in white. They both try on little plate samples with dessert forks and cold water to drink.

"Now this is so good, moist," Rea said.

"Right, not too overpowering, but delish," Solace agrees.

Time goes on. Marie of Cake Sensations arrives with a white orange blossom pudding cream-filled base cake, with butter cream frosting. They both taste it.

"Wow, this is so refreshing," Solace said.

"Light to taste, but creamy, bursting with flavor," Rea said.

Next up is Shimmer cakes by Slade and Brandy, a white chiffon strawberry filled cake, with butter cream frosting.

"Now this is light, and moist also," Solace said.

"This is good too," Rea said.

Next up, Cakes for all occasions by Champagne, her cake is a white mix berry fruit curd coconut cake.

"Now, let me," Rea said, she takes another taste and closes her eyes.

"This is so good," Solace said.

All the bakers leave but leave behind several cake samples.

"I think they should have all four of these cakes into one," Rea suggested.

"Why not? Because each one has an array of taste bud for everyone," Solace said.

"Because each one, someone will love," Rea said.

Time goes by. Challis calls.

"So how did it go?" He asked.

Solace puts him on speaker and said, "We agreed that you should order all four as one huge cake."

"Yes, because all them cakes was so delicious," Rea said.

"I agree, because I have tasted all, I just needed a second opinion, and that's what we're going to do," Challis said, "kids and adults, all will love it."

"You are having a reception with kids?" Rea asked.

"Of course, our kids are going to party with the best of them," Challis said.

"You can't have them up all night," Solace said.

"Why not, they've been asleep for 11 months," Challis said.

"Well he got you there, because this party is going to be spectacular," Rea said.

Three days passed, and its thanksgiving. All has hit the scene, China and Mac have arrived with all their newborns in toe, plus their grown sons.

MacArthur has arrived with his fiancé on her way. Lynn and Maximillian aka Maxie has arrived, with his fiancé who is already present, Gigi.

"Both of my parents will be here tomorrow," China said, as she hugs Solace.

Rea is just using a food processor chopping up stuff for, all the food she is cooking. Solace has already cooked all her food and Gigi is making her food as they speak.

"Babe let's head to the movies," Maxie said.

"In 2 hours," Gigi replied," I got to finish."

"Okay, I'll go take a rest," Maxie said.

Constance is let in by Security and she has her 2 sons with her carrying all her already made stuff. Gigi goes to her, hugs and kisses her. Constance and her sons speak, and Gigi shows them straight to the kitchen where the 4 Chefs are, Darren, Tinsel, Craig, Jackson.

Challis comes in with Sassy from school and yells, "We are doing it!"

Soon the Clark crew leaves as Gigi shows them out. Solace and Rea go taste her food. "

This is good, Brussels sprouts and bacon," Solace said.

"Let me get a taste, and these stuffed peppers, let me," Rea said, "where is Gigi?"

"Here she comes," Solace replied.

"I don't care," Rea said, "I'm hungry, and this little white bogey can cook."

Rea covering her mouth, and saying, "This is too good."

Time goes by, and all is at the huge table. Challis just purchased seats up to 100 so people can sit at the table, which is so long, goes into the front room with upholstered chairs.

"Well, your sons are huge, and your family still looking good," Mac said.

"Thank God, I 'm so ready for them to wake up, and for us to get it on," Challis said, "how's life new parent?"

"You know, I never thought this would be what we needed, but it is, because," Mac said, China has done a 360 and a Bal face, we just got work to do in enjoying us and really raising our kids."

"I saw Chasity and Chloe turning over and Miles sitting almost up," Challis said.

Mac laughs and smiles, "I know, they are trying to keep up with Challis junior, Caviars, Solace junior, and Sole a."

"Yes," Challis agreed.

"What have you been up to?" Mac asked.

"Nothing get your coat come on let's go view our property and my family's home," Challis said.

Each tell their loves they are leaving, and they bounce.

"Luckily, I got these dash cams because, you remember Sunny Edwards?" Challis asked, as they were driving.

"Always had the lightning rod part in his hair," Mac replied.

"Yes, his baby sister, Sheila, tried to say I hit and run her off the road," Challis said.

"What? Why?" Mac asked.

You're asking the wrong one," Challis said.

"It's crazy out here, people want a quick buck for free," Mac said.

"Right. Here we go," Challis said.

They have arrived.

"Damn son, you've been grinding," Mac exclaimed.

"I'm not playing Mac," Challis said, as he gets out of the circular drive, I love our home, but nature calls out here."

"All these trees, and surrounding forest," Mac said.

"This is why I'm going hard or staying home," Challis replied.

"You got to, I told MacArthur and Maximillian," Mac said, we all are in same area code."

"Damn straight, it's us against the world," Challis said.

"I just feel a particular way since all that shady stuff went down," Mac said.

"Not having it, we are going to live," Challis said.

"And not die," Mac completed.

They speak to all the workers. Challis and Mac goes in, he says," I like this, it's big but not too big because you are going to need all this space with 5 kids."

They both walk into the sunken family room that leads to the huge kitchen.

"I just pray that we can be," Challis said.

"Man, they are coming, we have lived all this truth and we know the real," Mac said.

"Yes, we do," Challis said.

"This is really pure fire," Mac said.

They walk the total of the home and then they admire the grounds, then they leave and go over where Mac is building adjacently next door. He was across the street, but they settled for a split and now just as many men are working at Macs as Challis. They leave and drive home and it's still a lot of people at his

CHAPTER 30

Christmas surprise

"Daddy, daddy," Sassy called.

"Okay, baby girl what?" Challis asked.

"Daddy, my brothers are awake, they said to get their hair cut, and they prayed on me, and auntie, and Uncle Mac's babies," Sassy said.

"Where are they?" Challis asked.

"Drinking soup in the kitchen," Sassy replied.

Challis junior with hair to the floor, with each two braids, everybody is amazed.

"Wow, hello," Mac said.

"Hi dad, and hi Uncle MacArthur," Caviars said.

Challis gets down. Challis junior says the same. Then they both say at the same time,

"Dad we awoke, because God told us to pray for Sapphire, our big sister, and our bro, Miles, and Chloe, and Chasity."

"They're your cousins," China said.

"Babe," Mac called.

They hug, she cries, they hug her again and lay their heads on her.

"I feel so warm, thank you God," China said.

"Dad, God said you should cut our hair," Caviars said.

"Well, let's get to it," Challis said.

Gigi comes in, and screams, the boys run to her and jump up on her, almost knocking her down. They kiss her cheeks.

"What's up?" Mac asked.

The boys just looked.

"Son chill, it's like that," Mac said.

"They don't know you, go get your brother, he's up," China said.

Maxie does. Gigi keeps kissing them.

"Okay time up," Challis said, he takes them and goes to back to cut their hair. He puts them in the chair, puts them each on a cloth that snaps in the back, and begins to cut them one at a time.

"Dad, God said It is finished, and stay the course, and don't worry about nobody," Challis Junior said.

"What, how I still got," Challis said.

"Luke 16:10 He that is faithful in that which is least is faithful also in much: and he that is unjust in the least is unjust also in much," Caviars said.

"You've been accountable dad, over a few things," Challis Junior said.

"Okay, I hear you God," Challis said, as he cuts a few.

He finishes Caviars. Time goes by, boys eat again and finally are sleeping. Challis carries them up.

"That's a lot," Mac said.

Challis shuts the door after he puts them back in bed, he puts diapers on each one of them and then gets down on his knees and just balls and sob's like a baby and pleads out.

"Lord, the world, I don't know how to keep them safe and out of harm's way, these people are always doing something, I hate it here," He cried.

The Lord speaks, "you and your family will live a long, long, loving, prospering, soft flowing happy life."

"Thank you, Lord, please help us, I can't take much more," Challis said.

"You are finished," The Lord said.

Challis said, "thank you again, and amen."

There's a knock at the door.

"Do you want me to hook the boys back up?" Nurse Karen asked.

Challis gets up and says, "I'll come get you."

He goes in, and showers, and dries off, oils and puts on a warmup and house shoes. Mac has retired and did the exact same thing.

Sassy knocks on the door, "daddy."

"Come in," Challis said.

Sassy does, and says, "Aww, they are really sleeping, I wanted to play with my little brothers."

Challis picked her up and said, "in time we all will."

Night falls, and it's dinner time. Just subs, pizza salad, and corn and cold pop and juice.

"You ready?" Maxie asked.

"Let me just grab my throw, and my purse," Gigi said.

Soon the car service comes, and they leave.

"I have not had Josee's-pies pizza, in a minute, it's hot and good also," Mac said.

"They make the best," Challis said.

"Daddy, can I eat upstairs?" Sassy asked.

"Why?" Challis asked.

"I got her a new movie," Gigi replied.

"Yes, please," Sassy said.

'You could put it on right in there, and she can eat on a tray on top of paper," Sugar said.

"Wait, I got her movie mat," Gigi said, she runs upstairs, and digs it out of one of Sassy's big bags, plus a blanket and comes back down, and it's a thick mat with movies all over.

"That's nice," Rea said.

"Thanks," Gigi said, and puts it out. Challis grabs her food tray plus her bottle water.

"Have your Nurse bath you," Challis said.

Within minutes, Nurse Kimmie and Jamia

bath her quickly, and Sassy went to the mat. Gigi turns on the movie. Now she and Maxie bounced, and Sassy chowed down with every bite she was into her movie.

"I am starving," China said.

She says grace and just eats and eats. Mac chows down as well. Challis has gone and joined his daughter.

"Challis is the best dad," Rea said.

"He needs to be trained," China said.

"He's trying, but that movie does look good, action flick," Solace said.

The night came and went, and morning stood tall. On Thanksgiving Day by 4pm,

"Well family come on in," said Challis.

Constance hugs Challis, and she kisses Sassy, who just ran up. Challis shook hands with Clark, their sons choose to go elsewhere.

"Hello," Solace said, she hugs Constance.

"Mommy, you made it, and Clark thank you for coming," Gigi said, she hugs him too. "Well hello," Rea said.

Everybody spoke back to her.

Mike, with his sons, his wife Cindy all speaks, say, "Hey auntie Rea."

They hug, and then they all spoke to Uncle Frank. They shake hands, fist bump. Jamarion II and his wife Karen and their sons all spoke to each one of their relatives; all was together on such a nice blissful day. All now is sitting at the table, even Karen, Maximillian aka Maxie, MacArthur, Mac and China all was present. Light soft jazz played in the background and the NFL football game on blast on mega screen, they all go and washed their hands, they all sat down. Jamarion Senior stood up and hits his glass for quiet; he turns down the soft jazz and the football game.

Jamarion Senior, "let's all stand."

As all the Chefs and kitchen staff waited in the background, grace was to be cast in the air.

Senior said, "Let's all bow our heads, close your eyes, and hold the one next to you."

They all do, "At this precious time, we want to give thanks to our Lord and Savior," they all say yes, he continues, "Lord at this time, we bless you, this union and we bless this food. Lord we know that you are here, and we thank you from the littlest to the oldest. Bless our union, bless our harmony. Lord we know you did not have to do it, but you did. Lord we thank your precious name amen." All said amen.

The night went on and it was family oriented to the core, not a closed mouth in site. As quick as it came, the evening pulled on as it went. Busy days, black Friday, the ladies and Sassy were out shopping full speed.

"Hey Senator," Sheila Edwards said.

"Yes," Solace said.

"I just want to apologize, I did not want my parents to know that I had veered to the side of the road, while on the phone, and banged up their brand new car," Sheila Edwards said, "but they found out anyway."

"That was terrible, you could had gotten Challis in a lot of trouble," Solace said.

"My parents have told me over and over to stay off the phone when I drive, but regardless I'm truly sorry," Sheila said, "tell him to please forgive me. I'm on my way to the airport. I'm getting married on Sunday."

"Well congrats," Solace said to her.

They went their separate ways.

"I like this, and it's so soft and delicate, I'll have to buy this chemise in every color, one, two, three, ok six," Rea said.

"Let me grab six of those also," Solace said.

"Do you like these stiles to boots?" China asked.

"Those are banging," Rea said.

"Those are really nice," Solace said, "you can still wear those that high?"

"Yes, these got some kind of leg support pad in them," China replied.

She walks all around, and says, "I love them," as she keeps prancing up and down like a model, while December happily followed.

As days left as fast as they came, Challis was just finishing up the finishing touches on their family home, as Mac was all throttled in his family home, but they had gotten quite comfortable at the Penthouse.

Challis's own they felt that it was plenty of quality and roomy, they felt they were just as good, and could live there, but they knew it was a new day in him and China's and their inner families livelihood this time around they wanted to just not give a different stableness, but they also wanted their older sons to know that a house matures. This time around they wanted an essential purpose, although both their sons would be jumping the broom any day now after Challis and Giselle's wedding of all time. Well, Challis was doing this, doing that, and finally, he and Sassy rested on three huge Trees off their land, that he had some of his construction workers on the job deliver, and put right up in the huge picture window. They also put one in his parents' picture window upstairs, off their balcony. He had all three professionally decorated but Sassy hung all her bulbs she made at school that were presented for her family. Challis was a little at whit's end, he knew his family was to wake and he ran in the church. All were getting set up, it's the week of Christmas. Challis felt like it was some sorrow set to fall somewhere, but he had an already made plan last session with Bishop Connors at the church, and he needed his sons to not awaken again to tell him nothing. All he knew was what the Lord had set in stone in him, hat his loves were going to wake up on time for Christmas.

Challis, as he sits in Bishops Connors office, he says, "I'm ready, and I just feel like the Lord told my sons to tell me I was finished."

"Well, you are now. I believe God," Bishop Connors said.

"I do too," Challis said.

Bishop Connors, "let's read Psalms 23!"

"(New King James Version)

SEASONS OF LIFE AND THE ALTAR CALL OF CHRIST

A Psalm of David.

The LORD is my shepherd; I shall not want.

He makes me to lie down in green pastures;

He leads me beside the still waters.

He restores my soul;

He leads me in the paths of righteousness For His name's sake.

Yea, though I walk through the valley of the shadow of <u>death</u>,

I will fear no evil; For You are with me;

Your rod and Your staff, they comfort me.

I have seen all you have done, and I see all that God has done in you."

"I feel new," Challis said.

Bishop Connors continued, "Luke 39 King James 2000 Bible

Behold my hands and my feet, that it is I myself: handle me, and see; for a spirit has not flesh and bones, as you see me have.

King James Romans 1:9 Bible

For God is my witness, whom I serve with my spirit in the gospel of his Son, that without ceasing I make mentions of you always in my prayers.

You did it, and now all you got to do is sit back and reap your harvest."

"All these people coming all at a particular time," Challis said.

Bishop, "don't you think God knows time, but

<u>Genesis 18:14</u>

Verse Concepts

"Is anything too difficult for the LORD? At the appointed time I will return to you, at this time next year, and Sarah will have a son."

"God is of truth 1 John 4:6 Spirit and truth. You've prepared and it's not in vain."

"I know that, but I'm not perfect," Challis said.

"But God is whatever beseech you, son," Bishop said, "the Lord is with you."

They went on that evening to talk some more till late at night. Both left and made it home safely. Challis just sat in the car for a minute; he wanted to pull his-self together. He had been crying he let sometime pass. His security did not dare disturb him, finally, he went in and crawled into bed, with his clothes on and only removed his shoes, he pulled Giselle to him, and she did not stir at all, just slept for the days left before the big day. Their family seemed like a picture of busyness just throttling through the emotions of daily life, Sassy was finally out of school, and off shopping with Mrs. Mustier. Challis was happy because he could have some time to himself to vent in pure silence. Their tree had gifts but not as many as Challis and his inner family's home. He hired a Santa the whole time the reception would go on, and they would open their gifts all the next day. Well, all went to bed early except Challis, he stayed up all night, crying to God to let the True King of Glory come in, he did not waiver.

<u>King James Bible</u>

Lift up your heads, O ye gates; and be ye lift, ye everlasting doors; and the King of glory shall come in. But anyway, blissful Christmas Glory day morning gracefully came in, at 5 am Challis takes his time to cut his sons' hair on his lap, he washes each off, put them back to bed, showered, and came downstairs. His entire family was still sleeping, Challis just tossed and turned. A couple more hours pass, Sassy wakes, they all agreed she could open 3 toys.

Sassy, "Daddy, daddy, its morning," as she danced around with such pure grace, she said, "its morning."

"I know," Challis said, "wait let me go down. I'll call you."

He wanted to make sure that fake Santa showed up. He had just an eaten a mini breakfast that the Chef crew had put out, then all came down, lights went out, just candles.

"Nothing," Challis said.

"HO HO HO," Santa said, and Sassy screamed, "Daddy!"

"Come down," Challis said.

Sassy was so scared. Gigi was there, she grabs her hand, and walked her down slowly. Sassy was too stoked. Christmas music played softly in the background, then lights hung on a huge tree, hung gazed in the biggest window in the house.

Sassy just screamed again.

"Hello," Santa said,

"Sassy you've been a good girl." Sassy gets behind Gigi, and says, "Yes sir."

"Because nice over by the tree is 3 red glitter gifts," Santa said.

Sassy ran, pulled the paper off one, it was the infant custom baby doll she wanted, next gift she opened was a huge box, which was a lighted beauty bar, and big dolls with wardrobe case. She went ballistic, then the last gift she opened, just a name, Stallion. Her dad said, "Come," he puts her coat on, and her riding boots on her.

He slips on his riding boots jacket, and to the left, their family looked on from the window. There stood a huge black horse that she and her dad got on.

They rode around followed closely by a trainer on a bike. After a while, they finished their exciting ride, and both came back to the beautifully decorated glittery tablecloth, with bowls of bells around, and candles in box glass holders. Everyone loved the dominant sparkle, they all had breakfast to candlelight as they prayed and ate. Time shot by; it was time to go to the church.

"I don't know what to do," Challis said.

"We are going on," Solace said, "God is going to come through."

4 pm comes, and still, no loves.

"Son please listen to me," Jamarion Senior said.

"No, I'm about to tell these people," Challis said.

"6 pm, two hours," Bishop Connors said.

"Okay, all these people, and they have not budged," Challis said.

"You stand at the altar at 6 pm," Bishop Connors said, "who cares about these people, this is about you, and God."

"Honey, we have to close this off," Lady Collette said.

People from all around, as snow fell, prayer teams Jesus news.

"See a circus," Challis said.

"Dressed in all red gold silk," Bishop Connors said, "preacher Rob stated that they were at capacity and our Mega screen can be on no new vans up close."

"No," Lady Collette said.

Dennis and Maurice got them to the back, but no parking for miles. The mayor, the governor they know," Bishop Connors said. More time goes by, and back home. "Nothing," Nurse Kelly-Anne said, "still nothing."

Thirty minutes pass.

"Call me if anything happens," she said, as she left.

"Will do, but is that Mr. Challis again?" Nurse Jammia asked.

"Yes," Nurse Kimme said, "Lord help that man if they do not wake up, I don't know what to tell him. Let me go get water."

"Get me a coffee," Nurse Jammia said.

Suddenly, they all woke up in their right mind, as the outside light of God's presence glistened off their faces. Giselle saw her wedding gown; she went in with her daughters.

She showered.

Nurse Kimmie comes into the room, and she drops her water bottle, and says, "OMG!"

"Hello," Challis Junior said.

"Hello," Caviars said.

"Where are your mother and sister?" Nurse Kimmie asked.

Giselle with their robs on says, "Right here," they all come out.

"Here's…" Nurse Jammia said, and they all stand still.

"I want to tell you both thank you so much," Giselle said.

"I'll hug you," Nurse Kimmie said.

"Come on," Giselle said.

They all hugged.

"It's been so long, God bless you," Nurse Jammia said, crying. She hugs her as well. China just arrived, she says a prayer, goes up saying, "Wake up before I have to kill Challis wake up."

"Come," Nurse Jammia said to China, she goes, and then she sees them, and almost faints. She grabs the door, and says, "Lord you know."

Giselle goes over and hugs her, then all the kids do. China looks at the time, it's almost 20 till 6 pm, she says, "Let's do this."

They all dress up. In 10 minutes, Giselle and her daughter's hair is all down, with natural brown auburn high lights. China did two braids, Giselle puts on her veil, and they said, "Let's go." She calls her husband, no answer.

"I 'll just thank them all for coming and they can go eat at the reception," Challis said. China has not called.

"My ringer was off," Mac said, she hung up, no message."

"At 6 pm, I'll…" Challis said.

'You just wait, God, my God is not a liar," Solace said.

'It's going to be alright," Rea said, "Christmas Glory is here set in stone."

"Daddy, daddy, will we still get married today?" Sassy asked.

"I pray so," Challis replied.

All the doors are opened; they hear some cheering, Challis runs to see, and it's nothing.

"I cannot do this," he said to himself, and then he goes to the podium, and says, "It's 6 pm."

"Go on Do not be deceived, God is not mocked; for whatever a man sows, that he will also reap. (Galatians 6:7, NKJV)," Bishop Connors said.

"I'm just so tired," Challis said.

He takes and puts the headphone around his ear, and the music plays, and Sassy sees the Lord's light pressing through the glass stain windows. She runs, and she sees them.

"See, it's the Lord's light pressing through, and through," Gigi said.

She runs to them and screams.

"They're here! They're here!"

"What?" Challis asked, and then he sees as all his loves.

The church goes wild. Challis just looks on in amazement, as he sees the loves of his life. All of a sudden, Solace junior and Solae takes off running, "Daddy, daddy," with all their long hair flowing, with their white rhinestone lace half train dresses to with their white satin rhinestone patents.

They reach him, he picks them up and just walks half runs with them both, as his sons' run-up in all-white tuxedo's matching their dad's own. Sassy wearing the same pattern white lacer hinge stone, with white rhinestone tights as her sisters and white satin rhinestone patents with white matching fur stow.

All their daughters have on one, just a smiling she stays with her lady G, who is wearing a dress Gigi made. It is white rhinestone fox fur, long hooded to the floor, coat and stiletto rhinestones with a body upper bodice fitting wedding gown, with the back out to the end of her back with a full bottom, and her train flowing behind her, with 4 tuxedo dressed Security guards.

"No more lady G, my mommy," Sassy said.

Giselle stops and squats down, and says, "Only if you want it that way."

"Yes ma'am," Sassy said.

They hug and kiss, and then they finish walking towards Challis hand in hand. Challis realizes that all, "My Hope is Built on Nothing Less,

My hope is built on nothing less

Than Jesus' blood and righteousness;

I dare not trust the sweetest frame,

But wholly lean on Jesus' name.

On Christ, the Solid Rock, I stand;

All other ground is sinking sand."

Edward Mote, 1834

He harnesses on that parable, and comes up, reaches out to them. He puts his daughters down, and then he softly grabs his love of his life, and hug, and kiss Giselle as he picks her up. Solae holds Sassy's hand and Solace's as they walk behind their parents, their sons also follow closely in pursuit, Giselle lays her head on her love, as her hand lays gently across Challis's chest, as they, as one walk. The light of God as The Seasons of Life and Altar, Call of Christ presses forward, though gracefully, as they all walk up to Bishop Connors. As the wedding-goers look on, they finally say their vows, which they never rehearsed, and within minutes they are married as one under the Son, the Father, and the Holy Ghost. They kiss, sealed the deal, music plays, and to God, the true Christmas, be the Glory of the Seasons of Life and The Alter Call of Christ.

THE END